The Grass Roots Fundraising Book

The Grass Roots Fundraising Book

Joan Flanagan
for The Youth Project

Contemporary Books, Inc.
Chicago

Library of Congress Cataloging in Publication Data

Flanagan, Joan.
    The grass roots fundraising book.

    Includes index.
    1. Fund raising—Handbooks, manuals, etc.   I. Title.
HV41.F49   1982   361.7′068′1   81-71078
ISBN 0-8092-5746-7 (pbk.)   AACR2

Published by Contemporary Books, Inc.
180 North Michigan Avenue, Chicago, Illinois 60601
Manufactured in the United States of America
Library of Congress Catalog Card Number: 81-71078
International Standard Book Number: 0-8092-5746-7

Published simultaneously in Canada by
Beaverbooks, Ltd.
150 Lesmill Road
Don Mills, Ontario M3B 2T5
Canada

Contents

Preface

The Youth Project first published *The Grass Roots Fundraising Book* in 1977. Its primary objective was to help thousands of community groups we aided over the years build financial self-sufficiency. Philosophically, and practically, we believed that dependency—on us, on other foundations, or on the government as sole sources of funding—was not the best way to achieve solid citizen organizations. Achieving greater self-sufficiency and staying alive have become urgent necessities. The current scarcity of resources, both public and private, have made The Youth Project's work unintentionally prophetic.

When the clamor for learning how to conduct bingos, membership drives, raffles, carnivals and coffees increased, our small supply of first-edition books decreased rapidly. Early in 1981 the demand for a second edition became obvious.

Joan Flanagan, along with other trainers, followed up the first edition of this book with workshops across the country to give additional assistance to groups committed to raising more of their own money. We've all learned a lot in the last four years. Our increased knowledge of what works makes this second edition brim with new but tested ideas.

Three attributes of this book make it especially appealing and useful. First is the level of commonsense detail. Joan is a person who

has been through the fundraising wars: *anybody* who can include
the caution to check the outlets before a potluck supper so that too
many coffee urns won't blow the fuse is clearly a veteran with firsthand experience.

Secondly, Joan shows that fundraising need be neither drudgery
nor activity that diverts the main objectives of a group. Organizational goals and fundraising strategies can be connected in a way to
further the group's mission while expanding its coffers.

Finally, her suggestions for fundraisers (staggering in their sheer
variety) leave you with the subtle reminder that, like quilting bees
of old, fundraising events can be a celebration of community, a re-
affirmation of the spirit of collective action.

Karen Paget
Executive Director
The Youth Project
February 8, 1982

The Youth Project

The Youth Project is a tax-exempt public foundation that supports a wide range of grass roots social change efforts. The Youth
Project seeks to identify emerging community organizations and
provide the financial and technical assistance that will help them
succeed. This emphasis on grass roots projects stems from ten years
of experience, which indicates that local citizens can have the most
impact on their own communities and can best achieve broader
goals by building on local success.

A decentralized field operation is the key to our effectiveness.
Seven full-time field representatives in Bridgeport, CT, Knoxville,
TN, Atlanta, GA, Chicago, IL, Minneapolis, MN, Portland, OR,
and Roswell, NM, work with the 200 organizations a year that
receive our help. The Tribal Sovereignty Program, a special
program of The Youth Project since 1977, became an independent
organization, Seventh Generation Fund, in January of 1985.

Foundation, church, corporate, and individual contributions
enable The Youth Project to provide modest seed funding and substantial technical assistance in response to local initiatives. We are
grateful to the Avon Products Foundation and *Newsweek* for their
grants in support of this second edition. The first edition was made
possible with support from the Edward Hazen Foundation, Max
and Anna Levinson Foundation, McDonald's Corporation, Nor-

man Foundation, Playboy Foundation, and the Veatch Program
(North Shore Unitarian Society).

The Youth Project
1555 Connecticut Avenue, N.W.
Washington, DC   20036

Acknowledgments

Grass roots fundraising is a team sport. "I couldn't have done it without you" is always true, and it should never go unsaid.

This book is also a team effort. It represents thousands of hours and mountains of advice shared by hundreds of people. Although there are too many to list here, I deeply appreciate each and every one of you. The book could only become a reality because so many people cared enough to ask the right questions and share the best answers.

It represents the vision and concern of The Youth Project staff and board of directors. They were my best advisors throughout the project. The Youth Project regional office staff and special program staff introduced me to the top grass roots fundraisers around the country. Special thanks go to Executive Director Karen Paget and Special Programs Director Patricia Rubacky for supporting the idea of an updated and expanded book. The current staff continue the fine work of former Youth Project staff members who backed the first edition of *The Grass Roots Fundraising Book,* especially former Executive Directors Margie Tabankin and Lenny Conway.

Major contributions to the expanded text were made by Jane Beckett, independent fundraising consultant; Kim Klein, independent fundraising consultant; and Jon Pratt, Field Director of The Youth Project Midwest Office. Many other experts offered their tested advice, inspiring anecdotes, and success stories. Groups all over the United States and Canada sent examples of their best money making ideas.

Most of all, thanks to my family and friends for their unfailing support and optimism. I couldn't have done it without you.

1982
JMF

How to Use This Book

You have a vision of how the world could be better, and you have a plan to make it happen. You have an organization to achieve the plan, and it has members to do the work to win the victories. What else do you need?

Money.

This book will tell you how to use your own common sense and energy to raise the money you need. You can create your own fundraising plan using the members and resources you have right now, so that you can pay the bills and build your organization at the same time.

It is not easy. But it is simple. Ask for money. Ask the people who benefit from the work of the organization to pay dues and make pledges. Ask the people who like the goals and achievements of the group to make donations. Then ask your leaders to devise other ways to ask for money from the general public.

If you do it right, you will get the good feeling that you can be sure of all the money you need this year and in the years to come. You will have a stronger organization that can accomplish higher goals. You will get more members and better leaders. And you will make a lot of friends and share good times together.

Grass roots fundraising will open doors to discover new people and new experiences. Each person can grow and learn something new every day. You will make memories you will cherish for the rest of your life.

This book is a distillation of seven years of advice from more than 2,000 successful fundraisers in the United States and Canada. All learned fundraising by asking for money for an organization that they wanted to succeed. They were all very generous in sharing their stories, their triumphs, and their occasional disappointments. All were eager to learn more. From all of them to all of you, here is the best current advice on grass roots fundraising. Use it, add to it, and share it with your friends.

This book is written for brand new groups that want to get started on the right track. It is also written for young groups that have done a little fundraising and now want to make more money in less time. And it is written for older agencies that have been dependent on grants in the past, but now want to launch a new program to make their programs self-sufficient. Any leader or staff person can use these principles to make money for his or her own organization today.

Grass roots fundraising gives you access to most of the money available for nonprofit programs. In 1980, foundations gave only 5 percent of the philanthropic dollars to American nonprofits. The other 95 percent came from the grass roots. Individuals gave approximately $40 billion, $3 billion came from bequests, and $2.5 billion came from corporations. There is plenty of money available for your organization if you ask for it.

A national survey showed that only 4 percent of those interviewed had contributed to political campaigns. However, *89 percent* said they would contribute *if asked*. The money is out there for your organization as soon as your volunteers begin asking for it. Use the advice in this book to train your leaders to make a plan to ask for money. Begin asking, use the know-how you gain to devise a plan that will work best in your community, then improve the plan every year so you make more money in less time. Then you will have the satisfaction of seeing more members, better leaders, a more successful organization, and greater self-sufficiency come from your commitment to grass roots fundraising.

The Grass Roots Fundraising Book

1

Why Do It?

Grass roots fundraising means asking for money for your organization. It is dependable, renewable, internally controlled money because it comes from the people who need and want your organization. The basis is dues and pledges from your members, but there are hundreds of other ways to raise money using your own people and your own resources. Ad books and auctions, bake sales and barn dances, carnivals and corporate donations are all grass roots fundraisers.

Grass roots has nothing to do with gardening. You can be a tenants' club in a big city skyscraper and still be grass roots. You can be a national environmental organization with a goal of $1 million or a high school ecology club with a goal of $100. You can be a block club that has just won its first stop sign or a statewide action league working on six issues in fourteen counties. *Grass roots* simply means you are ordinary people. You don't have to be a professional fundraiser, have a lot of money yourself, or know a lot of important people to raise money for your group. To do grass roots fundraising you need only a basic understanding of money and of people.

You already know a lot about money. Everybody works, pays taxes, buys things, and would like to buy more. When you outfit the kids for school or plan a vacation, you are managing money.

You already know a lot about people, too. Any group activity —
singing in the choir, working for a political candidate, playing on
the company softball team — has taught you about how people like
to do things together.

Now you are going to be the fundraiser for your group. As an active member of an ambitious organization, you know it takes money
to run your program. You can use what you know about money and
what you know about people to do grass roots fundraising. What's
more, you can intentionally strengthen the group at the same time
that you raise the money.

The dual goal of grass roots fundraising is to pay the bills and to
build the organization. Your fundraising program should fit in
naturally with the strategy and goals of the members. Every new
block club that joins a citywide program should increase the income
and the strength of the group. Just as you set goals for your group,
such as working for property tax reforms, or remodeling the church
kitchen, you can set specific goals for your fundraising program.
When you choose to do grass roots fundraising you can reach your
own financial goals and organizational goals.

THE FINANCIAL BENEFITS

There are a lot of benefits from doing your own fundraising
besides the cold, hard cash. When you map out your fundraising
strategy, consider all that you can gain from raising your own
budget through your own work.

You gain self-sufficiency. A well-planned, long-range fundraising campaign will guarantee that you can pay your staff, buy your
supplies, and run your program. It's a good feeling to know you can
take care of yourself, whether you are a not-for-profit corporation
or an individual.

You gain independence. When you have an income from the people who want and need your program, you know you have the talent
and the techniques to raise money. No one can threaten to cut off
your funds. You are free to plan and run whatever programs the
members choose.

You gain peace of mind. Knowing you can plan and control your
income will take away the anxiety of the leaky roof or the horror of

a missed payroll. You can use your energies to make things happen rather than worry about which creditor to put off. As any coach will tell you, "Winners decide what they want to do. Losers worry about what they don't want to have happen to them."

You gain pride. Remember how proud you felt when you got your own first paycheck? The pride of raising your own money, and sharing the success, will boost the morale of your group in the same way. Grass roots money is honest money. Everyone in the group can be proud of his or her part in raising the money. You can answer any questions from a new member, a donor, or the press honestly and easily from your own open, up-to-date reports. Raising your money from a variety of sources will also reduce the temptation to accept money from any single donor who could compromise the organization.

Never underestimate the moral advantage of raising your own money. Be proud of your independence and the support of your neighbors. When Kate Bradley was raising money for the Petros, Tennessee, health clinic, she learned the railroad was going to sell the land around its unused tracks. She wrote to the president of the railroad and asked for the first option to buy the land for the clinic building. Then the politicians in Morgan County learned the land was for sale and tried to outbid her. It was clear they could double or triple her offer. Coal companies in Tennessee are used to getting their own way by using county and state politicians. Kate drove 175 miles to Nashville to meet with the railroad president and the representatives of the coal companies. When she walked into the meeting, she saw she was the only woman in the room.

The president said, "You must be Mrs. Bradley."

"I am," she said, looking him straight in the eye. Without waiting to be asked, Kate Bradley spoke her piece to the older man:

"Sir, I know you are going to honor your letter giving the health clinic the right to buy your land in Petros. I know these politicians can give you a lot more money. But I just want you to know that our money comes from cupcakes. We've had a rummage sale every Saturday and held dinners and bake sales. Everyone in the community has given me a quilt, or a jar of beans, or put up some preserves to sell for the clinic. That's where my bid comes from." The railroad president sold her the land and adjourned the meeting.

Grass roots fundraising proves you have a lot of people who support your work. If most of your neighbors will buy memberships or make donations, you know, and the people outside of your group will know, that your people want the program enough to work for it.

This gives you a boost with other funding sources. Ironically, successful grass roots fundraising makes it easier for you to raise money from institutions. Foundations and national church giving programs are interested in groups that can show that their own people will support them. Corporations and United Way executives want to choose the best outfits from a flood of applications, and they need some way of judging your effectiveness. If you can go to corporate executives and show them that you signed up 60 new members last month, or had 500 people at your dance, or that you raise 75 percent of your budget yourself, they can feel confident that their money will be well spent if they give it to you. The depth and breadth of your grass roots fundraising is the most accurate evidence that the people in your community *want* your program.

Some foundations make what they call a *matching grant* or a *challenge grant*. They will give you a set amount of money if you will raise a specific amount in a given time period. For example, in 1981 The Youth Project's Midwest Office offered a $4,000 grant to the Nebraska Safe Energy Alternatives if they could raise $4,000 of their own. This organization was created to offer alternatives to a high-voltage powerline designed to run from Manitoba, Canada, to Nebraska. The leaders used this opportunity to ask farmers in the designated path of the powerline to join the organization or make contributions. First they announced the matching grant challenge in their newsletter, then went farm to farm along the powerline corridor in the evenings after their farm work was done. They recruited 134 members at $15 each for $2,010 and received another $1,922 in contributions. Then they organized a Christmas craft sale that raised another $130, bringing their total to $4,062! They collected the matching grant and expanded their efforts to inform the citizens about the dangers from the powerline to their health, welfare, and economy.

The foundations can test the strength of local support in this way. They do not want to invest money in a group that may become dependent on them year after year. The grass roots group gets the benefit of knowing that every dollar it raises is doubled. People don't always like "charity" from the outside; matching grants are joint efforts and help organizations work toward local independence.

Wily old Ben Franklin was the first person in America to use the matching grant. In 1750 he lobbied the Pennsylvania Assembly to create the first government matching grant—for his favorite project, the Pennsylvania Hospital. The assemblymen agreed to appropriate £2,000 if Franklin's volunteers could raise £2,000. As Franklin wrote in his autobiography:

> . . . the members [of the Assembly] now conceiv'd they might have the credit of being charitable without the expense . . . ; and then, in soliciting subscriptions among the people, we urg'd the conditional promise of the law as an additional motive to give, since every man's donation would be doubled; thus the clause work'd both ways.

THE ORGANIZATIONAL BENEFITS

You can use your grass roots fundraising to improve three major parts of the organization: the program, the membership, and the publicity.

Program Benefits

Grass roots fundraising proves the popularity of your program. Your program is your product; it is what you "sell" to everyone, members and nonmembers alike. If people give you money to run a sports program, or fight an expressway, or support the symphony, you know they support your goals. If they won't pay for it, they don't want it. This gives you a way to compare the popularity of different programs. If people support your campaign against the highway but don't contribute to the recycling center, you know which one to put first.

If contributions to a program have dropped off, it may be time to change the program or let someone else try it. For example, a civic club may be very enthusiastic about raising the money to set up a recycling center but then lose interest in running it every Saturday. It is time to turn it over to the Scouts or the local environmental club and move on to something new.

Membership Benefits

Grass roots fundraising can be a magnet to bring in new members. People are naturally more eager to join a group of people they met at a party or pot luck dinner. After they have had a chance to meet the folks they will feel more comfortable at a business meeting or an action. Everyone feels shy in a new group and afraid of being different from the old members. The more controversial your program is, the more timid potential members may be about joining unless they know a current member. The hoopla and fun of fundraising events give the new people a chance to learn who you really are in the most pleasant surroundings.

Fundraising work will deepen the commitment of the members who do it. If they go out to "sell" their club to their neighbors or local businesspeople, they must learn more about their group, its structure, and its goals. They will also be proud of the booty they bring back. Besides getting credit for their important work in supporting the organization, they must also get a bigger voice in how it is spent.

Grass roots fundraising is the most democratic way to raise money. For those of us who spend a great deal of our lives in meetings, democracy can be an irritatingly laborious way to make decisions. But it is also the fairest, the most reasonable, and the most productive way for groups to make workable, popular decisions.

The enthusiasm created by successfully raising your own budget will be reflected in all your meetings and events. You can tell the minute you walk into the room if a group has the vitality and confidence of members who raise their own money; you can see the sparkle in their eyes.

People who raise their own money will control their own organization. They can hire and fire their staff, they can expand, and they can make choices. He who pays the piper picks the tune; it may be a cliché, but it is also true.

Plan fundraisers that are fun for everyone. It is important to share good times together, to make your own fun, to sing your own songs, and to have an occasion to look forward to. The jokes, the food, the prizes at a good party build the friendships that are the glue of the organization. Even putting up posters or cleaning the gym can be fun when you do it with people you like. Throw a party for every victory, celebrate holidays, and install your new officers with a flourish. Some organizations hold birthday parties for themselves every year to bring together all their members and staff, publicize themselves to friends, and let their supporters know it is time to send in another donation. The clever entertainment and good spirits turn a potluck supper in a church basement into one of the most enjoyable, and profitable, events of the year.

Publicity Benefits

Good fundraising creates good publicity. Your event gives you many chances to tell your story to new people. If you are selling memberships in the bank lobby or shopping center, you are an ambassador for the group. When you run a hay auction you will reach all the farmers in the area; when you run a flea market in the town square you will reach all the shoppers. As you sell ads for the ad book to business executives, you are teaching the corporations about the importance of your work. So *all* of your efforts are productive. Even if you do not make a sale, you have made every person you talk to more aware of your organization.

Good publicity helps introduce you to others who would like to help. In 1975 the Runaway House in Washington, DC, gave a reception for *Washington Post* columnist Art Buchwald as "Runaway of the Year, 1943." (He had run away from home to join the navy when he was sixteen years old.) They invited society and news media stars. As a result of the good publicity and new friends they made, the Runaway House was chosen as the recipient of the profits from the 1976 annual pet show at Mrs. Ethel Kennedy's home in McLean, Virginia — a tidy $10,000.

Fundraising can also produce publicity to improve your image. The leaders of the gay community and the police department run a charity softball game each year in San Francisco. The profits go to send poor kids to summer camp and provide meals on wheels for shut-ins. More than 3,500 people come to see the game, and it always gets great press coverage. Both the gays and the cops get a better image.

A comprehensive grass roots fundraising plan produces a solid financial base, enthusiastic members, and colorful publicity. Created with care and imagination, it will get better every year and generate more money from less work.

2

How to Do It

How do you turn the dreaming into doing? Where do you start? You start with the volunteers you have, get them moving, and keep them going. Apply the physics of fundraising: take your people's potential energy—all their ideas and talents—and turn it into kinetic energy—planning events and asking for money. Then keep up the momentum. You know it takes more energy to bring a pan of water to a boil than it does to keep it boiling. The same is true with people. It takes an extra push at the beginning but gets easier once you're rolling.

The grass roots fundraiser's goal is to use the volunteers' energy most efficiently. Set high standards for yourselves so you can get the most money in the least time for your organization. Then all of the volunteers on the fundraising committee can use their time and talents to achieve the goals of the group.

GOOD FUNDRAISING IS GOOD BUSINESS

The idea behind good business practices is that you will make the most money by providing the best product most efficiently. Your product is your program—organizing ranchers against strip mining, lowering homeowners' utility rates, or keeping the art museum open. The more efficiently you sell your program, the more money you will make.

Successful grass roots fundraisers follow good business practices because they work. Unfortunately, some of the organizations opposing the exploitation of the big corporations have foolishly rejected what is good about business along with what is bad. Making money is not wrong, evil, or something to be ashamed of. Money itself is neutral — it is neither good nor bad. Only one's choices in getting and spending money have values attached. The difference between a healthy grass roots organization and a greedy multinational corporation is in how they make their choices. When people who share common values make their choices by an open, democratic vote, they are going to make moral choices about how they raise and how they spend their money.

You choose to spend your money on staff, supplies, and program to achieve the goals of the group. The more you have, the more good you can do. So you would be smart to copy those business practices that have evolved over centuries to produce the highest profits. These include preparing long-range plans, making the most money in the least time, and keeping clear records.

Maximize the Profit

One of the goals of grass roots fundraising is to make the most money in the least time. You want to make a lot of money quickly, so that the members can spend more of their time on the program, cleaning up the parks or fighting the nuclear power plant.

Always consider which fundraising events will be most economical in terms of the volunteers' time. It is much easier and quicker to ask for one $100 donation than it is to sell twenty $5 dance tickets or four hundred raffle chances for a quarter each. The time of your skilled members is your most valuable asset — don't waste it.

Respect your members' time and also respect your customers' time. If your volunteer goes to the bank and asks for $100 when she could get $1,000, it means it will take that member ten times as long to make the same $1,000. This volunteer would use her time better doing her homework to pinpoint the highest possible donation she could get from the bank. Then, when she goes to the bank and asks for $1,000 in a lump sum, she gets her $1,000 in one-tenth of the time. Also, asking for the higher figure tells the bank: 1) she's done her research on the community's resources; 2) she respects the bank; 3) she is serious about her program and serious about raising money.

It takes thorough research to calculate what will be the highest amount you can get from each giver, and it takes real courage to ask for it. Boldness pays off. The more money you can get from each meeting, the more time you will have left to prepare your testimony for the city housing committee.

Another tool to increase the profit per member hour is a detailed schedule to help you get control of your time. You can attract more workers to your fundraising program and increase each one's profits by preparing a complete timetable with specific deadlines for each stage of the project. The more efficiently you preplan and publicize the campaign, the more you can shorten the actual work time. When Bob Russell took over the Montgomery County, Indiana, United Fund, he inherited a corps of workers who usually took months to collect funds from local residents. In 1970 Bob did a brilliant precampaign promotion, including a contest for all the schoolchildren to design MUFFY (*M*ontgomery *U*nited *F*unds *F*or *Y*ou) and a kickoff parade with all the county high school bands and baton twirlers. The actual solicitation and collection of money was compressed into a fourteen-day blitz. The same corps of workers collected $84,000 in just two weeks, almost double the take from the previous year's twelve-week campaign.

Make Long-Range Plans

Serious businesspeople work systematically, set goals, and know where they are going. They make long-range plans, assume they will be in business for a long time, and try to make more money every year. You can do it, too.

The most efficient way to boost your profits is to schedule your big fundraisers so they can become annual events. Then you don't have to start from scratch every blessed year. There is no reason to reinvent the wheel every year for your big fundraiser, especially when you can make more money each year improving the wheel you have. The first time you hold an event is really training time — you are learning how to do it. Every following year you should make more money as you gain expertise.

The Women Employed Ad Book made $3,500 in its first year,

1972. In 1981 it netted $13,300. The WE leaders had ten years worth of trained volunteers and staff who were able to pinpoint the best targets, reduce costs, increase incentives, and streamline the sales procedure.

You can always find something extra to add new life to a proven winner. The Fourth and Gill Neighborhood Organization runs a street fair every summer in Knoxville, Tennessee. The fair originated in 1976 with food, music, games, events for the kids like a sack race and antique fire engine ride, and events for adults like a race around the neighborhood and voter registration. Every year the organization accumulated more experienced leaders, good ideas, and supplies. Through "trial and success" it discontinued the money losers and added money makers. By 1981 the street fair included the best music, food, and games as well as an ad book, T-shirt sales, an information booth for other agencies and organizations to publicize their work, a dunking booth for politicians, a radio van, a rummage sale, horseshoe and Ping-Pong tournaments, a bake sale, craft booths, and a raffle for a ride in a hot air balloon. The net profits were as follows: 1976, $25; 1977, $47; 1978, no fair; 1979, $126; 1980, $1,270; and 1981, $1,369.

Whether your organization is a small one that can raise all of its budget from members' dues or a very large organization with a very diversified fundraising strategy, you will make more money with less work each year when you make long-range plans. Some campaigns, like the membership drive, build on themselves since more members mean more salespeople. Others, like the street fair, literally build on their assets since every year they have more lumber, fabric, and tools to use. In either case, long-range planning makes fundraising more fun and more profitable each year.

Keep Accurate Records

Clear, complete records are the best tools to use to control your fundraising efforts and increase your profits. You will get the most renewals from this year's membership campaign if your renewal letters are compiled from last year's receipts and mailing list. You can be a better shopper and make more money if you know the expenses and profit from each part of last year's fish fry.

Clarity is desirable in all fundraising efforts; it is indispensable in your record keeping. A democratic organization must have clear records that anyone can understand. Reports that only the treasurer can decode or records written on the back of last week's agenda are confusing in the short run and lead to disaster in the long run. People invented numbers to communicate precise amounts. "It costs $15 to print 1,000 tickets" is specific and informative. "A lot of tickets don't cost much" is ambiguous and inadequate.

Your records are your recipe for future successes, so make them as precise as possible. Uncertainty causes wasteful guesswork and discouragement. It's like trying to cook with your grandmother's recipe: "Add enough milk to make liquid, stir for a little while, cook until almost golden, add some of the sauce, and cook till done." Clear reports, exact numbers, and current records will make all your fundraising more manageable. Ask for advice from veteran fundraisers, treasurers, and bookkeepers and order the books recommended in the Bibliography, Chapter 14, to help the treasurer prepare useful reports.

Find the Donor's Self-Interest

Fundraising is simply asking people to give you money to support your organization. What makes fundraising exciting is that each person gives for a different reason. The challenge is to figure out *why* they give. What do they want in return? What is their self-interest? Do they want their names in the newsletter? Do they want to be asked to join the finance committee? Or, more directly, do they want to improve neighborhood schools? There are no formulas to provide an easy answer. People are like snowflakes—each one is different. Each one will act—give—only if he or she believes there is a reason that is personally important.

MAKE IT PERSONAL

So *make* it personally important. Individualize everything as much as you can. Make each donor feel as though he or she were your most intelligent and most important supporter. If I have my choice of responding letters addressed "Dear friend," "Dear concerned American," "Dear fellow feminist," or "Dear Joan," I am going to respond to the "Dear Joan" letter.

Add a personal note whenever you send an invitation or make a call. "Will you sit at my table?" or "Can I give you a ride?" is much better than "I hope I'll see you there." The personal touch helps the shy people feel welcome and comfortable and makes everyone feel like you want him or her to become part of the group as well as give money.

Put the donors first, and you will understand more about them and why they support you. If you want to find a prospective donor's self-interest, all you really need to do is ask. Then listen. Besides learning a lot, you'll find there is nothing more flattering than sincere interest in someone's comments. Direct mail professionals tell you literally to count the number of *you*s and the number of *I*s in a letter. If the *I*s outnumber the *you*s, do it over. This is also an excellent rule when you ask for money person to person.

Asking *in person* is the best way to individualize a request for money. It is more pleasant and more profitable to discuss the program live than over the phone or in a letter. You can get a donation this year and lay a strong foundation for next year. The American Friends Service Committee does *all* of its fundraising through person-to-person visits—and they have a 100-percent renewal every year.

An extra advantage of asking in person is that the people who ask not only become better fundraisers; they usually also become better givers themselves. Since they know what it takes to ask for money, they will respond better to a fund request than someone who has never raised money. Volunteer fundraising produces more members who are both better fundraisers and better givers.

Plan for Success

A grass roots fundraiser plans a strategy with three goals: 1) Each person will feel good about his or her work. 2) Each campaign will be a success. 3) The whole organization will be stronger and more unified. The experienced fundraiser knows *nothing* happens strictly by accident. The profit, in terms of both dollars and satisfaction of the workers, has to be planned. A successful fundraiser sets goals to make measurable improvements in the group: more members, stronger committees, and better leaders.

Begin at the beginning: start raising money at the very earliest opportunity. Asking for donations at the first public meeting helps the audience realize that *someone* had to pay to print the agenda, rent the room, and make the coffee. Asking for volunteers for the fundraising committee tells people that this will be a serious campaign that will need an office, professional staff, and lots of supplies. If you are trying to get a stop sign on a dangerous corner, you may be able to win the stop sign quickly with few expenses. If your goal is to win twenty-four-hour free public transporation for senior citizens, it is going to be a long, expensive campaign. When you launch the fundraising immediately, everyone attending the first meeting knows you are serious about winning.

Actively recruit and involve everyone you can in the fundraising. Never turn down a volunteer. Use your imagination to think of a job for everyone. Senior citizens can be your official hosts and hostesses. Housebound parents can bake for the bake sale. Teenagers can put up posters, park cars, and run the checkroom. Even smaller children can help with decorations—they *like* to cut out leaves for the Harvest Moon Ball.

Each new volunteer gives you access to another family, another group of friends, new businesses, clubs, and churches. The potential of every member is multiplied by all of his or her friends and acquaintances. In the late Mayor Richard J. Daley's accounting, each city job was worth seven votes. I think each volunteer is worth more than seven new contacts. Clearly, the more volunteers you attract, the more potential givers you can reach. Professional fundraisers call this *donor acquisition,* organizers call it *building the base,* and preachers call it *evangelism.*

In addition, the volunteers themselves are more likely to give to your organization. According to a 1981 Gallup poll on volunteering, "volunteers are more likely than nonvolunteers to give monetary contributions. Ninety-one percent of all volunteers have made a charitable contribution, compared with 66 percent among nonvolunteers. The group most likely to give a charitable contribution in a particular area are those who have volunteered in that area."

Plan the Fun

Last, but certainly not least, decide to have fun while you raise the money. Plan the fun just like you plan the work. Make up your mind to have a good time, and your volunteers will be chomping at the bit to start the next project. In 1975 Lois Weisberg and Juanita Banez pulled together 125 volunteers to produce and sell a concert with Antonia Brico conducting members of the Chicago Symphony Orchestra and the women of the William Ferris Chorale. The proceeds went to Business and Professional People in the Public Interest (BPI), a Chicago public interest law firm. The fifteen-member organizing committee crowded into the tiny BPI conference room every Monday morning, did the work, and planned the fun. In three months they scheduled a brunch, a cocktail party, a champagne picnic, and a sold-out celebration luncheon, as well as forty-nine film showings. Starting from scratch to produce BPI's first special event, they sold out all 4,000 seats in the Auditorium Theatre and netted $25,000.

Most important, they decided to make many new friends for the public interest law firm, and they succeeded. They produced such an overwhelming feeling of goodwill that, like the five-minute ovation at the end of the concert, no one wanted the project to end. At the wrap-up meeting of the organizing committee, each one asked "What can we do next?" and "Who should we get for next year?"

Everybody wants to feel like a winner in a winning organization. The beauty of grass roots fundraising is that every member can improve his or her own skills and increase the budget at the same time. Each person will feel more and more self-confident, closer to the other members, and prouder of the organization as the fundraising campaign goes on.

GOOD FUNDRAISING IS GOOD MANNERS

Grass roots fundraising is volunteers asking for money to support their organization. The fundraiser's job is to arrange matters so that both the asker and the askee enjoy the experience and will want to do it again. Good manners are a basic tool to make any transaction go more smoothly.

Respect the expectations of the people you meet because everything is easier when you both play by familiar rules. Courtesy is not to be confused with hypocrisy. Courtesy is caring enough about the other person to learn how they want to be treated and then making the extra effort to act the way they expect.

Good manners are simply common sense and respect for others. Respect the time of busy people: make an appointment, be on time, get to the point, and do not stay too long. Treat other people as you would like them to treat you, and try to see things from their point of view. Address their mail correctly and, if you are not sure, take the time to look it up. Even if you think a letter to "Dr. Thomas Dooley, M.D." looks all right, Dr. Dooley knows it should be either "Thomas Dooley, M.D." or "Dr. Thomas Dooley."

A good impression may not always bring immediate results, but it will pay off in the long run. You will discover many people who are very interested in your work but have already spent this year's budget. Though they may not give money themselves, they may be willing to introduce you to other givers. If the potential donors remember you favorably as the courteous representative of an exciting project, they may contribute next year. Treat each person as an important, intelligent individual. If you slight someone even unintentionally, you are not going to be welcomed back.

Add a personal touch to your fundraising by sending prompt, individual thank-you notes. When Sally Berger and her partner called on Chicago executives to raise money for the Michael Reese Hospital Research Institute, each sent every exec a handwritten thank-you note for meeting with them. Then they each sent a handwritten thank-you note for the donation. The hospital staff also sent

---

* My favorite name blunder came in 1971 when I was selling ads for the Citizens Action Program (CAP) in Chicago. I went into a pub named Brian Boru's and arrogantly insisted on speaking to Mr. Boru. The bartender said, "That will be a little difficult, darlin'. Brian Boru was the king of Ireland who defeated the Vikings at the Battle of Clontarf in 1014. Would you perhaps rather see the manager, who is still alive?"

an official thank-you letter and receipt. Thus each donor received five thank-you notes. Sally got writer's cramp writing more than 700 notes — and increased the annual research budget from $260,000 to $1,400,000 in one year.

Be sure to thank your own workers, too. Cleveland Women Working, which organizes clerical workers in downtown Cleveland, ran a raffle as its first fundraiser and netted $950 in only three weeks. More than eighty women successfully sold raffle chances — and each got a handwritten thank-you note from the leaders.

Thank the people who do not expect to be thanked. Remember the workers who are doing their jobs but who do something extra for you. If policemen reroute the traffic, or a janitor comes in early to let you into the building, or secretaries stay late to get the mailing out, let them know, in writing, that you noticed and appreciated their work. Let their bosses know, too.

Good manners make every meeting easier for you and for the other person. Remember fundraising rule number one: people give to people. Since each transaction requires at least one meeting, make it easy on yourself and make each one a pleasure. Learn — and use — good manners and decide to enjoy every encounter. You will.

GOOD FUNDRAISING IS GOOD SELLING

All fundraising is really selling. You are selling your program — renovating Symphony Hall or preventing child abuse. There is a psychological advantage in selling the positives of the program: you get away from the feeling that you are begging. Be proud to offer an opportunity to support the most exciting program in town. Instead of saying, "Give me money because I think ecology is important," you can say, "Give me $50 and your children and 100 others can have a personal experience in learning at the bird preserve next month."

Any sales campaign begins by finding the customers for the product. Your customers include everyone who will benefit from your program. If your goal is to reduce pollution in Pittsburgh, everyone in Pittsburgh will benefit from your success, and everyone should support it. If your goal is to improve women's working conditions, your market is all women who work, as well as all people who care about women who work.

Accentuate the Positive

Always sell the program creatively and forcefully. A basic sales technique is to present any feature of the sales item as a benefit; that is, take the basic package and highlight each element as attractive and special. Copy the best sales techniques used by professional salespeople and advertisers.

Think positively. Always sell the best parts of your program and brag about your accomplishments. Never assume that everyone knows you built the playground because the story was in the newspaper. Clip the story to show them what you've done, then tell them about your new idea to build two more playgrounds and run a coordinated sports program after school.

Break down the costs of the program and tell people exactly what their money will buy. For example, the American Friends Service Committee Midwest Office's 1975 Christmas letter set out examples of what each donation could provide. They ranged from $5 to $1,000 to give an idea of the scope and variety of AFSC projects, while appealing directly to the donors:

$5 supplies sufficient yarn for sweaters for five Vietnamese children.

$9 provides a month's supplemental feeding for a child in a Santiago shantytown.

$15 enables a mother in prison to stay in touch with her children and arrange for their care.

$25 gives information and materials to a labor group wanting to know about the B-1 bomber and other military spending.

$50 provides counseling to senior citizens on Social Security income, food stamps, or Medicare.

$75 allows educators and parents to work together on teaching nonviolence or on the problems of suspensions in schools.

$120 enables an Arab and Israeli to meet for dialogue and join in a common search for better understanding.

$300 helps defray the costs of an international seminar to promote peace among nations.

$1000 gives five exoffenders room, board, and the loving counseling they need for a lasting reentry into society.

This gives the potential donor a picture of what his or her money will buy: sweaters, food, counseling. The donation seems much more important and tangible than if the AFSC had said something vague like: "Help us relieve suffering."

Always ask for a specific amount. I discovered when doing door-to-door canvassing that if I said "Any donation will help," I got contributions in the range of 25¢ to $1.50. When I asked for $10 to $25, I got an average donation of $12.50. When I said, "For a donation of $5 or more you can receive the newsletter," I got $5.

Always ask for a specific amount for a specific program; then appeal to the broader vision of the donor. For example, when you ask Father Reilly for $250 for scholarships for ten ghetto girls to take a self-defense course in their public housing project, the immediate program is the course. The intermediate goal is trained self-defense teachers to teach the rest of the women in the project to protect themselves. The ultimate goal is for every woman to be safe and confident wherever she goes and whatever she does. Tell Father Reilly that you are asking him to contribute both because he understands the immediate dangers in the housing project and because he shares the vision of a world where all can live with dignity and control their own lives.

One final note: never ask anyone to pay off your deficit or make a donation because you "need" the money. Everyone wants to back a winner. Political fundraisers have proven the importance of having their candidates seem to be the front runner in the first poll; it increases the donations. In fact, you will notice that if it is a close race, the second-place candidate will often produce his own poll to "prove" *he* is really in first place. People want to back a winner, to pay for successful programs. In politics, it is an investment which they hope will be repaid with political responsiveness when their candidate wins. If they donate to the Fairbanks Fair Tax Program, they hope their property taxes will be reduced when FFTP wins. Everyone wants to be part of a winning team, even if their part is only giving money. Sell your "most likely to succeed" program, and donors will give out of their own desire to share your success.

Be Prepared

Make the most of every opportunity. Be prepared to meet with potential donors at their convenience. If Mrs. Gotrocks is leaving for Nairobi for three months and the only time she can see you is tomorrow for breakfast at 7:30 A.M., be enthusiastic and prepared to see her at breakfast. She may be a lark who has already been up for two hours, jogged her mile, and done her paperwork, whereas you may be an owl who is a total zombie in the morning. So what? A professional will be up and ready to go. Even if you're like me and think that morning is only for farming and fishing, get up, drink coffee, run around the block, and be there — bright, alert, and *on time.* The same is true if you're a lark and have to meet Frank Sinatra after the last show at 2:30 A.M. Take a nap, stay hungry, don't drink, do whatever you have to, but be at your best when you meet him. A real professional makes the special effort to be at his or her best. Remember, you are asking *him* to do *you* a favor — to meet with you. Then you are going to ask him to commit himself to the organization with a large donation. Anyone with any money gets lots of these requests. You may get only one chance, so make the most of it.

Get control of your time. Own and use a watch and a calendar, start and end all meetings on time, and pay all your bills when due. Send your own invoices promptly. Respect the busy schedules of your volunteers and especially your donors. The best way to get more out of your time is to talk less and listen more. Read *Get Control of Your Time and Your Life,* by Allen Lakein, and ask the achievers you admire for tips.

Do your homework. Then you will be ready for any short-notice meeting. If you are to sell donors on your project, you need to know all about your organization, why it needs money, and how it spends money. It is good promotion to keep a donor informed through the year with news — especially good news: we saved the park or we got the mayor to give us permanent space in City Hall to do free blood pressure testing. While volunteer Nancy Klimley raised $900,000 for the Chicago Heart Association, she sat through lengthy (low-cholesterol) lunches with doctors, discussing their research. Each time she went out to ask for money she could explain the current status of each research project and what the Heart Association hoped to fund next.

When you know your facts and figures, practice talking about the group's work *and* asking for money. Be sure to practice both parts.

Some people can give a beautiful talk on the importance of their organization but can never bring themselves to ask for the money. Most potential donors will wait for you to ask for the money. If you don't ask, they can't respond. Don't leave it to implication — say exactly what you want.

Since that is the hardest part, practice it first and most often. Then you'll be more comfortable with "closing" — asking for the sum you want. Ask someone else to pretend to be the banker. Then the two of you can rehearse presenting your case and asking for his donation. The one playing banker should ask logical questions, and you should practice giving short answers. The banker should also try to divert you to other subjects — the state of the economy, the World Series, the renovation across the street — and you should practice gracefully returning the conversation to your topic, which is a donation for your organization. Never go in and ask for any donation without having practiced first. Alan Alda is better because he rehearses; so am I; so will you be.

A real professional always tries to get good advice. Solicit as much advice as possible. As Yuri Rasovsky, who produces original radio plays, says, "If I talk to two people, I get confused; if I talk to six or seven, I get enlightened." Your own membership is always the best place to start; ask questions and listen — you'll be surprised at how clever they are.

Don't be afraid to ask other volunteer or professional fundraisers and salespeople to brainstorm on your project. This book is the result of 800 people sharing their ideas with me. I found that the most successful people were the most generous with their time and encouragement, and I'm sure the best people in your community will be willing to help you.

Conquer Fear

Money is like sex. Everyone thinks about it, but no one is supposed to discuss it in polite company. Everyone has a lot of inhibitions about money, especially asking for money; think of all the cartoons of the office worker afraid to ask for a raise. In our society fears about money are *normal*.

Most people are afraid to ask someone else for money. They are afraid they will fail and afraid they will lose face. A few admit they are afraid, but most give other excuses: I can't make calls at the office; I don't know anyone rich; I can't get a baby-sitter. Or they postpone forever: I can't do it until after the kids are back in school, the holidays, the election. Volunteers often make asking for money sound like a bothersome chore, like taking out the garbage. It is not a chore; it is a challenge. Asking for money is like going out to beat up a bear. The larger the amount, the more frightening it becomes, because you have to beat up a bigger bear.

The job of a good fundraiser is to teach volunteers how to conquer their fear of the unknown. The first step is understanding that each person comes complete with his or her own set of fears and hang-ups, and the package of inhibitions usually includes a fear of asking for money. The second step is realizing this is normal and nothing to be ashamed of. The third step is working with the volunteers so they can get control of their own fears.

You must understand and appreciate your volunteers' real feelings, because when members succeed at fundraising they do more than bring in money for the organization. They have also overcome their own fear. When they raise money they have won a personal victory; they have conquered the bear. When people can raise money they can do anything.

WHY PEOPLE GIVE

Asking for money is actually a common transaction that happens all the time. Each of us is asked for money much more often than we ask others. Just think of how many fund appeals you get in the mail every day. How many do you send? We have all been in touch with fundraising since the days we carried our dime dues to Scouts or saved our allowance for junk food and death-defying rides at the county fair and the parish carnival.

To get over the feeling that fundraising is intimidating, make it familiar to each member. First ask everyone to think about why they themselves give. Have them write down on paper every contribution they remember, who asked for it, and why they gave. Cover everything: the Girl Scout cookies from your niece, your dues to the block club, the T-shirt from your alderman, the bumper sticker from the high school football team, the tickets to the firemen's ball. Figure out why you gave to each one. Most of the time, you give for one of two reasons. Either someone is selling a product you want anyway, or it is in your own self-interest to give. Once you understand why you give to people, you will understand why others will want to give to you.

For example, the easiest way to raise money is to sell a product people want to buy anyway. For example, what happened when you bought your niece's Girl Scout cookies? She was happy; it pleased her parents; it helped her troop; it reminded you of the fun you had as a Scout; and you got all those tasty cookies. When you sell something people want to buy, they too will get good feelings as well as a good product.

The other impulse is contributing to something that will clearly pay off in your own interest. When you bought the tickets to the firemen's ball, you not only had fun at the ball; you also knew you were supporting your volunteer fire department, which you want to be well prepared if you ever need it. A lively grass roots program provides something that is just as much in the citizens' self-interest — more power to influence the government, or decent housing, or innovative arts.

While buying something like the cookies gives you a product you want, contributing to a cause in your self-interest gives you a program you want: a better block club, halfway house, or museum. Either way you are making an investment to please yourself. The seller is neither begging nor bullying. He or she is simply giving others an opportunity to get what they want. Just as people look forward to getting a good product each year, like Girl Scout cookies or UNICEF Christmas cards, they will look forward to getting the good news about your program.

Fear is very expensive. Remember Flanagan's Fear Formula:

> Fear is the parent of procrastination.
> Procrastination is the thief of time.
> Time is money.

Fear causes inertia, which causes low morale and low income. The biggest fear of taking any new action — whether it is selling the cover of the ad book to the bank president or leading 200 people to confront the mayor — is the fear of losing face. This is why most people would rather be followers than leaders. They think, "How can I volunteer to sell the bank president? If I fail, everyone will know. I'll feel like a fool."

STRATEGY FOR SUCCESS

Get together in a group before and after each major sales effort. Frankly discuss the work, share the funny stories, applaud the successes, and cooperate on the hard cases. Remember, fundraising is always more imposing for the new members, so give them an extra boost. Even Jesus sent the Apostles out in pairs when they were starting their mission (Mark 6:7). Pair a new volunteer with a veteran and give them a sure-sell ad to renew from last year. Build on success. Let them sell a $20 ad to the hot dog stand and a $100 ad to the funeral home before you send them to the savings and loan for a $500 ad. Prepare attractive sales kits and give simple instructions. Above all, plan enough time so you can be available to answer questions, give advice, and listen.

To take control of fear, make it concrete. If you just let it spin around in your head, all you think about is the fear and not its consequences. Put it on paper and put down what you stand to lose and what you stand to gain. If you fail, you don't get the donation. However, you still get 1) experience, 2) the knowledge that you were brave enough to try, and 3) an introduction to make it easier next time.

Focus on your strategy rather than on your fear. Instead of sitting home being afraid, get out and do some research. Find out everything you can and use it to succeed. Maybe you will find out that the bank president is a graduate of the University of North Carolina. Then you can invite your group's treasurer, who just happens to be a former Tarheel football hero, to go with you. When you go in well backgrounded, you will feel more confident and give a better presentation.

Divide the difficulties instead of taking them all at once. First decide to call today to make the appointment. Tomorrow you can send a confirming letter with clippings about your group. The next day go to the library and do some research on the bank president. Then practice your sales pitch. If you lay out a schedule to make each part manageable, then you will have your homework finished and feel more secure when you do meet to make your pitch.

See if you can find some allies to put in a good word for you. If you know the bank president is unfamiliar with your group or uncertain about your goals, seek support from someone you know he respects. Ask the pastor of the biggest church or the most popular local politician to write a letter recommending you.

As a last resort, take the situation and turn it around. Think what will happen if you *don't* call to make the appointment. First, you are 100-percent guaranteed you won't make the sale. What's more, Frank is an usher at the bank president's church and may ask him if he has talked to you when they usher on Sunday. Soon everyone will know you never called. So it turns out the only way to really lose face is by being afraid to take a chance!

Reward Your Fundraisers

The whole organization should understand and appreciate the achievements of the fundraisers. Successful fundraising takes intelligence, concern, hard work, and courage. Fundraisers deserve a lot of applause and appreciation!

Reward each person who succeeds in raising money. In the business world the payoff is high salaries and special rewards like trips to Europe for the top salespeople. Maybe you can't offer that, but that's not what your people are working for, anyway. Spotlight the top fundraisers in your organization. Offer them public recognition. The Broadmoor Improvement Association in New Orleans puts the names of the ad sellers in its ad book for the annual Home Improvement Show. Women Organized for Employment in San Francisco gives its top salespeople flowers and applause at the theatre party where the ad book is distributed. Wilmington United Neighborhoods (WUN) in Delaware calls the top salesperson up to the stage at its annual convention to receive a framed certificate of appreciation in front of 600 delegates.

The thank-you note is the most important fundraising tool. Give the stars of your fundraising campaigns public recognition, but give *everyone* private recognition. Any volunteer who sells one membership deserves a thank-you note from the chair of the membership committee and the president. If you are president this year and want to win the hearts of your followers, send thank-you notes every day. If you want to be president next year, send thank-you notes every chance you get. It makes a bigger impression than you think, and people never forget getting a personal note from a busy person.

It is no small achievement to raise money. It requires overcoming deep fears and inhibitions about money, belief in the organization, and an appreciation of human values. Money is the oxygen of the organization's actions — it keeps the group moving. Fundraisers are vital to the life of the organization and must be appreciated and applauded to keep the group alive and growing every year.

ETHICS

The values of the members form the foundation of the organization; shake their faith, and the entire organization will crumble. An honest grass roots fundraising campaign must be run with standards of behavior built on the members' values. Being clear about your standards is critical to building a long-term trusting relationship between the people who give money and the members who spend it.

Your first responsibility is to see that you are raising money for an honest, ethical organization. This means one that has open access for any person who wants to join; open, democratic decision making; clear, complete, up-to-date reports; frequent reporting to all representatives; and sensible financial controls. An ethical organization makes sure that the people who raise the money have a say in how it is spent. Think of the photo of the president of the "Women's Board" presenting a check to the male president of the "Board of Directors" so the all-male board can decide how to spend the money. If volunteers are asked to raise money, but are denied a voice in spending it, that is simple exploitation. Never waste your talents on any group that will not allow you to help prepare the budget and vote on expenditures. If the staff or entrenched leadership refuses you access to the decision making, the real action, join a different group. There is simply no way you can honestly ask people to give money to support an organization that wants their money but not their ideas.

Be sure the board that runs the organization is democratically elected and representative of the members. A grass roots fundraiser respects the integrity of the members. Put your own people first. If you have a group of welfare mothers who want to build an after-school center for your kids, never deny one of your own members a place on the board so you can include the wife of the bank president. Although you must be pragmatic about the self-interest of the rich and powerful people, do not fall into the lure of finding the "right people" to "do it for you." It is immature to depend on even well-intentioned people outside the organization, and it is unethical to let anyone who does not have a real following in the membership make decisions for the group.

Your standards must include a genuine curiosity and concern about all the people involved. Consciously work to treat each person as an individual. Stereotypes are confusing, unprofitable, and often just wrong. It is a common mistake to exclude or ignore people as volunteers or donors because they have been labeled. We all do it. She won't help because she's "a limousine liberal" or "a suburban socialite" or "not a feminist." He won't give to us because he's "a rockbed Republican" or "a male chauvinist" or "a culture vulture." It's unfair for you to make someone else's decision by not asking for help because of your own stereotypes. It is also 100-percent unprofitable. Include everyone; you will be pleasantly surprised at the number and variety of allies you really have.

Set your own standards and be accountable to your own membership. Make specific, clear, and public criteria for donors that feel comfortable to the whole group. The Chicago NOW chapter sold the centerfold of its 1973 ad book to *Playboy* because it would be a humorous turnabout and the group would use the money well to fight for women's rights in Chicago. That was all right with the majority of the membership. On the other hand, Women Employed's ad book committee voted to refuse ads from any employment agency they knew exploited women. WE decided that making a clear distinction between the good agencies and the bad agencies was more important than collecting the money.

No one else can set your standards for you. Each group decides for itself what is proper. For example, Roman Catholics raise money from Las Vegas nights, liquor, and lasagna. Episcopalians think the gambling is wrong but will sell mulled wine next to the bratwurst booth. Methodists abstain from bingo and booze but sponsor lavish dinners. What you decide is less important than *how* you decide. The board must openly and democratically vote on where to draw the line, based on public organizational policy. It is better to return a donation than to lose members because it offends their values.

Never accept or pursue a donation that would restrict the choices of the organization. It is a common tactic of industry to try to buy off trouble before it arrives. Business people know when they're guilty, and they know you're smart enough to find out when they're guilty, too. They also know bribery has worked with other groups, and they may hope it will work with you.

Does this mean you can never accept money from the "enemy"? Again, this has to be decided openly and democratically by the leaders before the campaign. When the Citizens Action Program did its first ad book in Chicago, Co-Chair Father Leonard Dubi sold a full-page ad to Valentine Janicki, colorful trustee of the scandal-ridden Metropolitan Sanitary District and proprietor of a religious novelties store. Dubi was completely clear that CAP would continue its campaign to force the Sanitary District to stop polluting the southwest side of Chicago. CAP took Janicki's money, continued the campaign, and won without breaking stride.

Blackmail is the other side of bribery. It is just as wrong to tell a polluter your group will ignore his polluting plant if he agrees to make a big donation as it is to accept his bribe to leave him alone. If you choose to take money from a person or corporation you are attacking, make sure you both understand this donation will in no way affect your adversary relationship.

Ask for a written agreement of what the donor will do and what your organization will do to protect both sides. The best protection is a diversified fundraising strategy that raises money from your own members, other individuals, businesses, and churches. Independence comes from diversity in fundraising. If you control your own income from many sources, no one donor will be able to influence your decisions unfairly.

Each year the board of directors will plan the organization's program, budget, and fundraising strategy. Most of the planning for the fundraising strategy will focus on where you want to go to ask for money. After you make your choices of where to ask for money, decide if there are any specific places the board and members should not go to ask for money. This may be specific individuals, companies, institutions, or government agencies. Make your list, vote on it, then return to the positive side of your strategy. Say, "Here is the 1 percent we will not ask for money. Now let's look at the other 99 percent that we *will* ask for money."

You want to send your volunteers out thinking positively about their opportunities for getting money. Ask each member of the board to take a personal quota and to begin selling memberships or asking for donations the next day. That way you will focus their energies on what they *can* do rather than on what they *will not* do. The weakest members will want to dwell on where you should not ask for money; the strongest leaders will point out where you can ask for money, then go and ask. Keep the discussion of where you will not ask as short as possible and sandwich it between positive discussions of where you *will* ask for money.

The goal of grass roots fundraising is to build an adult, self-sufficient organization. A mature organization is like a mature person. It has learned to set its own standards, it respects the integrity of its own members and the individuality of those outside the organization, and it is proud of its own principles.

3

Who Can Do It?

Grass roots fundraising is do-it-yourself fundraising using the talents of your own people. If you are starting a new group, simply begin asking for money at every meeting. This will cover your expenses and show everyone at the meeting that you are serious about starting a group that will get results. As soon as possible, choose a structure, write bylaws, and create a way for the people who benefit from the group to pay money to the group every year. The most popular methods are dues and pledges, described in Chapter 4. Ask for donations at first; then sell memberships as soon as the group is incorporated. The people who raise the most money will naturally rise to the top as they show their leadership abilities, their commitment to the organization, and their convictions about the cause.

If you are starting a term of office as the leader of an older organization that has done a little grass roots fundraising in the past and now wants to do more, schedule one board meeting to evaluate your current fundraising strategy. Look at what works best and what your own members like the most. Ask every member of the board to come to the meeting with suggestions from their other organizations or from other local groups. Continue what you do best; then test new ideas that your leaders want to try.

31

STARTING IN THE MIDDLE

The most difficult way to launch a grass roots fundraising campaign is with leaders who have served on the board of an organization that was able to get all its budget from outsiders in the past. Since many organizations were begun in the '70s on foundation and government grants, many boards exist today that are really advisory boards. They have never planned a program, made a budget, designed a fundraising strategy, or asked for money. Because of this, they also have no power. The bylaws or the government regulations may *say* they have power, but in real life it is the people who raise the money and pay the bills who have the power.

If your organization has depended on grants in the past, but you would like to raise your own budget now so you can control your own organization, choose a bolder program, hire (or fire) paid staff, recruit more members, and get more accomplished, you can begin to teach the board how to do grass roots fundraising. It will probably take you from three to five years to switch from outside funding to your own internally controlled income, but you can do it if you want to.

First, ask the board of directors to set aside at least four meetings to plan the next year's work, especially the fundraising. If you want to have long discussions, it may take longer than this. The top officers can discuss their own plans before the board meeting so they are ready to offer some choices for the rest of the group.

At the first meeting, discuss the mission of the organization and your program goals for the next year. Most groups find it very helpful to write down their mission in one sentence, called their *mission statement* or *statement of purpose*. This helps the board agree on the purpose of the organization. Next discuss the programs for the next year. For a very large organization you may ask the chairperson for each program to bring in his or her own program goals. Review what has been the most effective in the past; what, if anything, you want to eliminate or give away; what to continue; and what, if anything, you want to start new. This meeting will produce an agreement on what you are doing, the mission statement, and how you intend to get results, the program goals. At the end of the meeting, ask the president, treasurer, committee chairs, and staff to prepare a budget for the next meeting.

The second meeting looks at the budget for the planned programs. This is your "shopping list" of what you need to buy to accomplish your goals. If you hire paid staff, the biggest item on your shopping list will be salaries, taxes, fringe benefits, and staff expenses. If you do not hire paid staff, your largest items will be rent, printing, telephone, insurance, and postage. Once the board has the estimates for expenses for next year, add 10 percent for everything you cannot anticipate; then add 10 percent more for inflation. Depending on the total, you may decide to add to or subtract from your shopping list. This meeting will produce an agreement on what it is going to cost to run the programs you want next year. At the end of the meeting, ask the president, treasurer, committee chairs, and staff to make up a fundraising strategy for the next year.

At the third meeting the board will adopt a fundraising strategy and take personal quotas to do the work. The strategy will show everyone where the money will come from. The personal quotas will guarantee that the board chooses a strategy that it intends to accomplish. For example, the board could say it will meet its budget next year with 50-percent foundation funds, 25 percent memberships, 10-percent corporate donations, and 15-percent special events. Each person will then make a commitment for his or her fair share of the budget. If your budget is $40,000 and you have eight people on your board, each one needs to raise or motivate other people to raise $5,000. If you assign paid staff to write proposals to raise the 50 percent from foundations, or $20,000, this leaves $20,000 for the board to raise. Then each person's quota is only $2,500. Before the end of the meeting, each person must commit himself or herself to raise that much money or something worth that much money. For example, if you budgeted $2,000 for your audit, and the treasurer persuades a local accounting firm to do your audit for free, then he can count $2,000 toward his quota.

At the fourth meeting, extend your plan over the next five years. Of course, this work will not come out exactly the way you plan it, but it will make your work easier if you know where you are going.

For example, the board could say that it wants to double the budget and eliminate dependence on grants in the next five years. So its plan could look like this:

Source of Money	1982	1983	1984	1985	1986
Grants	$20,000	$15,000	$10,000	$ 5,000	0
Dues	10,000	20,000	30,000	40,000	50,000
Corporate Donations	4,000	6,000	8,000	10,000	12,000
Special Events	6,000	7,000	8,000	9,000	10,000
Major Donors	0	0	2,000	4,000	8,000
Total	$40,000	$48,000	$58,000	$68,000	$80,000

This plan will help the board use its energies to make the most money in the least amount of time, especially if accurate records are kept so it can build on each year's plan results. See Chapter 13, "Fundraising Forever," for examples of a five-year projection for a small and a large organization.

ENSURING SUCCESS

If the people on your board have never raised money, they may try to avoid the job. They can postpone, make excuses, or, if there is a paid staff, try to delegate the job to staff members. If you are the leader who wants the board to begin fundraising, and succeed, you have to get them started in a way that will guarantee their success.

Veterans of other organizations that have moved from grant dependency to self-sufficiency say that it can be done in three to five years if the board wants to do it. So the first step is convincing the board that it is a good idea. Here are some hints on how to make the board want to try asking for money for the first time. After they experience success it will be easier to put together a one-year and a five-year plan to meet your goals.

First, choose events and fundraising techniques the board members *like* to do. Let them plan a special event or a membership drive and do it their way. If they plan it, it will succeed. Expert Jane Beckett observed this with the Rogers Park chapter of CAP on the northeast side of Chicago. They did plant sales that involved lots of hard, dirty work digging up and selling plants. But it was their idea, so they *liked* it. The sales succeeded and the fundraisers felt great about their work. If the majority of the board members want to do a fundraiser, let them do it, even if it seems like a lot of work to you. It *will* succeed.

Second, make it fun. You can take any job and make it fun if you want to. Successful walkathons use "billing parties" to send out all the bills after their annual walkathon. Because they are called parties, organized by creative people, and offer plenty of refreshments, they *are* fun and attract a lot of volunteers. Make your work fun, be enthusiastic about the activities, and your leaders will learn to like the work.

Third, point out that one of the big advantages of grass roots fundraising is that it can give you a quick "win." If your people meet their goals, they have an accomplishment to be proud of. Especially if your organization is involved in a prolonged action campaign or lengthy litigation, it is a great lift to do fundraising and organize a campaign that works and *ends!*

Fourth, realize that fundraising is a life habit for many people. According to a 1981 Gallup poll on volunteering commissioned by the Independent Sector, 52 percent of Americans volunteer in some way. Your own people already know about weekly contributions or pledges through their church; they know about dues from their union, professional association, neighborhood association, or club; they know about special events from other organizations. They have already learned skills that are transferable to your organization. Just ask them to start discussing their experiences in fundraising, and you will be excited by the pool of expertise you already have on the board. Best of all, try to find some senior citizens to give you advice. Then when someone whines that you can't raise money because the economy is bad, the senior can say, "Sure you can. Here's what we did during the Depression, which was much worse than this!"

Fifth, earmark the first fundraising campaign funds for *something the board wants*. Several groups have begun grass roots fundraising because they wanted to run ads on a particular issue in the newspaper. They were not allowed to use grant funds for advertisements, so they decided to raise their own money to run the ads. They were pleasantly surprised when they discovered how easy it was, so they went on to raise more money for the group!

Even if your board has never raised any money in the past, you can begin to raise money now. Decide you want to succeed at fundraising, make a plan, then ask for money. You too will be delighted at the difference it will make in your group.

WHO DOES WHAT?

Every organization works better if there is a clear plan stating who will do what for the group. If you are a small group, you can divide the fundraising tasks among the officers, the leaders, and any enthusiastic volunteers. If you are a larger group, you can set up more committees and assign certain work to the paid staff. Ask local organizations that do successful grass roots fundraising how they divide the work. Then make your own plan, try it out, and change it when you get better ideas. See the sample work plans for a small group without staff and a large group with staff at the end of this chapter.

SHOULD THE STAFF ASK FOR MONEY?

Power in any organization goes to the people who raise the money. For this reason, most groups recommend that the board of directors and the members raise the money, rather than paid staff. If the board raises the money, it can hire and fire the staff and can control the plans of the organization. When you start, you may want your staff to accompany you to give you support when you ask for money. But as soon as possible, the board can take over raising money and let the staff members do what they are paid to do.

Anyone who wants the organization to succeed can raise money. As organizer Heather Booth says, "If you don't have Scotch tape on your mouth, you can raise money." If you have the courage of your convictions, you can raise money. Why *pay* a staff person to ask for money when you can do it yourselves? Why not pay the staff to do work to accomplish the goals of the organization?

If the board does the asking, what can the paid staff members do? They can prepare the fundraising materials such as brochures, letters, and sales packages; they can do the record keeping; and they can train the leaders. Unlike writing grant proposals, successful grass roots fundraising is a team sport. You depend on a volume business and personal relationships to raise money, so you need to motivate as many leaders as possible to start asking for money. Local leaders are more effective at getting donations and memberships than a paid staff person, so the job of the staff is to encourage the leaders to ask for money and then keep them going when they get discouraged.

It is *much* more difficult to train someone else than to do it yourself. The best staff will tackle the more difficult job of training the leadership to ask for money. When they succeed, the organization will succeed, this year and every year in the future. Football coach Amos Alonzo Stagg, who won 314 games, used to say, "No coach ever won a game by what he knows; it's what his players have learned." Assign your paid staff to coach the board and other leaders until they are star fundraisers.

CAN WE PAY VOLUNTEERS?

There is nothing more persuasive than a volunteer asking for money because he or she believes in the organization. According to the Small Business Administration, the average cost for an in-person industrial sales call is $75 to $100. If that is what it costs for-profit businesses to sell person to person, that is what your volunteers are worth when they go out to sell the organization. The best way I've found to close a sale is to say, "I'm giving my time to this organization; all I want from you is money." It is much harder to say no to a volunteer, so the most profitable way to raise money is to use all volunteers. You will make the most money when all your fundraisers are unpaid volunteers.

Most groups will not give the volunteers money, but will give them something else they want. For example, if you volunteer to run the cloakroom at the opera, you get to see the show for free; if you volunteer to be a guide at the art museum, you get to see the exhibit for free. Fundraising volunteers get special advantages and a successful organization.

Some groups choose to compensate volunteers who miss a special event. For example, if you handle child care at a concert, you miss the performance, so you are given a free ticket to the next concert.

The choice for the organization is to ask for volunteers and give them tickets to the next event or hire outsiders so all of the insiders can enjoy the concert. In either case, the value of the tickets or the cost of the child care workers is an expense to the organization.

Some groups want to hire their own members to do fundraising. Several groups have hired unemployed members to sell ads in the ad book to corporations. Especially if all your members work at full-time daytime jobs, it can be difficult to sell to the right person at the corporation. Hiring an out-of-work member to cover corporate sales provides an excellent part-time job for the member and enables the organization to sell many more ads to corporations. Then your other members can focus on selling to their own friends, neighborhood businesses, churches, and other organizations.

If you do hire a member to sell ads or do other fundraising, be sure that he or she is then recognized as a member of the paid staff and *not* as a volunteer who is getting paid, or else the other volunteers will resent what looks like unfair treatment. Depending on the structure of your organization, you may require the person to resign from any elected role on the board or committee, then turn over that office to a new volunteer and serve exclusively as an employee during the time he or she has the job.

Although some kinds of organizations, such as labor unions, have a tradition of paid leadership, for most volunteer organizations it is a bad idea to let one person serve as a paid employee and as an elected leader at the same time. Your organization will benefit from greater clarity, more enthusiastic leaders, and more accountable staff if you keep a clear division of labor between the leaders and the staff members.

DO IT NOW!

The way to get started is to start *now*. Simply decide that you will start your programs and ask for the money you need to run them. You will get money as soon as you start asking for it. As the program grows, so will the number of people who want it enough to raise money for it. The more you do, the more effective your fundraising will become.

Even if you start small, if you have the courage of your convictions and a worthy cause, you will be able to raise the money you need. In 1975 *Chicago Tribune* journalist Vernon Jarrett interviewed "The Forgotten Heroes of the Montgomery Bus Boycott" of 1955. One heroine was Mrs. Georgia Gilmore, who helped raise enough money to run free car pools for 40,000 blacks for 381 days until they won the desegregation of the city's bus system. Here is an excerpt:

> The financial contributions of Mrs. Gilmore and her fundraisers represented much more than the actual cash they contributed each week, according to Dr. Benjamin J. Simms, sixty-two, a retired college professor, who once masterminded the boycott's free transportation system.
>
> "This fine woman and her team represented the grass roots type of support and enthusiasm that launched the boycott and kept it moving to the very end," he explained when we neared her new home on Montgomery's east side.
>
> Early in the boycott Mrs. Gilmore and several of her friends put their heads together and tried to figure out what they could contribute immediately — "what we could do best." All agreed they were experienced cooks.
>
> "Right then we collected $14 from among ourselves and bought some chickens, bread, and lettuce, started cooking and made up a bundle of sandwiches for the big rally.
>
> "We had a lot of our club members who were hard-pressed and couldn't give more than a quarter or half-dollar, but all knew how to raise money. We started selling sandwiches and went from there to selling full dinners in our neighborhoods, and we'd bake pies and cakes for people.
>
> "When we'd raise as much as $300 for a Monday night rally, then we knew we were on our way for $500 on Thursday night. Then other ordinary folks like us started doing the same thing in their neighborhoods — competing with us, trying to raise more than us."*

Small personal contributions also launched the National Organization for Women (NOW). In June of 1966 a dozen state

---

* Vernon Jarrett, *The Forgotten Heroes of the Montgomery Bus Boycott* (Chicago: DuSable Museum of African American History, 1975), p. 9.

leaders silenced at a federally sponsored conference decided to start
what Betty Friedan called "something so radical as an independent
organization." They each contributed $5 to cover mailings to plan
the organizing conference three months later. By October of 1966
they had 300 members and officially announced the creation of
NOW. By October of 1981 NOW had 200,000 members and an annual budget of $5 million raised from dues, donations, and sales.

Begin today with the skills and resources of your own leadership.
You can learn to be a great fundraiser only by asking for money, so
start asking right away. Then the board can analyze what works
best in your community and what it wants to do for the next year.
You will be on your way to making your organization powerful,
independent, and self-sufficient.

WORK PLANS

All leaders do a better job if they know what they are expected to
do and what the other volunteers will do at the same time. Here are
two sample work plans for the officers of a small group without staff
and a large group with staff. Your own leaders and staff can use this
to make their own work plans. Make a list of these and other tasks
that need to be accomplished over the year for the organization;
then decide who can do them best.

Neither of these plans allocates work to a vice-president, so you
could rearrange the tasks to give some of the jobs to one or more
vice-presidents, if you prefer. Or you could add more committees, if
you want to make more opportunities for leadership development.
This is only a sample to use to begin your own plan.

Sample Division of Labor: Small Volunteer Group

OFFICERS AND MEMBERS OF THE BOARD OF DIRECTORS:

1. Plan programs.
2. Make budget.
3. Make fundraising strategy.
4. Give money first.

5. Sell memberships and ask for money.
6. Review and revise budget and fundraising strategy every three months.

PRESIDENT:

1. Leads fundraising.
2. Asks for money first and most often.
3. Recruits and inspires other fundraisers.
4. Can cosign checks.

TREASURER:

1. Prepares monthly report on income and expenses.
2. Prepares quarterly comparison of income and expenses to budget.
3. Prepares annual reports for the Internal Revenue Service and state regulatory agencies with the help of a volunteer CPA.
4. Supervises annual audit.
5. Serves as liaison with bank and investment institutions.
6. Pays bills.
7. Deposits money.
8. Maintains journals, ledgers, and files.
9. Maintains petty cash.
10. Can cosign checks.

(*Note:* Another officer should reconcile the bank statement.)

SECRETARY:

1. Takes minutes at meetings.
2. Maintains mailing lists. Recruits and trains mailing committee.
3. Maintains donor cards.
4. Maintains files, including corporate records, correspondence, historical samples, and fundraising records.
5. Serves as liaison with post office.
6. Can cosign checks.

Sample Division of Labor:
Large Organization with Paid Staff Members

OFFICERS AND MEMBERS OF THE BOARD OF DIRECTORS:

1. Plan program.
2. Make budget.
3. Make fundraising strategy.
4. Take personal quotas.
5. Give money to the organization.
6. Ask for money from individuals, businesses, churches, and others.
7. Review and revise budget and fundraising strategy every three months.
8. Evaluate program, budget, and fundraising once a year.

IF YOU HIRE PAID STAFF, THE BOARD WILL:

1. Hire and train the staff.
2. Supervise the staff. Assign as needed to achieve your goals.
3. Evaluate the staff once a year.

PRESIDENT:

1. Recruits and inspires people for the board of directors.
2. Sets pace for fundraisings — sells first and most.
3. Leads major donor campaign.
4. Leads corporate campaign.
5. Can cosign checks.

TREASURER:

1. Prepares monthly reports on income and expenses for board meetings.
2. Prepares quarterly reports comparing income and expenses to the budget for finance meetings.
3. Supervises annual audit.
4. Prepares annual reports for the Internal Revenue Service and state regulatory agencies with the help of volunteer CPA.
5. Liaison with bank and investment institutions.
6. Can cosign checks.

TREASURER MAY DO THE FOLLOWING JOBS
OR MAY SUPERVISE AN ASSISTANT TREASURER OR A PAID BOOKKEEPER:

1. Pay bills and write checks.
2. Calculate and write payroll checks and deductions. Deposit all payroll taxes on time.
3. Make deposits.
4. Maintain journals and ledgers.
5. Maintain petty cash system.

(*Note:* Another officer should reconcile the bank statements.)

SECRETARY:

1. Takes minutes at meetings.
2. Maintains files of corporate records, correspondence, historical samples, and fundraising records.
3. Maintains donor cards.
4. Maintains special lists other than members or subscribers, such as the board of directors or district politicians.
5. Serves as liaison with post office.
6. Serves as liaison with other organizations.
7. Can cosign checks.

MEMBERSHIP COMMITTEE CHAIR:

1. Leads membership campaign.
2. Recruits and inspires membership committee.
3. Prepares membership brochure and other materials.
4. Organizes annual membership drive and year-round sales at meetings, parties, and actions.
5. Puts on victory celebration after annual membership drive.
6. Sponsors "just fun" events for new members, such as summer picnic and winter potluck supper.
7. Maintains inventory and keeps records of membership supplies.
8. Organizes salespeople to sell membership supplies such as T-shirts, hats, bumper stickers.
9. Recruits and trains committee to handle renewals.

PUBLICITY CHAIR:

1. Recruits and inspires publicity committee.
2. Places leadership on radio and TV and in newspaper and magazine features.
3. Serves as liaison with working press.
4. Maintains list of local, state, and national working press.
5. Maintains current file of résumés and black-and-white photos of officers and speakers bureau volunteer.
6. Maintains file of clippings about organization from newspapers and magazines and tapes of radio and TV shows.

THE PUBLICITY COMMITTEE MAY HANDLE THE FOLLOWING JOBS
OR MAY START SEPARATE COMMITTEES:

1. Newsletter — Publish and mail newsletter. Maintain list of subscribers who are not members.
2. Speakers bureau — Sell leaders to speak in public.
3. Slide show — Create and rent slide show.

CO-CHAIRS FOR FUNDRAISING CAMPAIGN, SUCH AS MAJOR DONORS,
OR SPECIAL EVENT, SUCH AS ART AUCTION

1. Plan campaign or event; divide the tasks.
2. Recruit and inspire volunteers.
3. Chair committee meeting to plan campaign or event, make timetable, divide work, and set deadlines.
4. Train and support new volunteers; encourage and improve veteran volunteers.
5. Chair meetings to make decisions and do work.
6. Prepare written records of campaign or event.
7. Send thank-you notes to all workers, donors, and volunteers.

PAID STAFF:

1. Help with record keeping and list maintenance.
2. Help produce materials for fundraising campaigns.

3. Train leaders and members to ask for money.
4. Do work to enable the organization to achieve its goals.

Note that paid staff members should not:

1. Serve on the board.
2. Sign checks.
3. Take a major role in asking for money. If they are good fundraisers, they can train the leaders to ask for money.

4

Raising Money from Members:

Who Needs What You Do?

Getting money from the people who need your organization is the foundation of all grass roots fundraising. It is the most dependable, renewable, and democratic way to raise money for your group. The most popular way to get money from the people who want your group is to ask them to pay dues. Dues are a set amount per year paid by each member to support the organization. There are also other proven techniques you can use to raise money from the people who need your group. One of the best is pledges, which is a system to get larger amounts of money from members by asking them to pay more often. Even the poorest member can give you 25¢ a week; in a year that pledge will amount to $13. You can also ask your members to pay for the goods and services they use from the organization. This is the fairest way to raise money for your work; the people who get the benefits pay a fee.

WHAT IS A MEMBER?

For the purposes of this book, *members* are those who need your organization and who give their time and talent in addition to their money. Some organizations call anyone who gives them money a member, even though the vast majority of them never *do* anything for the organization except make a contribution. For your own planning, the board must be clear about what is a member.

For clarity, I call the people who give you time and money members. These are the people who need what your organization does, so you know you can depend on them to show up when you need them. Other people will give you money because they like the idea of your goals, but they will not give you their time. In the next chapter we will discuss all the ways you can get money from people who believe in your goals. But first you need to find the people who need your program and ask them to join your group.

WHO NEEDS US?

Begin by asking yourselves, "Who needs us?" The people who are already getting the benefit of your program are the people who need you. If you are just planning a program, selling memberships will tell you precisely who needs this program and who does not. If your program has been going for some time and you already have members who pay dues, you know who needs you now. You can find more people like them to increase your membership sales and renewals. If your organization has never asked anyone to pay dues because you had some sort of third-party payment, such as foundation or government grants, then you have the most to gain when you begin asking your own people to pay for the programs.

The answer to the question "Who needs us?" will depend on the purpose of the organization. For example, for a day care center the people who need the center are the children, their parents, and the employers of the parents who are able to work because of the day care center. These people get the most obvious benefits, so they are the easiest places to start selling memberships. But there are many other people who also benefit because the day care center is in your community, and these people may also be eager to join the group. These would include the other relatives of the children — grandparents, aunts, uncles, older brothers and sisters, and godparents; people who make money from the center — the employees, the suppliers, the bank that has their account, and the landlord of their building; and other educators in the local elementary and secondary schools who will get the benefits of children who are easier to teach because they attended the day care center. If your center has been operating long enough, be sure to ask your alumni who are now grown up to be members; they *certainly* know why you are needed in your community! Last are the people who simply like the idea of a day care center: clergy, politicians, feminists, or other working parents. These people may not buy memberships, but they can certainly be asked for donations. The active members can do the asking.

After the board discusses who needs your program, set aside one meeting to talk about the advantages of dues and to set the amount of dues. If your organization already has dues, discuss again why they benefit the organization and consider whether or not it is time to raise the dues. If you have not raised your dues in the last two years, they are worth about 25 percent less than two years ago. Go through the same steps a new group would use to set dues, and see if it might be better to raise the amount you ask.

ADVANTAGES OF DUES

Dues are the most popular way of raising money for volunteer organizations because they produce dependable income that will build the organization at the same time that it pays for your program. Ask the people on your board or fundraising committee to make a list of every other organization to which they pay dues to be members. Then ask them to list the amount they pay each group, and how much time they give each group. You will probably discover that the groups that ask for the most money also ask for and get the most time. The best example is churches. Most ask people to attend a service and pay their dues once a week, or *52 times a year!* Because of this, churches get the lion's share of individual contributions, 46 percent in 1980. Dues will increase the time your people give.

Dues increase the commitment of the members. As one group says, "If they pay in, they stay in." Ask your group to look again at the list of other organizations they pay dues to. How long have they been members of these groups? You will probably find that the organizations that ask their members to pay dues keep the same people active for decades. The best example, again, is churches, which always ask for money from their own members. Churches are institutions that people join for a *lifetime* and ask their family and friends to join. Or turn the question around and ask people to think about organizations at which they volunteered for a year or less but then stopped giving their time. When you look at this list you will probably see that they are mostly agencies that gave away their services. There was no way to give your time or money, so there was no reason to stay involved.

Dues give the organization a reason to want to find and keep new members. More people mean that you will get more money and a larger, more powerful organization at the same time. If you take your money from people outside the organization, you have no built-in incentive to grow.

Dues are dependable, renewable, and democratic. Look at lists of organizations in your community. The ones that ask for dues from their members have probably been serving your community for decades. If dues from your own members are the foundation of your budget, you can be sure that your organization will stay in business through recessions and all kinds of political changes.

Dues give you a foolproof way to find out who likes you, who doesn't, and who has not decided yet. Especially if your organization works on controversial issues such as family planning or urban renewal, you need to know exactly who supports you and who opposes you. The people who need your work will buy memberships; the people who need your organization the most will *sell* memberships; the people who are unsure can give you a donation but will not buy a membership; the people who oppose your work will tear up your membership form and call you names! When you are through with the membership campaign, you will have a clear up-to-date list of who likes you a little, who likes you a lot, who is undecided, and who represents the opposition. This will enable you to design better program plans, publicity campaigns, and political strategy. Without a membership drive, you have no accurate way of knowing where your friends and foes are.

Dues give the leadership an accurate reading of what the members like most. It gives you a foolproof way to measure the most

popular programs, the most effective leaders, and the most industrious staff. You can eliminate all arguments from your planning
meetings. If four people want the organization to work on nuclear
waste and four others want the organization to work on solar green-
houses, send all eight out to sell memberships. The four who come
back with new members have a program the community wants. If
both groups come back with enough new money and new members
to do their programs, then do them both. If four come back with
excuses instead of new members, you know that they are the only
four people in your community who want this program now, so it
would be smart to wait for a better time to start. Keep testing the
market every three months to see if the idea has developed any
following. But there is no reason to allocate organizational
resources or staff to a project with no local support. If they want it,
they will pay for it. If they don't pay for a program, they don't want
it, no matter how good or right or important it may seem to the few
who like the idea.

Dues remind your own members every year of the value and importance of this organization. For the people who give you money
every year, and even more, for the people who *ask* for money every
year, they must reconfirm their faith in the organization and their
desire to be a part of it. Because your own people are asking people
they know to give their own money, they will demand up-to-date accounting they understand. This is an incentive to improve your
bookkeeping.

Dues are quick. You get money the same day you start selling
memberships. For a new organization, this means you immediately
get cash to begin buying supplies and holding meetings. For an
older organization, it means that you have a quick way to put cash
into the treasury whenever you need it. Of course, the best system is
to create a year-round plan to recruit members, but if you ever need
cash in a hurry, you can simply sell more memberships.

Best of all, dues make your organization self-sufficient. As long as
you deliver the results the members want, you will always have the
money you need. Again, ask your members to think about the organizations they know that exist almost entirely on dues, such as their
church, their labor union, their social clubs and professional associations, and their neighborhood associations. What advantages do

these groups have? Your committee will notice that the groups that
raise most of their money from dues are permanent, independent,
and run by people they know. They may run one or two special
events for fun, fellowship, publicity, and extra money, but they do
not depend on special events to pay the bills. Dues work.

HOW TO SET DUES

Roxanne Conlin was one of a handful of leaders who began the
Iowa Women's Political Caucus in 1971. By 1975, when I met her,
she had developed a system for starting new groups that worked so
well that she had a successful caucus working in every city in Iowa
except Fort Dodge. (Now they have that, too.) Any organization
that wants to be self-sufficient can follow her recommendations on
dues:

Dues Must Support Structure

Our membership must be willing to pay sufficient dues to at least
maintain their own organization. Special event fundraising is fine for
extra projects or programs, but whatever your group decides is to be
a regular function (newsletter, annual meeting, expenses for delegates, whatever) should be budgeted for and paid by membership
dues. You will never achieve a firm fiscal existence if you have to
have a panic special event to pay your running expenses.

It is impossible to set dues so low that no one is excluded through
inability to pay. It's better to have a reasonable dues level that most
can pay without real discomfort and that will cover those who cannot
than to set dues so low that you loose your appeal as an effective
force. Almost everything political except your vote costs money (and
even that, if transportation or child care is needed, costs something).
It is better to lose some prospective members because your dues seem
too high than to lose many more because your group never does anything more interesting than put on special event fundraisers.

When your board decides to set (or raise) your dues, you must go
back to the beginning of your planning and work from there. First,

review the goals of the organization. What do you want to accomplish in the next year? Second, review your budget. What will that program cost in the next year? Then pick out the bare minimum that you need to accomplish your goals. This is your core budget. If your group decides it wants to hire paid staff, their salaries must go into the core budget because the staff must know that they can count on you to raise that money during the next year. The core budget is the amount that must come from the people who need your work. Their dues and pledges will cover this program as long as it is something *they* want.

Next discuss how much people pay for other organizations that run on dues. Ask people how much they pay for their church; even $1 a week adds up to $52 a year. Ask how much they pay for union dues; even $5 a month adds up to $60 a year. Many people pay much more than that for their church or their union. Then discuss the advantages they see for those groups such as permanence, independence, power, high-quality staff, and the ability to get results. Begin with local examples of high dues; then plan your own. This will help you avoid setting your own dues too low.

One-Year Plan

First devise a one-year strategy for selling memberships based on the amount of money you want. Then plan a five-year strategy to sell memberships based on the number of members you want.

If your group wants to raise a core budget of $10,000 from dues, consider the choices, then create a sales plan. If your dues are $20 each, you only need to sell 500 memberships. But the board says it thinks that $20 is too much for this community. If your dues are $5 each, you have to sell 2,000 memberships this year. The board says that is more work than it wants to do. So you choose $10 a month, which the board members know they can sell, the community will buy, and will mean they have 1,000 sales to plan.

To make it easy, let's say there are ten members on your board. Divide the number of members you want, 1,000, by the number on the board. Each person is responsible for selling 100 memberships to make your goal of $10,000. You can design any plan that makes that easy. You could say that each member of the board will sell two a week except at Christmas and Easter to yield 100 new members per board person per year. That will appeal to the people who like to do a little work each week. Others will say they would rather do it quickly and be finished. They can sell 50 memberships per month for the next two months. To make their goal they will ask four of their friends to host membership parties. Each host will invite 15 to 20 friends. The board members will sell the memberships. These sales plus their own family and friends will fill their quota of 100 in two months.

It doesn't matter what plan you choose, and not every member of the board needs to choose the same plan. But the board as a whole and each individual member must choose a plan and a timetable to sell their quota before they leave the meeting. The president (and anyone who wants to be president next year) will fill his or her quota first, then give the rest of the board encouragement to meet their quotas.

Five-Year Plan

After you choose a plan to make your goal this year, look at a five-year strategy for selling memberships. Of course, the first year is much more difficult because you are starting with only ten salespeople. Next year you will have 1,000 members and scores of possible salespeople. So you can plan to expand your membership sales rapidly after the first year. Then your plan can be based on your political goals as well as your financial goals.

Get the List

According to organizer Bill Pastreich, the way to begin any organization is to get the list of people you want to join that organization. The same principle will work for you. If you want to build a group that can get results, you must know how many potential customers there are for your membership sales (the market) and then make a plan to get whatever share of those people you want.

If you are starting a self-help group that wants to remain very small, your costs will be low enough and your purpose simple enough that you can recruit the number of members you want through word of mouth. On the other hand, if you want to influence local politics, then you will want to sell memberships to a significant percentage of registered voters. Fortunately, in this case it is easy to get the list, so it is easy to make your plan. For example, in a big city the wards are divided into precincts of about 600 registered voters each. If your group wants to get power in your ward, you can find and train two people per precinct to sell your memberships. They can get a free list of all registered voters from the city board of elections. If your goal is 50 percent of all of the registered voters in the first five years (more than enough to make the politicians pay attention to you), it means that each pair of volunteers needs to sell 300 memberships in five years, or 60 per year, or 5 per month. This way even a very ambitious goal can be broken down into a manageable plan. Any pair of enthusiastic salespeople can sell 5 memberships per month. They know *who* to sell to (the names on the list of registered voters), and they know how fast to work. So they get the people you want at the pace you want. If your organization is a general interest group, why not set your goal at 1 percent of your community's adult population per year? After five years you will have 5 percent of your community as paying members. This sort of plan is well worth the work, because you get more people and more power at the same time that you get more money.

If you are beginning an organization of one type of person, then you have to get the list or at least an idea of the size of the list of your target population. Ask local investigative reporters, social workers, researchers, or the librarian in the reference room at the library to teach you how to find the current numbers and names. Then, if you know there are 90,000 tenants in Baltimore and you want to sell 1 percent each year for the first ten years, the board will want to sell 900 memberships the first year, or 75 a month. At the end of ten years you will have 9,000 dues paying members.

The reason you want to set your dues and make a strategy is that you get a personal quota and commitment from the leadership with a plan and timetable to get it done. Each person can see how to do his or her work. The plan connects the price of the dues to your goals and your budget so any leader can tell any prospect how you chose that amount.

The easiest way to get started is simply to set your dues, then begin selling the same week. Have weekly turn-ins the first month to keep up the enthusiasm and get off to a fast start. Ask all the new members to sell memberships to their families, friends, coworkers, and neighbors. Then the new members will know that you are serious about building an effective organization, and your membership campaign will be more successful every week.

Alternatives

Although it makes tidy arithmetic, there is no reason why everyone has to pay the same amount. Your group can set different levels for dues. Here are some alternatives.

DUES RANGES

Set a range. For example the Metropolitan Milwaukee Fair Housing Council set dues categories of $10 to $24 for individual memberships, $25 to $99 for sustaining memberships from individuals, and $100 to $1,000 for sponsoring memberships from organizations, corporations, and churches. Most of their members pay an amount in the middle of the range.

SLIDING SCALE

This gets more money from the people who have more money. For example, Cleveland Working Women, which organizes women office workers to win rights and respect, set its 1981 dues as follows:

Category	Dues
Income less than $10,000	$10
Income more than $10,000	$15
Sponsor	$25

The Chicago Council of Lawyers, an alternative bar association organized for "the advancement of the law, not the advancement of lawyers," set its 1981 dues as follows:

Category	Dues
Out of law school less than two years, public interest and government lawyers, and academics	$40
Two/five years	$60
Six/ten years	$75
More than ten years	$90
Law students	$8
Cooperating members	$150
Sustaining members	$200
Life members	$1,000

DISCOUNTS

Discounts offer real financial incentives in return for dues. The Arkansas Community Organizations for Reform Now (ACORN) developed food buying co-ops that sell food at substantial discounts to ACORN members. The Senior Federation in Minnesota offers its members the lowest prices in town at its own drugstore. Many art museums give members discounts at the museum stores and special preview privileges for shows.

PERCENTAGE OF INCOME

Some churches ask their members to pay a tithe of 10 percent of their income for the work of the church. One Methodist minister claims he saw a bumper sticker saying, "If you love Jesus, tithe. Any fool can honk." Church members just assume that part of their income belongs to the church; it is not theirs to spend. As their income goes up, so does their donation to the church. The church also reminds us that, for some people, tithing is selfish. The people who make the most money ought to give away more than 10 percent. Similarly, some organizations have voted not to spend time doing extra fundraising, but instead to focus 100 percent of their

energies on their program. So, instead of doing fundraising events,
the members work at their regular jobs and donate a percentage of
the income to the group.

DIFFERENT RATES

Set different rates for individuals and families.

AFFILIATE DUES

Some umbrella organizations have each affiliate group pay a
lump sum based on either the number of members or their ability to
pay. Voting power may or may not be proportionate to the size of
the dues. Some groups also give the affiliates the means to raise the
dues, such as selling ads in the convention program or newsletter.

EQUIVALENTS

Make the dues equal to some other expenditure. Political organizations tell prospective members that good government is one of
the basic necessities of life, just like food, shelter, and clothing.
They ask people to give what they would spend on one pair of shoes.
Then the people who buy $30 shoes give $30 and the people who
buy $100 shoes give $100.

THIRD-PARTY PAYMENT

You can get a for-profit company to offer your memberships as a
premium to attract people like your members. For example, the
Metropolitan Senior Federation in Minneapolis–St. Paul, Minnesota, had negotiated a deal with seven banks to buy its memberships for senior citizens. The banks gave anyone over sixty years old
a gift membership in the Federation for opening a new bank account. Since seniors are good customers for banks, the banks were
glad to have the chance to buy memberships to draw in new senior
accounts. The senior citizens wanted the memberships because they
enable Federation members to get discounts on drugs, medical

care, and insurance. The cost to the banks was only $4 for an indi-
vidual account or $6 for a joint account—much less than other
typical bank premiums like blankets, toasters, and calculators and
worth much more to the senior citizens. In the first three years the
Federation got 12,000 new members. The advantage of this plan is
that everyone benefits: the banks, the seniors, and the Federation.
The disadvantage is that, like any third-party payment, it is a
fragile system. Any year the banks can choose to stop buying or renewing memberships. But as long as the banks are satisfied, the
plan delivers large numbers of new members with no sales effort by
the Metropolitan Senior Federation.

Exceptions for Low-Income People

LOWER RATES

Some groups choose to give a special rate to people living on a
fixed income, such as a $5 rate for senior citizens, students, and
unemployed people. Depending on where you live, this is the cost of
one movie or half a carton of cigarettes. If they pay for those, they
can pay for your organization, which is entertaining *and* good for
them!

SWEAT EQUITY

Some groups offer to let you give work in lieu of money. If you
work sixty hours a year, you do not have to pay cash dues.

HARDSHIP DUES

Some groups offer "hardship" dues. In this case, people who cannot pay the regular dues but want to be members of the group and
want to pay *something* meet with the treasurer to choose a hardship
rate or a time payment plan. Hardship cases are usually allowed to
pay a small amount per month, rather than the total dues in one
chunk, which would be too much. So someone who cannot pay your
$16 dues at one time but wants to be a member can work out a plan

to pay you $1.25 a month. They get all the privileges of member-
ship for the year at a rate they can afford to pay. At the end of the
year the organization will have $15. This is much more work for the
treasurer and membership chair, so it is fair to ask the hardship
cases to give you a hand with the paperwork for the membership
drive.

SCHOLARSHIPS

You can begin a scholarship fund to raise money to provide dues
for people who cannot pay. Then the people who like the organization the most can pay their own dues as well as make an additional
contribution so a low-income person can also join the group. For
example, the American Conservatory Theatre of San Francisco offered four levels of dues, then asked for an additional $10 gift "as a
gift membership for a Bay Area senior citizen."

COMPLAINTS ABOUT DUES

Affordability of Dues

An inevitable part of any discussion about dues is the declaration
by someone that the organization should not have dues (or the dues
should be *very* low) so "no one is excluded." Someone will argue
that, if you set dues, some people won't join. That is true. The people who won't join are the people who *do not want* your organization. If people want your group, they will pay for it.

Especially in a low income community, it is important to ask
members to pay dues. Poor people, better than anyone else, know
that if you want something, you have to pay for it. If you can't pay
for it, you can't have it. Usually the only institution that low income
people control is the church because it is the only one they pay for.
If you do *not* ask for dues, your organization will be seen as simply
another welfare program that does not respect the people in the
community and does not intend to accomplish anything.

Ask someone who has participated in a citywide or statewide
coalition made up of groups from both low income and high income communities. They will probably tell you that it is always the

low income people who pay *first,* because they *want* to be equal members. It is usually the wealthier people you have to hound for their dues!

Actually, complaints about other people's inability to pay is really a disguised way of saying that the speaker does not want to ask for money. It is perfectly understandable that middle-class people, especially paid staff, are reluctant to ask poor people for money. The solution is simple: let the low income people plan their own membership campaign and ask each other. They will be much more enthusiastic salespeople and make much more money for the organization. The middle-class person can sell to other middle-class people, and everyone will be happy. Never let one committee member's timidity discourage the group from choosing dues. Ask for dues, and you will get the income and the independence you need to accomplish your goals.

Other Complaints

Someone will say, "But I already give my *time!* You want money, too?" The answer is, 'Yes!' Time and money are not the same. Of course, we value the energy and talent that you give to this organization; we could not exist without them. But we also need to pay the phone bill, the rent, and the post office. They will not take your time for their bills; they want money. If we want to accomplish our goals, we need money to buy the supplies and staff we want. Those of us who give the most time should be the *first* to give our money, too. Who knows better than we do the value of this group?"

Someone else will say, "But it is already costing me a lot to belong to this group. I pay for a baby-sitter; my phone bill has doubled since I joined; I drive to local meetings every month and to the statewide meetings each quarter. Now you want dues on top of all this?" Again the answer is "Yes!" You can only develop as a leader because you have a group to lead. If you do not pay for the organization itself, you cannot participate in the activities that you love, you can't meet the people you like, and you can't win the victories you need. Paying your own bills and paying dues to pay the organization's bills are both necessary for a successful volunteer organization.

YOU ONLY GET THE NET

When you plan your strategy for dues, remember that you get only the *net*. You can spend only what is left *after* you subtract the cost of member services. In our earlier example, the dues were $10 per member. What are some options we can give the members, and where does that leave our net?

1. We decide our members get a right to vote.

Dues	=	$10.00
Vote	=	− 0
Net	=	$10.00

2. We decide to give each member a membership card (5¢), a button (25¢), and a four-issue mimeographed newsletter mailed first class ($1.00). Our costs per member are $1.30.

Dues	=	$10.00
Costs	=	− 1.30
Net	=	$ 8.70

3. We decide to give each member a window decal (25¢), a twelve-issue printed newsletter mailed bulk rate ($2.50), and a consumer guide to local businesses ($2). Subtotal $4.75.

   We pay a staff person to coordinate the membership activities, maintain the mailing lists, help prepare the newsletter, and provide clerical services. Salary, benefits, and expenses add up to $12,500. We have 1,000 members, so the cost per member for paid staff is $1.25. The total cost per member is $6.00.

Dues	=	$10.00
Costs	=	− 6.00
Net	=	$ 4.00

For every item you decide to give the members in addition to the vote, you need to estimate whether it will increase the number of new members enough to pay for what it costs you. It is always better to sell membership material like buttons, decals, and research than to give them away.

RAISING DUES

If you set your dues too low in the beginning, or if you have not raised them for five years or more, it is time to raise the dues. First, review your goals and your budget. Based on your mission and need for money, you may choose to raise your dues. If you decide you want to raise the dues, create a plan to let everyone share in this decision. Send out a notice in writing, including a copy of this year's program plan and budget to show why you need to raise the dues. Ask everyone to come to one meeting to discuss the dues. At that meeting the top officers can explain why you want to raise the dues. Describe the difference in terms of what the group can *do* with the money. If you have $5 dues, you can run the program as it is now. If you raise the dues to $15, in the same time you can hire paid staff and double the program! Let everyone discuss the proposal, encourage suggestions, and announce that you will vote at the next meeting. Between the meetings, line up more support and meet in person with the people who need more persuading. At the next meeting, vote to raise the dues. It usually works best if you set the new rate to begin in about three months. Then use every meeting and newsletter during the next three months to sell dues at the "old bargain rate." Encourage everyone to sign up before the new rate goes into effect. Then you will get a flurry of new members to give you extra income until you can start sales at the new rate.

HOW TO HANDLE RENEWALS

If you are a small group, you can handle renewals in person. The easiest way is to buy a receipt book with carbons at an office supply store. Each time a volunteer sells a membership, you write one receipt with two carbons. Give the original to the new member, send one carbon to the office or membership chairperson for the permanent files, and keep the other copy. That night, write a thank-you note to the new member and welcome him or her to the group. Then file the receipt in a file or envelope bearing the name of that month. Next year, simply pull out the "March" file and you have the name and address of all the members up for renewal in March. Ask them in person to renew, and you should get close to

100 percent. If one fundraiser moves or quits, the chair of the membership drive can use the office copies of the receipts to assign those renewals to a new salesperson. Since renewals are so much easier to get than new sales, it is the best way to give new people confidence.

For a larger group you can ask for renewals through the mail. Create a system to keep track of all your members by the month in which they joined. Two months before their dues expire, send the members a reminder letter from the chair of the membership committee, asking them to renew. Tell the member what you accomplished with his or her dues last year and what your goals are for next year. If you have not received their dues, send a second reminder in a month, and a third on the month they expire with a handwritten "Last notice—please stay with us because we have a wonderful year ahead!" If your committee is large enough, you can ask volunteers to call or visit the few people who don't renew through the mail. If you have a large number of people who do not renew, find out why, because it is a good indication that you need to change your renewal letter or your programs.

In rural areas the membership committee has to be more ingenious to get renewals. Ask other local organizations how they get their renewals. Here is some advice from Denise Scheer of Minnesota COACT, a dues-paying organization. They raised $8,000 from dues in 1979, $12,000 in 1980, and $24,000 in 1981.

Membership Dues in Rural Areas, by Denise Scheer

Minnesota COACT is a dues-paying organization. Dues are $12 per year per family.

COACT's recruitment and renewal system had to be adjusted to accommodate isolated and unpopulated areas, like many of the farming and logging communities where COACT is presently organizing.

Even in small towns, COACT is able to go door to door for recruitment and renewals. However, this is not possible outside the city limits of these towns. In these cases, COACT relies heavily on networks that it taps into (where they exist) and/or creating networks where they aren't already defined.

Key network people then take on the responsibility of recruitment and renewing. As they bring in new members, the dates are recorded in the office, plus the name of the member who brought that new person in. The next year at renewal time the key network people get a list of who needs to be renewed, and the network people follow up for the renewal.

In many of the more isolated areas, renewals (names of people) are printed in the newsletter. If there is no response, the people to be renewed receive phone calls, either from the network person or one of the members of the executive board, reminding people to send in their dues. If there is still no response, there is a personal visit by the network person or the executive board members.

Because of the distances involved, it becomes more difficult for a staff person to shoulder the responsibility of recruitment and renewals alone. It becomes imperative that members be actively involved in the process.

In addition, active dues solicitation occurs at all meetings, both at general membership meetings and committee meetings, because of the distances involved in tracking people down. It is consistently built into the agendas of all meetings.

USE OF CREDIT CARDS AND BANK COLLECTIONS

Ask your treasurer to ask your bank about using major credit cards to collect your dues. Then shop around at other good local banks to see if they will give you a better deal. Most banks and credit card companies treat your dues collection in the same way as a retail business. They will charge you a rate based on your volume of transactions and the per-ticket amount. This usually ranges from 3 to 5 percent. So you can allow your members to charge their dues to their credit card, then pay the company 3 to 5 percent for collection. One advantage is that many people like to pay their bills this way, so you are making it easier for your members. The big advantage is that you speed up the cash flow from the donor to you. Their dues are deposited in your account as soon as you bill the credit card company. The company in turn bills the member, but you do not need to wait until the member pays the company. Instead, you already have the value of their dues.

Large groups say that it is worth the fee to the company to get the value of the dues sooner and to offer a convenience to your members. Some organizations also offer their members the choice of paying directly from their bank account like their mortgage. The opportunities for using the banks will vary with every state and every bank, so ask your own bank and other local banks how they can help you collect your dues.

MORE ADVICE

See the Bibliography, Chapter 14, for recommended reading on getting and keeping dues-paying members.

Ask your committee to bring in some samples of brochures from groups that ask for dues. Notice how they offer a variety of dues levels and opportunities for volunteer work, too. This way they get both the money and the talents of the people who need their group.

BEYOND DUES

There are several other ways to ask for money from the people who need your work. You can use these in addition to dues or in place of dues. Two popular and profitable ways to make money from your own people are pledges and fees for services. Ask your leadership to think of groups in your own community that make money this way. Then ask one or two people to interview their leaders to find out how they make the system work.

PLEDGES

Pledges are a time payment plan for dues, which allow the donor to pay in several installments and allow the group to get more money. As expert Kim Klein says, "Pledges allow even small givers to become major donors." If members pledge $5 a month, they are giving you $60 a year; if they pledge $10 a month, they are giving you $120 a year. Pledges can come from members first, then from people outside your membership.

Talk to other groups that use a pledging system to make up your own system. Churches use this system best, because they are most important to their members' lives and they can collect fifty-two times a year. Most community organizations work on a monthly pledge system. In that case, they create a pledge committee that can be part of the membership committee or part of the major donors committee. Their job is to handle the record keeping, billing, and soliciting of pledges.

Asking for Pledges

A fundraiser can ask for pledges every time he or she talks to someone who is eager or able to give a donation larger than the amount of the dues. Of course, people who make their own pledges always make the most persuasive salespeople. So always begin by asking your own members to pledge, especially the volunteers who will be asking others to pledge.

Many groups begin by asking everyone to join as members, then asking the most committed members to pay a monthly pledge instead of a yearly membership. For example, Cleveland Working Women (CWW) recruits women office workers who pay from $10 to $25 per year in dues. The leaders then ask members to join the "CWW One Hundred" and pledge $100 per year by paying $8.25 per month. Although few office workers would give $100 in a lump sum, many are willing and able to make twelve payments of $8.25 each year to support the work of the organization.

You can use a pledge system to collect larger donations from your major donors, as described in Chapter 5. Whenever your leaders give speeches they can end by asking the audience to pledge their support for the organization. Any special event fundraiser gives you an opportunity to ask for pledges. Always have pledge cards available and enthusiastic volunteers ready to sell the plan. The pledge system works especially well at house meetings, described in Chapter 8.

Once you have pledges for money, organize the donor cards so that you can efficiently mail the reminders (also known as *the bills*) each month. Ask the secretary or office manager of a local group to recommend a system for you or order *Survey Savvy,* listed in the bibliography, for an explanation of a cheap sorting system that uses cards, a punch, and a knitting needle. To begin, choose a system that will let you retrieve your cards by the person's name, zip code, and the amount given. When you can, expand the system so you can retrieve the cards by the name of the fundraiser and the special interests of the donor. See Chapter 13 for a sample donor card.

Once a month, write up a one-page letter telling the pledgers what your group did this month. This can be signed by the president or the chair of the pledge committee. Print or mimeograph it on your stationery; then add personal notes to each copy. Ask your committee of volunteers to help with the notes and the mailing. Two people can write and produce the letter one day; a committee of four to eight can write the notes, fold, stuff, seal, stamp and send the letters the second day. Include an envelope for the next month's pledge. When the pledges come in, the committee sends a thank-you note for the pledge. This is a lot of paperwork; it requires volunteers to be very dependable, well organized, and competent, so they never get behind on the work.

A pledge system provides great volunteer opportunities for people who are too shy to speak in front of a group or lead a committee but care deeply about the work of the organization and want to make a contribution of their energy. Capable volunteers can run the pledge billing and renewals in the office or the chair's home at night or on the weekends. Enthusiastic leadership can persuade people to make the pledges, but it is the conscientious workers behind the scene who make the money come in and keep it coming in.

Here is a sample of a pledge card used by a battered women's shelter and counseling service for their major donors. You can find other samples in your own community, too. Ask your volunteers to bring in samples from their church or other volunteer organizations that ask for pledges. Then design your own cards and begin asking for pledges.

Besides your own system of reminders, you may want to use a credit card company or a bank billing system to collect your pledges for you. These will add to the costs of the pledge system, but they appeal to busy people who pay their other financial commitments that way. Check with your bank for more advice.

Mid-Peninsula Support Network

Yes, count me in as a Friend of MPSN!

I enclose:

☐ $500   ☐ $250   ☐ $150   ☐ $100   ☐ $75

☐ Other $_____

I would like to pledge $_____ per

☐ month   ☐ quarter.

Please send me convenient reminder envelopes.

Name _____

Address _____Zip_____

Phone_____

Your donation is tax deductible and greatly appreciated.

Make checks payable to Mid-Peninsula Support Network
655 Castro Street
Suite 6
Mountain View, California 94041

One last note. A pledge system will get more money from everyone who uses it, but it will not interfere with your other money makers. Some people are afraid to start a pledge system because they think, "If she pledges $60 a year, she won't support anything else." This is not true. The veterans say that pledgers are the *most* supportive of your work and your activities. They are usually the first ones to buy tickets for special events and show up at benefits. This is only natural, since they have so much money invested in your group; they must believe your organization is wonderful and want to meet the people who make it all happen!

Pledges work especially well for organizations that have a bold program that gets a lot of publicity but have a closed membership. For example, the Farmworkers Union used pledges to create a dependable fundraising base during their lettuce strike in 1978. For two days a month of office work, and requests for pledges at *every* meeting, party, and action, they brought in between $600 and $1,000 per month in cities outside California. Obviously most urban people were not migrant farmworkers, so they were not able to join the group as members. But many people believed in the goals of the organization and pledged their money to support its work when they were asked to do so.

Advantages of Pledges

Pledges let you target the amount you ask for to the person you are asking. Dues are democratic because everyone pays the same amount. This is good for the spirit of the organization. Pledges are fair because they allow the people who have more money to give you more money. This is good for the treasury of the organization.

It is much easier to raise the amount you ask for from pledges each year than it is to raise your dues each year. Some groups wait five years or more to raise their dues. For the last three years before the increase they are getting much less than they planned on in terms of what that money can buy. Inflation is a fact of life in the 1980s and must be considered in your long-range planning. The great thing about pledges is that you can raise them easily each year to keep up with inflation. Since the amount you ask for is based on the donor's ability to give and enthusiasm about your work, as the donor's income or enthusiasm goes up, so should the amount you ask him or her to give. As my pastor Father Reed says, "There's no such thing as the same thing as last year. That sounds like Gilbert and Sullivan, but it's really the *Wall Street Journal!*" Be bold and ask your pledgers to increase their pledge each year. You both know how good your work is and that they are getting a bargain for their investment — they should be glad to pay!

FEES FOR SERVICES

The last source of renewable money from the people who need your work is fees for your services. If they get the benefit of your work, ask them to pay for it, or at least part of it. This is the system used by most private and alternative schools, health clinics, adult education programs, and arts organizations. Never insult your program by giving it away free! If you ask people to pay, they will take it more seriously and value it more highly. You can also ask people beyond your membership to pay fees for what you do, using a speakers bureau as described in Chapter 5 or training as described in Chapter 6.

See Bob Wagner's excellent book *Fee Management,* listed in the bibliography, for good advice on making money from fees. Based on his experience of taking an adult education program from 0 to $350,000 gross revenue a year, Bob shares his tested advice for making a profit from fees.

Many groups use a combination of these fundraising techniques to get money from the people who need their work. For example, a health clinic can ask for fees on a sliding scale from the people who use the clinic, ask the people who have used the clinic in the past or could need it in the future to become dues-paying members, and ask the people who can pay more to give monthly pledges to support their work. Pledges could come from doctors, nurses, pharmacists, social workers, and other concerned citizens who want to support community-controlled health care. The more you diversify your fundraising base, the more independent and powerful you will be.

5

Raising Money from Believers:

Who Wants What You Do?

The second major source of dependable money for a volunteer organization is the people who believe in the purpose of your organization. Ask yourselves, "Who wants what we do?" The answer is the people who support your goals and your philosophy. These people will be able to give you money year after year just like your members do. The difference is that they will give you little or no time. A member is someone who *needs* the organization and gives time as well as money. A believer is someone who *wants* the organization to succeed and gives money but little or no time.

Although most groups have a limited number of people who will need the organization enough to be members, they can sell the value of the organization to a much larger group of people. This is an obvious advantage to any organization that has very few members or very poor members. Those members can use their time to get more money from the people who admire the organization.

Asking for money from believers allows the people who have more money to give you more money. Most groups set their dues relatively low so many people can join and everyone will pay the same rate. Asking for money from people outside the organization allows you to ask for larger donations. You only need to do your homework to match the size of the request to the donor's ability to give and enthusiasm for the organization's program.

Your goal in designing a strategy to get money from believers is to get the most money in the least amount of time and to get it from sources that can give to you year after year. You are looking for dependable, renewable money. All of the methods of fundraising discussed in this chapter will enable your organization to ask for renewable money every year.

The first method of fundraising from the people who want your program is door-to-door canvassing. This fundraising technique is what for-profit companies call *cold canvass selling*. Your salespeople knock on doors and ask people to give money to your organization. It is a very profitable way to make money in dense urban areas for high-visibility organizations. Dozens of community organizing and advocacy organizations run year-round canvassing operations staffed by professionals. Similar organizations in small to medium-sized towns run a three-month canvass by paid professionals during the summer. Many organizations run weekend canvasses by their own members. We will look at the advantages and problems of professional year-round canvassing and the volunteer canvass by members.

A second dependable source of money from believers is donations from the for-profit businesses and corporations in your area. In recent years corporations gave away more money than foundations to nonprofit organizations. Many older organizations have received donations from local businesses for years. We will discuss how to find the businesses that are most likely to want to support what your organization does and how to ask them for money so they say "yes!"

The third way to ask your believers for money is through the mail. Direct mail fundraising is a business that uses a volume approach to find the people who like what you do, then ask them for money. Direct mail fundraising copies all of the science of for-profit mail order sales, then adds some artful touches of its own. If your organization has a purpose that will appeal to a very large number of people, you can use direct mail very profitably. If your organization has a purpose that appeals to a smaller local audience, you can use a volunteer member mailing approach to make money. A large-scale professional direct mail program costs more to get started, involves some risk, takes longer to make a profit, and can make more money in the long run. The volunteer approach can work for more organizations, more quickly, with less risk and less profit. We will discuss both professional and volunteer direct mail fundraising so you can choose which is best for your group now.

The fourth sector is called *major donors*. These are simply people who like your organization so much that they give you large amounts of money when you ask for it. What you consider a major donor depends on your organization. Some groups say that anyone who gives more than $50 is a major donor. Other organizations that have many wealthy supporters will set up several categories of major donors, such as patrons ($150 to $249), associate members ($250 to $499), sustaining members ($500 to $999), friends ($1,000 to $1,499), guarantors ($1,500 to $2,499), sponsors ($2,500 to $4,999), and benefactors ($5,000 and above). We will discuss how you design a campaign to get money from major donors, how to train your fundraisers to ask for large donations, how to find wealthy people who would like your cause, and how to make the program work year-round. This is based on one-to-one asking and shares the tested advice of Kim Klein. Kim began with four novice volunteers and built up a major donor giving program that produced 25 percent of her organization's annual budget. Any organization can adapt this plan to set up and run a successful major donor program.

The fifth vehicle for getting money from people who like your work is the newsletter. Most organizations publish a newsletter that is a money drain for the organization. We will talk about how you can use your newsletter to *make* money for the group, through subscriptions, advertising, and direct mail techniques. Any group that publishes a newsletter can follow this advice.

The sixth example is payroll deductions. This is a system by which people choose to give you money where they work. The employer takes the designated amount out of each paycheck, then sends one check to a group of organizations that forwards your part to you. The oldest organization making money from payroll deduction is the United Way; the first modern United Way was started in Cleveland in 1913. In 1981 there were also thirty-five alternative payroll deduction plans operating in addition to the United Way drives. These allow more innovative organizations to use payroll deductions to raise dependable money every year for their work. Jon Pratt, Field Director of the Midwest Office of The Youth Project, has researched these newer payroll deduction plans and will share the advice of the people who set them up. Your organization may also want to join an alternative payroll deduction plan.

The speakers bureau is the last example of using what you already have to make money from the people in your community who share your goals. Any organization that has leaders with expertise in a subject can set up a speakers bureau to make money. Especially if your organization is the first of its kind in your area, if it is on television often, or if you can combine excellent speakers with an aggressive salesperson, your group can make money by asking the public to pay to hear your speakers. Any organization that is asked to supply speakers to schools, colleges, clubs, and other organizations can add to its income by simply asking for money when a speaker is booked.

It is also possible to combine two or more of these forms of fundraising. For example, many groups collect money and names of supporters through the canvass teams going door to door and asking for money. Once those names are on the subscribers list, they are asked for money again through the direct mail campaign. The next year they can renew when the canvasser comes to their door again, or they will get a request through the mail to renew their support. When the speakers go out from the speakers bureau, the host organization has already paid for their presentation. Each speaker can also ask for donations from the audience or simply circulate a list for names to be added to the newsletter list. Once you have their names you can ask these people for money through the newsletter and the direct mail campaign.

INCLUDING MONEY FROM BELIEVERS IN YOUR FUNDRAISING STRATEGY

The basis of your budget and fundraising strategy must be the dues and donations you get from your own members, the people who need your program. Money from believers, the people who want your program, can make up the second part of your fundraising strategy. Before you design your campaigns to get money from believers, look at your complete fundraising strategy to see how you want this income to fit into your plan.

You can set a goal for your fundraising from believers in terms of a dollar figure, a percentage of your total budget, or a percentage of your income from dues. This is especially important for the fundraisers like canvassing or direct mail, which can produce great income from a professional staff. Since this money does not come from the work of your board, you do not want it to represent the majority of your income. Most successful groups recommend that you limit your income from a professional fundraiser such as canvassing or direct mail to less than half of your budget. Then you will be sure that the elected leaders rather than the paid staff keep the real decision-making power in your organization.

Putting a limit on income from believers at the beginning of your planning will also relieve the fears of any member or leader who is afraid to ask for money from local businesses or wealthy individuals. New fundraisers may try to avoid asking for money by introducing the fear that taking money from corporations or rich people might make your organization look as though it had sold out. Plan your fundraising strategy right from the beginning to eliminate this fear. When you make up your plan for the year, choose a limit for funds you will take from corporations or major donors. Some groups say any amount is all right for them; other groups set a limit of 25 percent of their budget or 50 percent of the income generated by the members. In other words, if your budget is $40,000, then $20,000 could come from the members, $10,000 from corporations, and $10,000 from other sources. As your membership income grows, you can increase your goal for corporate donations. If your membership funds grew to $30,000, you could ask for up to $15,000 from corporations. In this way you guarantee that your core budget, especially salaries, comes from money from your own members. You know and can show your members and donors that only a quarter of your budget comes from corporations. This way no one needs to worry about real or imaginary strings on the money, because the organization has enough dependable money that it can reject any donation that comes with strings that are not acceptable to the leadership.

MONEY FROM BELIEVERS—GRANTS

One other source of money available to your organization from believers is grants from foundations or government agencies. When you get grants you are getting money from people who believe in your work; they will never give you time. But grants are not discussed here because they are not grass roots money. They are not dependable, renewable, or controlled by your organization. Grants run out. If you want to get the most money for the least amount of time and effort, concentrate on the sources of money that can give to you every year. Then you won't have to keep starting over every year.

The only time it is worth your while to go after grants is for a one-time purchase that can be supported by income from your grass roots fundraising program. For example, if you run an emergency food warehouse and you want a forklift, you can go to the manufacturer and ask for the truck, or you can write a proposal for a grant for $12,000 to buy the truck. This is a one-time purchase, so it doesn't matter that the grant will not be renewed next year. All of the other expenses connected with the truck — gasoline, oil, parts, service and repair, insurance, and depreciation — will occur every year, so those expenses must come out of your dependable grass roots fundraising.

If you want to learn more about getting money from grants, visit the Foundation Center's Regional Collection library nearest to you. These are free libraries staffed by professional librarians who can help you learn to research foundations and write proposals. See the list of these free libraries in "Fundraising Forever," Chapter 13. For more advice, get the recommended reading listed in the bibliography, Chapter 14, or ask someone from a similar type of organization who has received foundation grants to tell you who to ask and how to get started.

BUSINESS CONTRIBUTIONS

If your organization is getting results that benefit your community, you can ask local businesses and corporations to support your work. Any for-profit business can give a donation to your organization. Legally, for-profits may give away up to 10 percent of their pretax income; the national average is usually around 1 percent. In 1979 and 1980 corporations gave more money than foundations to nonprofit organizations in America. The business community gave $2.4 billion in 1980. This is a growing and dependable source of money.

The corporation does not have to be large in order to give you money. In fact, many large corporations usually give small amounts. Ninety-four percent of the corporations that make gifts to nonprofits gave a total of $500 or less. Most of this money is going to the United Way or local nonprofits that ask for support, such as the local hospital, college, or Little League. Your group can also get this money, if you ask for it.

Most businesses want to support groups that benefit their employees, that make it easier for them to make a profit, or that will help improve their image with customers or investors. When you begin your corporate campaign, ask yourselves:

- Who benefits from our work?
- Where do most of our members work?
- Where do they shop?
- Where do they spend their money?
- Where do we as an organization spend our money?
- Who wants what we do?

First, you have to find the corporations and businesses that want your work. If your group works in a specific geographic area, get the *Yellow Pages* for that area and make a list of the companies that took the biggest ads. They will be the easiest to sell because they all benefit from the victories of your organization.

If your organization does not have a specific geographic base, you can begin by asking for money from any corporation that makes money from you or your members. In that case, make a list of all the places the organization spends its money. All of these companies can support your work. Second, ask all of your members to make a list of all the places they spend money. Tell them to keep a card in their wallet or checkbook and, each time they spend money for the next month, write down the name of the business or store that got the money. When you combine the lists you will see which businesses are making a profit from your members. These are the easiest to start selling, because your volunteers already know the stores. You can use the same system when you are looking for prospects to buy ads in your ad books as described in Chapter 10.

Make a list of every place your members work, either full time or part time. Add a list of where they worked in the last ten years. All of these companies make money from the talent and energy of your members. They ought to contribute to the program run by your members.

Next ask other organizations for the names of companies that gave them donations. If a company is giving money in your community or to your kind of program, it is a logical place to ask. Do not be too concerned about competition. Most companies that give money are eager to support good programs; they probably give to several arts programs, health care programs, and educational programs. They can give to you, too.

Last, simply find out which are the most profitable companies in your area. Recruit a stockbroker to tell you the latest business gossip about local companies. (They call it *market research*.) Read the *Wall Street Journal*, your local business paper, the financial columns in your daily newspaper, and the business magazines such as *Fortune* and *Forbes*. This can tell you which of the large publicly held companies are thriving. For smaller companies, your research will be done by word of mouth from the people who work there. Your own members are the best source of information on small local businesses. Ask them.

Once you have a list of local companies you want to ask for money, you can prepare a package of information and begin the research to find the right person in the company. Two people from the business contributions committee can research and write a draft of your corporate package while the rest of the group finds the best people to sell.

What to Ask for

The easiest thing to get every year, surprisingly, is money. If you prove you are a good investment, give the company lots of credit in print, and send an enthusiastic salesperson, you can get money every year from local businesses. But for-profit companies can give you a great deal in addition to money. You get what you ask for, so your committee should plan carefully what it will ask each company to give.

In some cases, you may be better off getting talent. A top-notch advertising firm can design your advertisements, your logo, even your T-shirts so they make more money for you. An accounting firm can give you a free audit if your fiscal year is set up so your job falls in the summer. A department store can host your next benefit. Some companies will even give you one of their staff members to work full-time on your project for a specific length of time. They pay the salary; you get the skills.

According to the new tax law, for-profit companies can now write off their equipment in four years. This means they can choose to depreciate the value of their new equipment in four years, then give it to you, take the current market value of the equipment off their taxable income, and buy something new. Since the technology of word processors, personal computers, and other office machinery is advancing so swiftly, profitable companies usually want the newest equipment and are glad to give you their old models.

You can also get office furniture when a company redecorates, plus supplies such as stationery and envelopes whenever it moves or hires new executives. Remind all of your members who work for a big company that you always need office supplies, equipment, and furniture. Make sure they put your organization first in line when the company needs to "find a charity" for its discards.

The Package

The purpose of your corporate package is to make your organization look like a good investment. Use up-to-date financial records and document every program with facts and figures. Include a copy of your budget, your last financial statement, your fundraising strategy, one or two good clippings or fan letters from celebrities, and a copy of your tax exemption letter from the IRS. If possible, include a copy of the auditor's opinion letter from last year.

Unlike a foundation proposal, which emphasizes needs and programs to be done in the future, a good corporation package emphasizes results and accomplishments. Tell the executive why, dollar for dollar, you are the best investment in your town. Show what your organization was able to do on last year's budget and how much more will get done on this year's budget, including the business's contribution.

The Right Person

Once you decide which companies would be good prospects for your fundraisers, you have to find the best person inside the company. This is just like any other kind of organizing or selling job. You have to find the person who can say yes, the person who can buy. As salespeople say, "Never talk to the monkey when you can talk to the organ grinder." This research will be largely word of mouth from the other organizations that get money from these companies.

Ask local groups who they talked to who gave them money. The individual recommended may be a top executive or may have a job that includes philanthropy for that company. Ask what the company person wants to hear and does not want to hear. Try to get three or four readings on each individual, since this information is obviously very subjective and may be colored by differences in personality or style.

The Committee

Once you have chosen your prospects and the package, match your best salespeople with the companies. The first year it is best if the board of directors leads the corporate campaign and asks for the biggest donations first. After the first year you can recruit volunteers to renew last year's contributions and use the members of the board to ask for new contributions. This is the best way to use the board's time, because you can make the most money in the least time, and it is all renewable money. Set a goal for the first month, such as having each board member call on five businesses. If you have twelve board members, they can ask sixty companies for money. If a quarter of them say yes, and you get an average donation of $500, you will net $3,500 the first month of your corporate campaign.

Send a letter from the board member explaining who you are and why you want money. Include the corporate package. Ask for a specific amount of money that is in the range of the company's giving record. Most will not give anything less than $25; average donations may range from $100 to $5,000, depending on the size and success of the company. Find out the company's average gift by asking other groups or reading the company's reports. At the end of the letter, say that you will call for an appointment.

Call back in a week to confirm that your letter has been received. It is your responsibility to call. Don't assume that if the company likes it, its representative will call you or that, if they don't call, they don't like it. You are selling your program to them, so you have to be the one to call.

Try to set up a personal meeting. It will probably have to be during the regular business day. You can also take your president, the person chairing the proposed project, or the staff member assigned to the project.

Then go and sell your program. The best corporate programs have staff people who may come out to a meeting or to a project, but for the majority, the only thing they will see of your organization is you.

Send a note right after the meeting thanking the corporate officer for meeting with you. If you get the contribution, be sure to keep in touch and ask the officer for advice on approaching other corporations. If you are not funded, keep in touch anyway, because they may simply be taking a wait-and-see attitude. They may fund you next year if you show some progress this year. Also, policies change, so they may turn you down this time and put you at the top of the list next time.

It is well worth the time of the board to begin and to maintain a good relationship with the business community because they are able to give you contributions year after year. In 1981, the Texaco Oil Company began its record 42nd consecutive season sponsoring "Live from the Met" on radio and its fifth year sponsoring the operas on television. If your leaders do the work this year to win support from local businesses, it can pay off for decades.

Also see "Selling Training" in Chapter 6 for advice on selling your skills to businesses. It describes a profitable system to sell your products or services to businesses as part of their employee benefits. If you want, you can sell training to benefit their employees on the jobs and also ask for a donation to support the accomplishments of the organization that benefit their employees off the job.

See the bibliography, Chapter 14, for recommended reading with more detailed advice, tested samples, and case histories of corporate campaigns.

DOOR-TO-DOOR CANVASSING

Professional

Door-to-door canvassing is a labor-intensive, high-profit, recessionproof method of raising money. It is copied from profitable door-to-door sales methods that have been used for decades to sell encyclopedias, vacuum cleaners, and cosmetics. The most profitable canvassing programs are run by professionals all year-round. Your organization hires a person to direct the canvassing program, then he or she hires and trains from four to thirty canvassers to go out and ask for money for your group. The canvassers are paid a salary or commission, depending on your state laws. If your organization has a program with mass appeal and high publicity in a medium-sized to large city with a large pool of available labor, you can consider beginning a professional canvassing program. For smaller communities, you can canvass with volunteers, as explained later in this section.

First check with the charitable trust division of your state attorney general's office to get the laws on canvassing in your state. Ask your city or town attorney if there are local regulations that will also affect your canvassing team. Ask a lawyer to review the laws to make sure that you can operate your canvass according to the current laws.

Second, get the current census data from the nearest large library that is a federal depository. This will tell you the number and location of households in your area with an income of $10,000 per year or more. A professional canvasser can reach from fifty to seventy-five homes an evening. Divide the number of households by the number of canvassers times fifty and you will learn the number of days it will take to canvass your target area. Then you will know if you want to set up a professional year-round canvass, a professional summertime canvass, or a volunteer weekend canvass.

Next try to work with a successful canvassing team for at least a week, to get a firsthand understanding of the labor involved. If the board chooses to begin a canvassing program based on your research, hire an experienced canvassing field manager from another profitable program or arrange for the director of your canvassing program to intern with another program at least a month before beginning your program.

Advantages

Although it takes a lot of very hard work to run a successful canvassing operation, there are many payoffs in addition to the income. It gives you a chance to reach fifty to seventy-five homes every evening to get an immediate and ongoing reading of the public's reaction to your work. You can find out firsthand what the public thinks are the pressing problems of your community.

In addition, it offers a superb training ground for prospective leadership or organizing talent. The skills you need to be a good canvasser are also the skills you need to be a good leader or a good organizer — the willingness to work long hours, the ability to explain the issues quickly and clearly, the skill to solicit a reaction to the problem, the capacity to listen, and the courage to ask for money.

Because the canvass is a business, it is only profitable if it runs efficiently. The best canvasses have copied the tools that make money for the most successful for-profit businesses, such as written job descriptions, long-range plans, teamwork, incentives, quotas, and strict accountability. All of these can be copied by the organization's noncanvass staff and leadership to get more results for the organization.

Problems

Although a professional canvassing operation can bring in dependable money each year from the people who believe in your work, it also can produce problems. If the board and top staff discuss these problems before they begin the canvassing program, they can devise a plan to avoid the problems. Be sure to interview the experienced leadership and staff of older organizations that have run canvassing operations for five years or more to get the best advice on avoiding the problems.

One of the most typical problems is the temptation to let the canvassing operation take over too much of your responsibility for raising money. Since canvassing can be so profitable, it is easy for the leadership to think that it can relax and let the canvassers do the fundraising. This produces two problems. First, power in any organization goes to the people who raise the money. If the staff raises money instead of the leadership, the staff will in fact become the decision makers, regardless of what the bylaws say. Second, the canvassers will want the organization to choose those issues that are easy to canvass on, like utility rates, and avoid those that are difficult to canvass on, like welfare rights. (The same things can happen if you begin a professional direct mail campaign.)

The way to avoid these problems is to get control of the organization's overall fundraising strategy right at the beginning. Before the board chooses to begin a professional fundraising operation such as canvassing or direct mail, it should plan a stategy that calls for limits on the amount of money to come from the professional canvassers. Most groups recommend you limit your canvass income to less than half of your budget. If the canvassing income surpasses your original expectations, the board can choose to slow down the professionals, step up its own fundraising efforts, or give away the extra money to help start similar organizations.

The second problem is a feeling of isolation on the part of the canvassers. It is important that the board work with the canvassers to explain the goals of the organization. The canvassers must realize that raising money is a means to an end and not the end itself. Most people who choose to canvass for a living are young and idealistic; they want a personally and politically fulfilling way to earn money during school vacations or until they get a "real" job. The organization gets all the benefits of this idealism and energy, so it needs to keep the canvassers involved in the purpose of the organization. The board can take turns talking to the canvassers once a week at a briefing. Some boards sponsor thank-you potluck suppers once a year for the canvassing staff members to let them know how much their work matters. Best of all, one week can be chosen for the board to go out and canvass with the canvassing staff. All will become better fundraisers, and the canvassers will *see* that their work matters to the leadership because the leaders are there sharing it with them.

The third problem to anticipate is reorganizing your lists and structure to handle all the names you collect at the door. The board must decide in advance if these people are going to be considered simply contributors so they get only a receipt, subscribers so they get the newsletter and direct mail requests, or members. Some groups call the people who give money to the canvassers *at-large members*. Thus they are distinguished from the active members who are involved in local groups and called *chapter members*. This allows the people who give money to canvassers to believe they are part of the organization, and it gives the organization a larger list of people they can claim to represent. The at-large members can be converted into chapter members when the organization begins a chapter in their area or if they choose to volunteer their time in some other way, such as working in the office or at bingo. (The same problem arises when you ask for money through direct mail and tell donors that if they send in money they will become members.) Be sure your planning clearly distinguishes between active members and mail or canvassing members.

Review and revise your bylaws to anticipate other problems, such as representation at your convention. Most groups require that convention delegates be elected through a local chapter so they have done some work and represent a certain group of people. The at-large members who gave money to a canvasser or through the mail may come to the convention as observers but are not allowed to cast votes until they are elected by a local group.

For more advice on professional canvassing order *Knock, Knock . . . Who's There? A Citizen's Guide to Canvassing,* listed in the bibliography, Chapter 14.

Canvassing by Members

Any organization can run a door-to-door canvass by its own members. Instead of hiring professionals to work for you for several months, you find and train volunteers to do the canvass in a few weeks. The volunteers go door to door and ask for money from everyone to support the work of your organization. In some locations it may not be possible for your volunteers to go door to door, such as urban high-rise apartment buildings that are too difficult to get into and rural areas where the homes are too far apart. In that case, your volunteers canvass the people where they can be found in relatively large numbers. Set up a booth or table in your target area, then canvass the people who stop at your table. This also works well for groups doing workplace organizing who are unable to ask their supporters for money at work. Urban groups run successful canvasses near busy subway stations or bus stops, supermarkets, big churches, and street fairs. Rural groups make money with booths at the county or state fairs, rodeos or sporting events, sales or auctions, busy stores, or election day polling places. Stop people by asking them to sign a petition supporting the goals of your organization. Ask the ones who sign for money.

The co-chairs of the volunteer canvass can ask for advice from other people who have canvassed in your community, such as professional fundraisers, political candidates, or large charities. Some of the large disease associations run a volunteer canvass every year using volunteers who do nothing else all year except ask for money on their block or in their building. These people can give you advice on the time of year, the time of day, and the sort of sales pitch that work best in your own community.

Line up a team of volunteers. Canvassing is more profitable and much more fun if you send your canvassers out in pairs. So, if you want ten teams, you need to recruit twenty volunteers. The top officers of the organization should be among the volunteer canvassers to show it is important work.

Training

The co-chairs will test your sales pitch and materials before you train the volunteers. You can work as a pair or separately to learn what brings in the most money the fastest. Once you have found a sales pitch that works well, call together your volunteers and train them to ask for money at the door. An experienced sales manager or sales trainer can help you here.

The key to success in sales is attitude. If your volunteers believe they can sell this organization, they will do it! Act out several successful sales and then act out some problem questions with answers that work. Pass out written materials and let each person practice asking for money. Give the pairs their assignments and send them out. You may want to work only one hour the first day so everyone can come back and share their stories. Applaud the successes, offer help on problems, and recheck your pairs. If one pair got much more money than everyone else, while another pair did poorly, regroup the pairs so each pair has one strong person and one weak person. They will both do better, and the more timid person will learn how to fundraise.

Give each pair a timetable and a map of their turf. They can cover their own block or precinct or building, or they can hit new territory. Remind them that your organization does valuable work that benefits the entire community. Everyone ought to give you money! You can send out your teams on a weekday night, on Saturday or Sunday afternoons, or on a combination of both. Try to recruit enough volunteers so they can cover your territory if they go out once a week for four weeks. Even better, double your volunteers and cut the time in half. Then you could cover your area in two weeks. Recruit more people each year and cut the time needed. Each year it will be easier to get volunteers.

How to Ask for Money

It would seem that asking a total stranger to give money to your organization would never work. However, you are going to be pleasantly surprised once you get your teams out asking! People *do* give to strangers, and they certainly give to a cause they believe will make their own life better. Canvassing works because of a universal sales principle: people are all the same. If you believe that your organization is so wonderful that you will give your money *and* your time to it, then won't other people feel that way? Of course! *Especially* when you can say that you are there as a *volunteer* from your organization. You are giving your time; all you want from the other person is money.

You get what you ask for. So tell the person at the door or at your table that you want a donation. Say it in your first sentence, such as "Hello, I'm Dick Davenport from the Maryland Audubon Society. We're here today to get signatures and donations to support the new bird sanctuary." Then tell them what you want them to do: "We hope you will sign this petition to the county board and give us $10." Show them the list of names and say, "Will you please sign the petition?" After they sign, say "Most of the people on your block are making donations of $10 or more. Will you please give me your tax-deductible donation for $10 now?" Answer questions briefly and pleasantly, then ask for the money again. Keep asking until you get the money. Keep asking in different ways even if they say no the first time. Your conviction will persuade them that your cause is a good investment.

Canvassing by members works best in communities in which people recognize your canvassers or believe they have received some benefits from the work of your organization. Most people find that they enjoy canvassing once they try it, because they can reach many new people, inform them about your work, and raise money at the same time.

Variation: The Every-Member Canvass

Another type of volunteer canvass is copied from small Protestant churches, known as the *every-member canvass.* In this system, 20 percent of the most enthusiastic members ask the other 80 percent to renew and increase their pledges to the church. The members' pledges make up the majority of most churches' budgets, and the pledge itself is usually the largest part of the family's charitable giving. Asking for pledges in person helps the church get more money and helps the family feel good about its investment. Since the most enthusiastic members of the church do the asking in person, the renewal rate is close to 100 percent each year. Any organization with a small membership that wants them to make a major financial commitment every year can copy this system.

The church chooses one Sunday every year to be its canvass Sunday. Everyone in the church is notified through the newsletter, church bulletin, and announcements from the clergy. About six weeks before the canvass, co-chairs of the stewardship committee recruit volunteers to ask. Depending on the enthusiasm of the volunteers and the size of the parish, each person can call on four to six families. The volunteers are all invited to a training meeting the week before the canvass, given all the necessary materials, and inspired to raise money. Each of them is asked to make his or her own pledge before canvassing the other members.

On the stewardship Sunday, the minister makes a moving sermon about the need for money to help the church accomplish its goals. The canvassers make their calls in the afternoon of the same day. Follow-up is handled by the best canvassers. This way the church meets every family every year to find out what they like most and least about the church right now. Then the board of directors can revise the program plans and the budget each year to provide what the members want most.

For more advice on volunteer canvassing, get *Helping NOW Grow—Fundraising,* listed in the bibliography, Chapter 14.

DIRECT MAIL

Professional

Writing letters to ask people to give you money is called *direct mail.* Many political campaigns and large national organizations use direct mail to get their message into people's homes. Once you find the people who believe in your work, they will continue to give you money through the mail. The trick is finding the believers and getting the first donation.

Although the returns will vary according to the importance of the issue, the quality of the package, and the currency of the lists, there is a formula that generally has proven to apply to direct mailing efforts. This is:

For the first mailing to all lists, expect a 1 percent return. This means one person in a hundred will give.

Of the people who give, 60 percent of them will give again when asked a second time.

Of the people who give twice, 75 percent will give when asked three times or more.

As you can see, it is very expensive to get started because it costs a lot of money to do the volume of mailing necessary to find the people who give. But it pays off handsomely in the long run.

If you can afford or can borrow the money to launch a direct mail program, probably a minimum of $30,000, and if you are doing work that will appeal to a national audience, hire a professional to advise you. Successful direct mailing requires many, many decisions on the package (the letter, the envelope, the response device, and other enclosures) as well as the many, many decisions on the actual mechanics of mailing (dates, lists, type of postage, repetition, and testing alternatives). Ask the big institutions and top politicians in your area to recommend the best professionals.

The reason you need the professional advice is that every part of a direct mail campaign can be tested and measured so there is an accurate way to know what works best. It is expensive to begin your program because you need to invest so much money to "capture" the names of the people who want what you do. Then you need to test your letters and enclosures to find out which ones make the most money for you. So you will probably need to reinvest any profits you get the first year back into the direct mail campaign. After the second year you can start drawing money off.

The payoff is the names you capture for your cause. Once you know the names of your supporters, your board members can ask the biggest givers in person to make a larger donation. Careful work with your list will turn small donors into major donors.

Volunteer Mailings

Because there is only about a 1-percent return when you begin direct mail, a professional mailing program is only a good choice for the groups that have broad goals to appeal to a large audience. For smaller groups, you are better off copying the techniques that work for the professionals but using your own labor and talent.

Many small organizations ask for money through the mail. Some ask their regular contributors once a year in an annual campaign. A team of volunteers writes a one-page letter on its personal stationery to a list of 20 to 100 people. They follow up with phone calls, collect donations, and send the thank-you notes. The return is usually 80-90 percent and the cost to the organization is only the postage.

Other groups use an annual holiday mailing. In October each board member is asked to bring in his or her own list of likely prospects, updated for their own Christmas or Hanukkah mailing. Also, test the lists of any clubs or organizations you believe would support this group. These lists are combined with the organization's master list to eliminate duplicates. A simple request with a nice photo or drawing is designed and printed. Include a reminder that donations are tax deductible, if true. Send your request with business reply envelopes and a simple reply card suggesting the amount to give.

In November a committee of the board and other volunteers hand-address the requests and add personal notes to everyone they know. The mailing goes out the second week of November, so people get them in November if they are mailed first class or in December if they are mailed third class. Be sure that your own names are on the list so you will know when your requests arrive. (Someone in my zip code said our postal service is so terrible it could be called *indirect* mail!) Follow up with phone calls to your best prospects to make sure your request is not lost in the holiday shuffle. Code the returns so you know which lists to use next year, send personal thank-yous, and count the money!

You can also alternate your volunteer mailings with requests for money in your newsletter, if you use the same list for both. Stagger the newsletter and direct mail requests so the donors get them at least two months apart.

See the bibliography, Chapter 14, for recommended reading from the experts to start your own direct mail program.

MAJOR DONORS

Fundraiser Kim Klein developed a profitable campaign to get her organization's volunteers to ask for large donations from individuals. She began in 1978 with four novice volunteers. When she left three years later the organization had fifteen volunteers and six staff members trained to ask for big donations. Their work produced a net income of $20,000, from donations of $50 to $5,000; this was 25 percent of the organization's budget. From 1978 to 1981 the organization's budget tripled, and its thoroughly planned individual donor system was the primary factor in this success.

Any organization that wants to ask for large donations from individuals in your community can imitate this plan. Use it to get more money from the people who have more money than your members. You can ask people with inherited wealth, business executives, and successful professionals such as lawyers and doctors. This article tells you how to ask donors one at a time. For advice on asking for money from rich people in small groups, see "Cocktail Party" in Chapter 10. For more advice on setting up a pledge system, see Chapter 4.

In the following article Klein shares her tested system on setting up a major donor campaign. You also get foolproof advice on how to train your people to ask for big money.

Setting Up an Individual Five to Thirty-five Donor Program, by Kim Klein*

One route to self-sufficiency for a nonprofit organization is to develop a funding base of individual donors.

An individual donor program differs from common dues-paying or subscription-oriented arrangements in several key ways. In a dues program members give a certain amount or a certain fixed percentage to the group to join. All members give either the same amount or the same percentage. In a subscription program, people pay a certain amount in order to get something—usually a newsletter or magazine. The subscriber is primarily interested in the product, and the pitch for new subscribers is geared more toward selling the product than the organization. Subscription rates are usually fixed as well. In an individual donor program, on the other hand, each person determines his or her own donation based on personal criteria and sense of commitment to the program.

An individual donor program allows the curious the opportunity to experiment, while it encourages the highly motivated to give as much as possible.

---

* Reprinted with permission from *Community Jobs*, Vol. 4, No. 1, February, 1981, pp. 9–11 and with permission from the author.

PREPARING A CAMPAIGN

An individual donor campaign takes careful and detailed planning. One or two people should take responsibility for coordinating and monitoring the campaign. Ideally, this should be a paid staff person, and it should be clear that his or her primary responsibility is fundraising. This person (hereafter referred to as "you") should have a small committee of volunteers to help with the planning and work.

Sit down with this committee, and, with a large calendar, begin to plot out your campaign. Be sure to allow two to four weeks for planning the campaign.

WHO TO ASK

Your major donor campaign has to be planned with the same thoroughness as the rest of your fundraising strategy. Be prepared for the fact that this will take longer than any other aspect of your fundraising efforts.

First, meet with your board of directors or other decision-making body, with the staff, and with anyone who has been around your organization for a while. Go through your lists of potential major donors. Keep a sheet of paper for each person on these lists (these people are called *prospects*). Write down whatever you know about them that is not hearsay or gossip. Facts such as, "interested in X" and "friend of Y" are important. "Just bought a house," "just had a child" are also important because they are facts you will want to take into account when asking for money. Note who in your group knows which prospect and can ask him or her for a gift.

Generally, your prospects will be of two giving abilities. Some will be able to give $50–$250 because they have salaries above $15,000. The other giving ability is much higher: $500 and up. These people will either be very successful, such as businesspeople, lawyers, and doctors, or people of independent wealth. Once you have all this data written down, determine a range of gift that you will ask from each prospect. Write that down on their sheet.

ASKING FOR MONEY

By now you will probably have noticed that you have some difficulty in getting people to volunteer to ask for money. You may experience difficulty yourself. Before you get any farther into your major donor program, you and your volunteers should discuss your feelings about money and about asking for money.

Asking for money is not that difficult once you get past some traditional reservations and understand some of the dynamics that surround the topic of money. Money is second only to sex in the number of prohibitions, myths, lies, distortion, and ignorance that surround it. Women, in particular, are often taught never to talk about money. Consequently, women often find it particularly difficult to ask for money.

But let's look at some of the excuses there are for not asking someone for money. One big excuse is, "I don't know her well enough." Seems legitimate until the next excuse is, "He's my best friend. I feel like I am taking advantage of him." This neatly eliminates having to ask anyone for money, since you either know them too well or not well enough. There are many other excuses that are variations on this theme: "It will put him on the spot," or "She already gives so much time," or "I would just be too embarrassed."

Stop and think of all the times you ask people to spend money and you are not embarrassed. You ask your friends to go to the movies or to try out a new restaurant. You have no guarantee that the movie or the food is going to be good, but you ask them to spend their money. Why not then on your organization?

You know that your organization is good, and you know that the money will be well spent. In fact, you are giving people an opportunity to invest in something worthwhile. In this world of sleaze, plastic and rip-off, having a place to spend money where the money is well used and where it makes a difference is a real pleasure. You will be surprised at the number of people who are flattered when you ask them for money. They are pleased that you want to include them in your work and are often happy to make a contribution.

People with money have something you need — their money. But you have something they need — a worthwhile group making significant social change that they can be a part of.

Try to imagine the worst thing that would happen if a friend of yours asked *you* for money for a cause in which he or she was involved. In most cases, the worst thing that could happen is that you would simply say no. As you think about what happens when your friends ask you for money, you will realize that you often say, "yes, I'll give." Statistics show that when asked face to face by someone they know, most people will give what is asked for.

The best way to get over a fear of asking for money is to make yourself do it. Practice first. Set up role plays. Practice what you are going to say. Be prepared for hard questions and think through the answers.

Common questions are: "But isn't the government taking care of this?" and "How effective is your organization?" and "Why should I give to you? I give $10 to a lot of good causes, so why do you think you deserve so much more?" If you are well prepared and know your organization, you should get what you ask for.

There is one way that is guaranteed to increase your chances of getting a prospect to say yes. **Give a donation yourself.** Give what is for you a significant gift. It may be $10 or $1,000, but give something. Money is powerful, and you cannot expect people to do something for you that you are not prepared to do yourself. Even if you don't tell someone that you haven't given, intuitively they often know. You will not come across as enthusiastic or as committed, no matter how much time you have spent with the organization. For this reason, many top fundraising consultants make a donation to all the organizations that hire their services. It sharpens their wits and makes them more interested. Don't try to be the first on your block to disprove this proven fundraising rule. You won't succeed. And your organization will suffer.

ASSIGNMENTS

When people begin to feel comfortable with the idea of asking for money, assign prospects to the people who know them best. Two or more people can write or call one prospect. People may also want to go in pairs.

Prospects who have given before — People who have given before are the simplest to approach. In a letter, phone call, or visit, simply remind the person that he or she gave a large gift once before and ask the person to renew. Remind everyone that inflation has driven your costs up and note that if it is possible to raise his or her gift, you will appreciate it.

Prospects that someone knows personally who have not given before—In the case of these people, most of the weight rests on the prospects' respect or friendship with the person they know. Ideally, the person should just ask the prospect. If that is not possible, then a letter using the name of the person who knows the prospect will help get the gift. Use it right in the first sentence of a letter. Say, "Jane Friendswithyou gave me your name. She knows you will be interested in learning more about our worthy cause. We hope that you will consider joining our work with a financial contribution." Then make your case and state why you need this prospect to give more than $50.

People that you don't know— People whom no one in the organization knows are the trickiest because you are making assumptions about these people that may not turn out to be true. In the case of people who have given before, you can safely assume that, unless they have fallen on hard times, they can give that much or more again. In the case of people that someone knows personally, part of your knowledge is how much they might be able to give. In the case of prospects you don't know, you can't assume very much beyond the fact that they *might be able* to give.

In your letter, tell this prospect that you have a goal to reach, say $15,000. Tell them you want to raise this money in denominations of $50 or more. You hope Mr. Rich will see himself in that category. If Mr. Rich does not, he will ignore your letter or send you a smaller gift. The difference in approach is that you don't say anything to the prospect about himself or herself, only about what *you* want.

FINAL TIPS ON ASKING

There are several things you should never say to a major donor (or to any donor, for that matter, though most of these tips will only apply to major donors).

• Never imply or state anything like, "Since you have so much money, how about sharing it?" (If this is your attitude, you would do well to let go of it. It will come through, and your donors will feel insulted.)

• Never admit to having deficit unless you know the donor well and know that she or he is not going to spread this information around. Operating at a deficit is not a disgrace, but it does lower morale. People don't want to put their money into a losing cause, and if you confess that you need the money to meet a deficit, you will find your number of donors (both small and large) dropping dramatically.

- Don't be obsequious, either in writing or in person. Although wealth may be intimidating to you, try to be as natural as possible, and you will soon discover real people under wealthy exteriors.

- Don't write or call the donors by their first names unless you know them well enough to do that. Most people are not offended by this practice, but some find it intimate and resent it. Practically no one is offended by being called Mr. or Ms.

- Don't try to make prospects feel guilty. The "less fortunate than thou" route for appeal is rapidly disappearing, and thank goodness. It is offensive and condescending, both to those who are more fortunate and to those who are deemed less fortunate.

All letters asking for money to major donors should include a brochure and a postage-paid return envelope. This is a sign of respect more than any effort to save the person money. All letters should be typed and personally signed by someone. Form letters asking for major donations, no matter how clever, will get you nothing.

WHAT NOW?

Now that all your appeals are out and gone, what should you do? Many people will be sending money in, and these donations need to be recorded.

Cards should be kept on all donors (large and small). The card should note the correct spelling of the donors' names, as well as information gleaned from their checks—phone numbers, professions, correct addresses. Also, note the amount of the donation, the date, and what the donation was in response to. For example. "John Jones, Green St., $50, 6/80, new office appeal." Or, "May Smith, friend of Nancy Faith, $250, holiday mailing."

The most important part of all donor solicitation and the major part of keeping donors giving year in and year out is the thank-you note. *Always, always, always thank everyone for every type of donation.* Even if you have to stay up all night writing these notes, do it!

Thank-you notes make the donor feel appreciated, and she or he will remember that the next time you ask for something. Feeling appreciated is important for anyone who works with social change groups. Since the society at large often does not appreciate your work, the people inside the organization must help bridge that gap and make everyone feel good about the time they spend with you.

In a more pragmatic sense, thank-yous loosen up money. Many times donors will send in an extra donation after receiving a thank you. For example, one organization had a donor who gave $50 and never got a thank you. The next year, when this donor heard from the group again, she told a friend, "Indeed, I will not give to that group. They don't even observe the most simple courtesy." The friend prevailed upon her to give them another chance, so she sent $25. She received a simple handwritten thank you, and four months later she gave the group $1,000. This is a true story. It could happen to you.

HOW TO KEEP THAT MONEY COMING YEAR AFTER YEAR

Major donors need more attention. When you have invested as much money as a major donor has, you want to know what is happening to it. Once or twice a year, send major donors a well written, concise, upbeat look at your financial structure. Spell out for them your goals and where you are in relation to your goals. Let them know how important they are in this plan. Have this report printed nicely (not on slick paper or in an expensive way) and send it *with a personal note* to each major donor.

In addition to this, your major donors should get some free gift for giving that much money. Each donor should hear from you — in a personal letter — at least three times a year. This can be with their gift, with a midyear financial report, and with an end-of-the-year financial report.

In addition to these times of being in touch, if you find out that one of your major donors has had a child, or if you know their birthdays, send a note. Keep in touch with them as often as you can without being annoying. Generally once every two months is good.

In order to ensure that your organization continues to grow and continues to be supported by a broad base of donors, you will need to conduct a campaign like the one described here every year. Each campaign gets easier as you understand more about doing it and as your systems are set up and operating smoothly. Every year you should solicit new mailing lists, new major donors, and generally keep a "membership drive consciousness" alive in your board, volunteers, and staff.

Setting up and maintaining an individual donor program is hard work and requires a lot of attention. But a successful and well-run program is very rewarding because it means that your organization is needed and supported by the community you serve, that you will exist past the end of any grant, and that you are inflation- and recessionproof because you are financially stable.

NEWSLETTERS

Most membership organizations have some sort of newsletter they use to communicate with the members, publish original research, and promote the organization. You can make money with newsletters three ways: sell subscriptions, sell advertising, or use the list for direct mail requests.

Selling subscriptions is the most difficult way to make a profit. If you include the subscription price in your dues, it must be less than the dues. If you choose to keep your dues low to make it easy to sell memberships, it will make your newsletter subscription price even lower. If your price is low, you have to keep all your costs even lower. If you are now paying staff to work on the newsletter or the mailing lists, you may be losing money on your newsletter. If you use all volunteer talent and low-cost production, you may be making a small profit. So you will need to sell many subscriptions to make the newsletter a money maker.

As expert fundraiser Richard Steckel says, "Never retail when you can wholesale." Try selling groups of subscriptions to local businesses, institutions, or churches. For example, you can ask a local business to buy 200 subscriptions to give to their employees as an employee benefit. Unless you can find a way to sell large numbers of subscriptions quickly, the revenue from subscriptions alone will not make much money for your group.

The way to make money with a newsletter is to sell advertising space. This is how almost all magazines make money. When you start you can have members volunteer to sell the ads. Build in some competition among clubs or committees to promote sales. You can even divide the ad displays by area, which is another incentive to make each chapter want to sell more.

Two chapters of ACORN (Association of Community Organizations for Reform Now) in Detroit sell ads in the $15 to $60 price range. The *Gratiot-Gunston-6 Mile Neighbors for Action* covers local issues and how to join GG6. Four smaller groups jointly produce the *Southwest News* in English and Spanish for the Southwest side. Both papers net more than $500 per issue from ad sales.

For an ongoing money maker, after you have worked out the most profitable newsletter format and advertising price arrangements, hire someone to sell the ads. This makes a good part-time job for a member and gives the responsibility of selling a monthly amount to a professional rather than volunteer fundraisers.

Low Overhead

The way to keep your profits up is to keep your costs down. Local merchants and politicians advertise in your newsletter because they want to support your work and reach your readers. They never assume that a nonprofit organization's newsletter will have a circulation or frequency to rival for-profit publications.

Calculate how much it costs you now to send out your newsletter. Be sure to include the cost of the salaries you pay any staff to maintain your lists; type, write, or edit the newsletter; and handle the mailing. If you include salaries, the cost of your newsletter is probably higher than you thought. If you want to make your newsletter a money maker instead of a money loser, replace the paid staff with volunteers. Many people already have newsletter experience from school, their job, or another organization and can do the work with little or no training. Since many volunteers like to pretend they are Brenda Starr or Lou Grant, it is easy to get volunteers for the newsletter committee. Then you can reassign your paid staff to get more results on the mission of the organization.

After you find volunteers to publish the newsletter, look for free printing and postage. Some companies and labor unions have their own printers and printing presses that can do your newsletter in between their regular work. The cost is trivial to a large company or union but can be a major savings to you.

Ask if they will also cover the postage. If not, you can ask another business to contribute the postage. Point out that all the talent and labor is supplied by volunteers, printing is donated by union A, so a donation of postage by company B will make the newsletter a real money maker.

Evaluate how often you need to mail the newsletter. Pull out samples of your last ten issues. How much of the copy was really "news" that your readers would not have been able to read except for your newsletter? How much was social notes, reprints, and filler to complete the issue? Calculate how much of the contents of the newsletter was not important news, then cut your circulation by that much. If only half of the copy of the last ten issues is truly important, then you can cut your frequency in half. If you mailed every month last year, you can mail every other month this year. If you published quarterly last year, you can publish twice a year this year. If you get a hot story in between issues, you can always put out an extra edition. But most organizations spend too much time and money mailing out newsletters that have too little news. Mail less often, and you will get better reading and less expense.

Direct Mail

A cardinal rule of grass roots fundraising is: Never miss an opportunity. Never print *anything* that does not include a request for funds from the people reading it. Your newsletter goes to people who believe in your work. Ask them for money!

If you have dues-paying members, always include an application for membership in every issue. Every organization can report on the success of its fundraising since the last issue and ask for more money. Most groups make enough money from the request to pay their production expenses; some make much more.

Even a very small organization can publish a newsletter in the spring and the fall including a request for funds. Then mail to the same list once before Christmas and Hanukkah to ask for holiday funds and one other time during the year to ask for an annual contribution or sell a benefit ticket. This way your newsletter fits into your larger direct mail campaign, so you get more money for the same amount of work.

See the bibliography, Chapter 14, for recommended reading on publishing great newsletters.

PAYROLL DEDUCTION FUNDRAISING

Asking for money through payroll deductions at the workplace has proven to be one of the most efficient ways to raise funds. The most common payroll deduction fund is the United Way that runs collections through employers in almost every city larger than 25,000 people. In the last decade new federations of charities have also begun asking for money through payroll deductions. In 1981 there were eleven affiliates of the National Black United Fund, eight combined health appeals, seven united arts funds, seven coalitions of alternative organizations, and two women's funds successfully soliciting money through payroll deductions. Like most high-profit fundraising techniques, payroll deduction is expensive to start but pays off in the long run with dependable income from workers who want to support your group.

The best place for your group to start is at your local United Way that collects money from businesses and state and local government employees and the Combined Federal Campaign that collects money from federal employees. Ask two members of your board to get the applications for each and interview local groups that have been accepted and rejected for each. Consider if these would be the best way for your organization to get money from employees. Only after you have researched the advantages and disadvantages of your United Way and Combined Federal Campaign should you consider starting or joining an alternative fund. As Frank Blechman, director of The Human Endeavor, A Fund for Positive Growth in South Carolina, says, "All grass roots groups should apply to the United Way. If they're accepted, good, they get funding. If they're rejected, good, that makes the case for an outside campaign. Also, the Combined Federal Campaign may be a major resource and should be reviewed. Because creating an alternative fund is so difficult, it really should be seen much more as a last resort than as a cornucopia."

Starting a new payroll deduction fund is a four-step process. First, local nonprofit organizations form a federation to solicit gifts, share the administrative expenses, and distribute the income. Second, they ask employers to let them ask employees to give to the federated fund. The employer agrees to let the federation solicit its employees and receive the deductions from the paychecks of its employees. Third, the federation asks the employees to pledge a certain amount from each check. Through this system, even small donations will add up over the year. If the employees are paid every two weeks they get twenty-six checks a year; if they are paid twice a month they get twenty-four checks a year. If a worker pledges just $2 per paycheck, the federation gets $52 in the first system or $48 in the second system. The employer takes out the money and forwards the total amount due to the federation each quarter. Fourth, the federation deducts a percentage for its administrative overhead, then distributes the net income to the members of the federation or charities designated by the donors.

There are three reasons why federated fundraising works so well. First, the overhead is very low since several organizations share the expenses. Depending on who does the books, the costs of federated fundraising usually run about 10 to 20 percent, leaving 80 to 90 percent profit for the member groups. The only fundraising method that makes more money is simply having volunteers ask for money in dues or contributions. Other fundraisers that make as much profit are ad books, services, training, and speakers bureaus. Other big professional fundraisers make much less, at least in the beginning. Canvassing nets 50 to 70 percent; direct mail can *lose* money the first year, then nets about 50 to 70 percent.

Second, like all pledge systems, the collection allows small givers to become major donors. The Combined Federal Campaign is the payroll deduction plan for federal employees. In 1977 it collected almost $80 million from 3.8 million employees. The average contribution was $39 per employee when payroll deductions were used and $12 when cash contributions or pledges were used.

Third, it is easy to give because the donor never sees the money. It is taken out of the paychecks before they ever get the money, just like their taxes and Social Security. So their donations go directly to the federation, rather than to them, and *then* to you.

Here is more tested advice on federated fundraising from Jon Pratt, the Field Director of the Midwest Office of The Youth Project. His article tells you how to begin, what to expect, and where to get more advice.

Payroll Deduction Fundraising, by Jon Pratt

Asking for money through payroll deductions at the workplace has proven to be one of the most efficient ways to raise funds. Where the employer agrees, a federated charity can solicit employees to have a regular sum deducted from each paycheck, and sent to the charity. The pioneer of this method, and its largest beneficiary, is the United Way.

The total money pledged for payroll deductions in 1980 was $1.3 billion. Of this, more than 90 percent went to United Ways and the remainder to Combined Health Agencies Drives (CHADs), united arts funds, Black United Funds, and other service and alternative funds. Each of these funds share common elements: 1) They unite many different organizations into a single appeal for contributions. 2) They focus their workplace solicitations on a limited campaign in one month or less. 3) The majority of their funds come from payroll deductions from individual employees.

HOW IT WORKS

Contributions made to federated funds are handled in three ways. Some funds have a committee, rather than donors, decide allocations. Some allow the donor to designate specific federation member organizations for support. A few allow the donor to designate any nonprofit organization—member or not—to receive the contribution.

The efficiency of payroll deductions comes from the use of employer-computerized payrolls, the ease of locating employees, and larger average contributions than one-time cash gifts. First an employer must agree to accept a federated fund to seek employee contributions through deductions. Then the fund need only get the employee to sign a card, specifying a certain amount per paycheck, usually from $1 to $5. From there on the employer deducts the amount from the check of each employee who signed the fund's pledge card and forwards the total amount to the fund. The fund, in turn, makes an allocation of the collected funds to its member or recipient groups.

The campaign to convince employees to pledge part of their pay to the fund is the main task of the fund in the fall. The campaign consists of brochures, posters, presentations to groups of employers, and one-to-one solicitations of employees by fellow employees appointed as volunteer solicitors.

The United Way of America is itself a federation of United Ways around the United States. It provides funds to a great variety of direct social service providers, including the Boy Scouts, Girl Scouts, Red Cross, Salvation Army, religious-sponsored social service organizations, YMCA, and YWCA. While these are important services, the United Way has been criticized for not funding women, minorities, advocacy groups, or organizations that do things other than provide services in the traditional charitable fields of health and welfare. Since most United Way funds are committed to traditional charities, very few new organizations are accepted for United Way funding.

BEGIN WITH UNITED WAY

Given the large amount of funds now raised by the United Ways, often $1 million to $12 million in a metropolitan area, an organization's first effort should be put into applying for United Way funding. United Way allocations are made by citizen review panels through a lengthy and detailed application process. Recently, some United Ways have responded to criticism and the threat of alternative funds and have supported battered women's shelters and minority agencies. Only if new funding from United Way is not possible, or if an organization does not meet United Way direct service criteria, should the option of helping organize an alternative fund be considered.

ALTERNATIVE FUNDS

An alternative federated fund can seek access to payroll deductions in the same way as the United Way but can be organized by groups sharing the same goals, such as health care, the arts, social change, women's issues, or minority rights. Several funds have been organized in the last five years, including the Cooperating Fund Drive in St. Paul, Minnesota; The Human Endeavor in South Carolina; the Women's Way in Philadelphia; and the Black United Funds in several cities.

These funds conduct fall campaigns, transfer money to organizations, and combine forces to communicate the message about needs of member organizations. They respond to a market for donations not served by United Ways. The appearance of new federated funds at the workplace is not competition for the same dollars, since in most cases after the new fund appears, total giving goes up so there are more dollars to go around. However, a local United Way may view a new federated fund as a threat to its reaching its goal.

HOW TO SET UP A FUND

Establishing an alternative fund requires a great deal of work and broad-based support, more than any single organization can handle. In addition, a new fund requires the investment of several years of outside support to cover the administrative costs that cannot be assessed against the pledged contributions. The mechanics of setting up a new fund must be tailored to each individual situation, but the following sketches the basis of such an effort.

The first step in organizing a successful payroll deduction campaign is to form the federation. Care should be taken to bring together a broad representation of groups to attract broad community support, employee interest, and employer acceptance. Federated funds have been formed around specific groups—women, minority groups, or social change, with membership from seven to forty-two agencies.

Two examples of successful alternative fund memberships are in South Carolina and Minnesota. The Human Endeavor: A Fund for Positive Growth in South Carolina (THE), was formed in 1978 to provide an efficient fundraising vehicle for small community organizations. THE now has forty-two member agencies, including the American Civil Liberties Union (ACLU) of South Carolina, the Brown Lung Association, the Charleston African Dance Ensemble, and the Horry County Grass Roots Association. The Cooperating Fund Drive in St. Paul, Minnesota, has twenty-two social change organizations as members, ranging from tenants unions and the Gray Panthers to alternative health clinics and the United Handicapped Federation.

The fund can be organized as a coalition of organizations incorporated as a separate nonprofit organization that will be able to pull off a campaign. Each organization should have representation on the board, and it is also useful to have at-large representatives from unions, the business community, and government. The new fund should have a common statement of purpose defining what it is organized to support and setting criteria for inclusion of new members.

In order to persuade employers to include the fund in their payroll deductions, the new federation should compile a listing of member agencies, the services or activities they provide, and the people whose needs are met. Because of the greater openness of government and its responsiveness to public support, it is generally easiest for new funds to begin with city, county, state, and federal employees. Endorsements from employee unions, other organizations, and local officials are helpful in obtaining access.

Some state governments and the federal government (through the Combined Federal Campaign) have set procedures for new funds to qualify for access to payroll. City or county governments, which in metropolitan areas employ as many people as the state and federal government, generally do not have a set method for admission of new funds. Corporations must be approached individually, but some have adopted open contribution policies, including TRW Defense and Space Systems Group, Crocker National Bank, and Cummins Engine Company.

The work of alternative funds is divided into two phases: 1) gaining access to employers and 2) the campaign—getting the message across to employees and asking them to pledge. Often, the campaigns are held at the same time in the fall as is United Way, sometimes in a joint campaign (with shared materials) or simultaneously (with separate brochures and presentations).

Member organizations contribute volunteers to make presentations to employee groups. Presentations can include slide shows, speeches, and question-and-answer sessions. Try to reach as many employees as possible through presentations and ask for support from supervisors.

Costs. Operating costs for a federated fund are met by retaining a percentage of money raised. In the first years outside grants can support start-up expenses. The United Way states that its administrative costs range from 9 to 14 percent, while The Human Endeavor charges 10 percent. Major expenses for a fund include office space, materials, and staff time.

The best guide for projecting income from alternative funds is to look at United Ways, since the new funds are still in their initial years of development. The United Way has found that it can raise $10 per working person in a given area. This translates into $4.5 million in a 1-million-population metropolitan area where 450,000 are in the work force. Of course, not every worker contributes, but the average payroll contribution of about $35 per person brings the total up.

The following chart projects the growth of a new federated fund over four years, showing the increasing number of workplaces participating, employees contributing, and total contributions.

Advice. Organizations interested in exploring the potential for payroll deduction fundraising can get more information from several groups working in the area. The National Committee for Responsive Philanthropy publishes a quarterly newsletter that covers national trends in the area. Order from NCRP, 2001 S Street, NW, Suite 620, Washington, DC 20009. NCRP memberships are $20 per year for individuals. Other funds that have information include the Cooperating Fund Drive, Liberty Bank Building, #215, Snelling and Selby Ave., St. Paul, MN 55104, the Women's Funding Alliance, 119 S. Main St., Seattle, WA 98104, and the National Black United Fund (NBUF), 2090 Adam Clayton Powell Blvd., Room 821, New York, NY 10027. Or call the National Black United Front at 1-800-223-0866.

Growth of a New Federated Fund

	Organizing Year	Year 1	Year 2	Year 3	Year 4
Workplaces Participating	0	3	7	16	25
Employees Solicited	0	10,000	25,000	50,000	80,000
Employees Contributing	0	700	2,500	6,000	10,400
Percent of Employees Contributing	0	7%	10%	12%	13%
Average Contribution	0	$25	$25	$25	$25
Total Contributions	0	$17,500	$62,500	$150,000	$260,000
Percent Administrative Fee	0	12%	12%	11%	10%
Administrative Income	0	$ 2,100	$ 7,500	$ 16,500	$ 26,000
Net Contributions Distributed to Organizations	0	$15,400	$55,000	$133,500	$234,000
Campaign Expenses	$18,000	$19,000	$25,200	$27,200	$ 29,200
Deficit to be Raised from Foundation Grants, Individual Contributions, and Member Organization Dues	$18,000	$16,900	$17,700	$ 10,700	$ 3,200

THE SPEAKERS BUREAU

When you need more money, one question to ask is: "What are we giving away now that we could be charging money for?" In other words, "What are we good at?" and "What do other people want?" Some examples might include charging a fee for giving advice on welfare regulations, tenants' rights, property tax changes, credit rules, or job possibilities. You can also charge money for people to hear your leaders speak about your issues.

A speakers bureau takes advantage of the fact that you have an exciting organization with something to say and someone to say it. Begin with a publicity campaign to make your group *the* source of expertise on your issue and make your leader the authority. The second is more important than the first for selling speakers. There are hundreds of consumer organizations, but Ralph Nader gets all the invitations. The key to success is TV. When your leaders are recognized from TV they become "somebody"—an expert. Of course they must also *be,* or become, experts on the issue before their first speeches.

When you are just getting started, place your leaders on as many TV and radio talk shows as possible. Your local publicity guide should list the shows that take guests. If you do not have a publicity guide, make your own list of talk shows from the newspaper's TV directory. Call them all. Tell the producer who you are, who your leaders are, and what topics they can discuss. It is best if you can link it to a current event—"Mrs. Gonzales, who will be testifying on nursing home abuses at the Senate hearings tomorrow. . . ."

In addition to the TV and radio talk shows, fill all the free speaking engagements you get to give the leaders experience in giving their speech and fielding questions.

After your speakers have some experience and the organization has built its reputation through research, exposés in the press, and testimony before government bodies, you can launch the speakers bureau. Get copies of the brochures from the professional bureaus listed in the phone book under "Lecture Bureau." Use these as models to make up your own brochure using photographs of the leaders, provocative titles for their speeches, short descriptions of the speakers, and a history of the group. You can also offer slide presentations and training workshops as well as speeches.

Selling the Speakers

Give your service a name and buy a listing under "Lecture Bureaus" in the phone book. Print about 200 brochures and mail them to the program chairpeople of all the civic organizations, professional associations, churches, and schools in your area. They are all listed in the phone book. You can also mail to the director of student activities and student government president at all the colleges and universities in the state.

Follow up with telephone calls to confirm that they have received your brochure and to sell your speakers. The best people to work with over the long run are the student activities people and the student government leaders. They get a large amount of money each year from student activities charges. Since they have to spend all of it every year in order to justify taxing the students, they are ideal sources of speakers' fees for your group.

Fees

Make a sliding scale based on the number of people in the audience, the group's ability to pay, and the type of presentation they want. A dollar a head works well for group charges, unless the group is a professional association or business group, in which case charge a minimum of $50. You will have to learn what the market will bear in your area, but most groups charge from $25 for appearing on a panel to $500 for running a daylong workshop.

The advantages to you of having other groups pay for the leaders are:

1. You raise money.
2. You really do limit the demands on the leaders.
3. You have a criterion for determining who is serious about wanting to learn more about your issues and hearing your speaker. If they will pay, they want it; if they won't pay, then they don't want it, regardless of what else they tell you.

4. Your speaker will speak to larger audiences. If the chamber of commerce pays $200 to hear your president, the chamber's program chairperson has to justify the expenditure by turning out a big group to hear the speech. If the speaker comes for free, it doesn't matter to anyone—except perhaps the speaker—how big the audience is.
5. Since we all suffer from consumer brainwashing, we "know" that the more something costs, the better it is. This works both ways. The audience will pay more attention knowing they paid for an expert, and the speaker gets a real ego boost knowing someone will pay $200 to hear him or her.

HANDLING COMPLAINTS

Common complaints about your fees and the answers that work are:

1) "I thought you people wanted to help the public."
A. We sure do. It costs $50,000 a year to run our program. We raise all of our money ourselves, and our program will help you, too. So we will have to ask you for an honorarium.

2) "Con Ed is sending Peter Power and we don't have to pay for him. Why should we pay to hear your side?"
A. You already paid for Peter Power. His *job* is to give speeches for Con Ed and his salary comes out of your rates. Our leaders are all volunteers. They donate their fees to the work of the group so all the citizens of Metropolis have someone to speak for them against Con Ed.

3) "But this is a real opportunity for you to talk to us! You want money too?"
A. We get more requests for speakers than we can handle. All our leaders are volunteers. They do all their work for the group in addition to their regular jobs. So the only way we can limit the demands on their time is to ask people to pay.

4) "Why should we pay for Mrs. Washington? She's just a housewife."
A. That's right, she is a housewife, which is why she will be able to communicate with your audience better than some academic

egghead who will put them to sleep. She is also president of the Metropolis Concerned Citizens by virtue of her election by 1,500 people at our convention in October. Can 1,500 people be wrong?

EXCEPTIONS

There are times when it really *is* an opportunity to address a crowd, such as the keynote at an important convention. In this case, the publicity and the goodwill of the other group are more important than the money. This is a political decision rather than a fund-raising decision.

More Money

At the end of every speech the speaker can ask the people there to give you money. At the very least, you can ask for donations that day. Even better, bring along a volunteer to help sign up people for ongoing donations. If the audience is mostly people like your members, ask them to join the organization. Point out your smiling volunteer, and both of you can sell memberships after the speech. If most of the audience has more money than your members, ask them to pledge monthly support for your group. Then you and your volunteer can get them to sign pledge cards. If the audience includes both kinds of people, bring two volunteers to sell membership and ask for pledges. Madeline Rogero-Pitt trained speakers for the United Farm Workers. As she says, "The measure of the success of your presentation will not be the amount of applause but the amount of pledges you sign up!" Never shy away from asking for money just because the organization gave you an honorarium. Every person in that audience ought to support the work you do. *Ask* them so they can all share in your victories!

PAYMENT

Checks should be made payable to the organization. If for any bookkeeping or political reason the check must be made payable to the leader instead of the group, the leader endorses the check to the group and is reimbursed for the difference it will make on his or her income taxes. Leaders may be reimbursed for any money they have to spend to make the speech, such as carfare, baby-sitting, or meals.

See the bibliography, Chapter 14, for recommended reading on speakers bureaus.

6

Raising Money
from the General Public:

Who Wants Something
Else We Can Offer?

After you establish a dependable system to get money from the people who need your organization and the people who want your organization, you can consider ways to get money from everyone else. Think about the talents of your own members. What are they good at? What do they like to do? What kind of fundraisers do they handle for other organizations? Then decide if you want to choose a method to raise money from the general public. This is sometimes called "external fundraising.

There are many ways to raise money from people beyond your own members and believers. Some of the most popular are the special events you hold once a year such as parties, dinners, and bazaars. These are described in chapters 8, 9, and 10. This chapter will discuss the fundraisers your organization can run all year-round to produce a steady income from the people in your community.

These include bingo and other forms of legal gambling, businesses, selling products, services, and training. All of these can make money for you from the general public.

There are four big advantages in raising money from the general public. First, you do not need to keep going back to your own people to ask for money. No matter how much they love the organization, you can tax the same people only so much before they revolt. Second, it broadens your base of income so you get donations from many more people. This makes your fundraising more dependable because it comes from more people. Third, it allows people of limited income to make large amounts of money for the organization. In some cities a team of twenty volunteers can run a bingo game that will net $60,000 per year for the organization. None of the volunteers could donate $3,000 to the organization, but the bingo game allows each one to raise that much money in an enjoyable way from four hours a week of work. Fourth, you can get money from anyone. These people do not have to like your organization or even its goals. People are getting something they want; you get the profits because you do the work. Everyone benefits.

BINGO

Bingo is a game of chance enjoyed by millions of Americans in church halls, fraternal lodges, and county fairs. In the game's simplest form, bingo players buy cards with a grid of twenty-four numbers and a free space in the center. Each card is different. A caller calls numbers drawn at random, from one to seventy-five, and the first player to get five numbers in a row on the card yells "Bingo!" and gets a prize. Charity bingos ordinarily give prizes of cash from $5 to $500 or merchandise like small appliances, dolls, or decorative knickknacks.

Bingo is currently legal in forty-two states. These states have recognized that their citizens are going to gamble anyway, so they might as well make it legal and tax the revenues. This is verified by the three-year study summarized in a 413-page book entitled *Gambling in America* (1976). The federal government spent $3 million of our tax money to find out what any citizen could have verified for free. The first sentence says "Gambling is inevitable."

Gambling is both fun and profitable, very profitable. If you choose to run a bingo game, you can get a big return for the effort involved.

First, the board of directors should discuss among themselves and with the entire membership whether or not to sponsor a gambling operation. The negative is that some people have strong moral objections to gambling as a sin and as a regressive tax. The positives are that it is profitable, most people want to gamble, it produces a convivial social atmosphere, and the occasion can also be used organizationally to reach new people. If the board decides to do it, get a copy of your state laws and read them thoroughly. Every state has different rules, and you must follow them scrupulously. Even if you know St. Bastion's is stretching the rules, it is a bad idea for you to deviate from the law in any way. Especially if your organization is controversial or sometimes has conflicts with the state government, remember that one way the state can retaliate is by inspecting your fundraising program with a microscope. Keep your record squeaky clean.

If the board chooses to run a bingo game, and if the organization meets the state requirements, apply for a license. Get advice from the people who currently run successful bingos. Play at several different halls before yours opens to learn how they entertain the crowd, get people to come back week after week, and offer special gimmicks. You may be able to use the hall and equipment of an existing group that already runs a bingo game on a different night. Otherwise, look for the best place in terms of conveniences, appeal to a crowd, and access to your workers. You can usually buy your equipment on the installment plan. It may be a good idea to own your own equipment anyway to use for other events.

The key to success with bingo is the appeal of the caller. The best callers have a following who come to play because they know he or she runs a fair game. When the star caller of Chicago bingo, Bernie Willow, jokingly told his crowd that anyone who brought him a valentine would get a free card, he was overwhelmed by the creativity and care of his audience. One woman gave him a valentine made like the bingo board, one gave him a decorated can of beer, and one dressed up her little girl as a valentine. The rapport between player and caller draws the crowd. Since every state law sets a ceiling on the total prize money, your caller is your drawing card.

The caller is also the best person to give you advice on types of games and gimmicks. For example you can run a friendship bingo game where the people on either side of the person who bingos get prizes or cash. This builds up team spirit. You can have the crowd sign the back of this week's card and put it in a box when they leave. Next week draw out three cards and give them extra cards, prizes, or cash if they show up. This will help build repeat attendance. You can also run a concession stand and sell supplies.

Rotating teams of workers sell the cards and verify the bingos after they are called. They also serve as the hospitality committee to assist the players so they don't need to leave their cards to get change, more chips, or an ashtray. Working the bingo can be a very rewarding job as the teams get to know the customers and vice versa.

In addition to the income, some groups use their bingos to introduce political candidates, circulate petitions, recruit new members, pass out issue papers, and pick up information on local problems. But the big payoff is financial. People come to play because they love bingo and hope they will win big. They do not need to support your program to support the bingo game. Although you can anticipate a loss while you build up a regular crowd, after the first six to twelve months a successful weekend evening bingo can bring in $40,000 to $80,000 a year—enough to support a medium-sized to large organization.

STARTING A BUSINESS

One way to make money for nonprofits is to start a business that is a for-profit. It is organized and run as a for-profit business, and all the profits go to your organization. The most common example of a business venture to support a nonprofit is a thrift shop or resale store. Many hospitals run gift shops, flower shops, and restaurants; art museums run gift shops, restaurants, and rental galleries; colleges run restaurants, bookstores, and adult education classes. Newer examples include a motel run by a battered women's shelter, a blue grass music festival run on the Oneida Indian reservation, and a drugstore run by senior citizens. The Baltimore Theatre Project opened its own cabaret "Ethel's Place" to showcase jazz singer Ethel Ennis and other local jazz and ethnic musicians. Movie star Jane Fonda opened a string of exercise salons to raise money for her husband's political party. Your organization may also choose to use a for-profit business to support your work.

Choose a business that makes sense to your own people. It should be something that uses the talents and the interests they already have. The way to guarantee that the business fits into the goals of your organization is to ask the leadership itself to plan the business. Ask two or more people from the board to head a committee to research possible business ventures for the organization. Allow the committee about three months to interview successful for-profit and nonprofit business managers, your lawyer, accountant, insurance agent, banker, and other financial advisors. Then ask them to bring the board a short report describing the types of businesses your own people would like to run, the financial advantages and disadvantages, the organizational advantages and disadvantages, the number of paid jobs, the number of volunteer opportunities, the amount of money needed to get started, and the projected time needed before you make a profit.

At the same time the board can assign two other members to research other kinds of high-return fundraising, such as direct mail, door-to-door canvassing, bingo and gambling, corporate solicitation, payroll deductions, or major donors. Then compare them to determine which is the best choice for your organization to meet its financial goals. The following chart gives you some average times for different sorts of fundraisers to make money for the group. Update this information with current results from your own community, then decide if starting a for-profit business is the best choice for your group and, if so, which business.

Average Time Needed to Make a Profit

Fundraisers	Time from Start of Asking for Money to First Profits Available for Spending
Dues	Today
Individual Donations	Today
Corporate Donations	1–6 months
Special Events (Benefits)	1–6 months
Selling Services	1–3 months
Canvassing (professional)	3–6 months
Foundation Proposals	3–12 months
Major Donors	3–6 months
Speakers Bureau	3–6 months
Selling Products	3–6 months
Selling Training	3–6 months
Bingo	6–12 months
Newsletter	6–12 months
Direct Mail (professional)	1–2 years
Government Proposals	1–3 years
Businesses	3–5 years
Payroll Deductions	3–5 years
Deferred Giving (Bequests)	3–20 years

Planning

Like any other planning, you need to begin with a clear definition of your goals. If the *only* goal is making money for your group, then you can choose the business that will make the greatest profit from the resources you have available. If you want to combine making a profit from the business with meeting other organizational goals, you have to choose all your goals and decide which one is most important. For example, a battered women's shelter that plans a for-profit answering service can say it wants the service to provide a safe, sheltered, supervised work experience for its women; to give the women the chance to earn their keep, raise their self-esteem, and update their job skills; and to produce an income for the shelter. In some cases, the organizational goals will be just as important as the financial goals. In that case, you may choose a business that is less profitable but more useful for your group's work. Just be sure that all of the board members agree on the goals and their importance. Write them down, in order, vote on them, then give each member of the board and staff a copy of the goals. Then begin the research on business possibilities.

First, ask for advice from local business leaders and nonprofit organizations that run profitable businesses. If you want to start a thrift shop, talk to the owners and managers of the most successful department stores in town and talk to the managers of the most profitable thrift shops. Use this research to decide if this would also be a good venture for your group. Make yourself a list of *do*'s.

Next talk to at least three people who started the same kind of business that did *not* make a profit. As Disraeli said, "There is no education like adversity." Ask the people what they would do differently next time, and make yourself a list of *don't*s.

Now ask for advice from your local Small Business Administration (SBA) office. The SBA is the federal agency mandated to help new small business ventures with advice and loans. Like any government agency, the quality of the SBA varies from city to city, but its services are free. There are 100 SBA field offices, most in large cities. You can find them listed in large telephone directories under "Small Business Administration" in the white pages or "United States Government" in the blue pages. Or ask the office of your member of Congress for the nearest SBA office.

Many SBAs offer low-cost ($2) workshops on starting a business. These cover management, financial basics, legal organization, business records, marketing, selling, and taxes. Their advice will help you set up your books and taxes right the first time. The SBA can also point you to people who tried the same kind of business and failed; the SBA is left holding their loan.

The SBA runs the Active Corps of Executives (ACE) and the Service Corps of Retired Executives (SCORE) to give you introductions to active and retired executives. Thirty cities now have branches of the Executive Service Corps which can give nonprofits introductions to retired executives. Professional Associations, trade associations, business schools, and the business or economic departments of local colleges or universities may also be able to help you find useful advice.

In any case, you get what you ask for, so be very specific about what you want in terms of a volunteer advisor. Especially for

SCORE volunteers, you can often get an old geezer who is full of quaint anecdotes but has little current or applicable advice for you. Remember your tax dollars pay for the SBA; persist until you get the help you need. If the first volunteer is not helpful, be more specific about your needs and ask for another. If you have to ask ten times, do it. Keep throwing back the lemons until you get a winner because that person can give you the advice and the introductions to make your business a success. He or she may stay on your advisory committee and repay your persistence many times over.

WHICH BUSINESS?

Once the board has collected advice on the dos and don'ts of starting a business, decide what you want to do. Ask yourselves these questions.

1. *What do we already do that we like and that we use to make a profit?* For example, many groups start out doing a rummage sale once a year. Then they make it quarterly, then choose to open a thrift shop using the trained talent they have from holding rummage sales. Another group may have dinners for senior citizens every month. They use what they already know to open a restaurant.

2. *What are our goals for this business?* This is the most important question, so spend the most time on it. All of the board members must agree on the goals and their order of importance for the business to succeed. For example, an alternative school that teaches juvenile offenders wants to start a business that will employ its students who have very low skill levels. If it chooses a business to make money, it will have to choose a business that can use workers with low skills, such as a car wash. If it chooses a business to train the teenagers in reading and arithmetic skills, then it could open a retail store. The teenagers will get a chance to learn new skills and gain a job experience they would not get otherwise, but the store will not be able to compete with other for-profit stores and will probably not make money. In that case, it is a training center instead of a for-profit business. It does not matter what the board

chooses, as long as you all understand and agree on the goals. If you choose to run a for-profit business, it must put money making first and your other goals second. If you choose to use a business for training or other goals, realize that it will probably be a money drain and will add to your budget money that you must raise from other sources.

3. *How much will it cost?* Get accurate current figures for what it will take to start from your business advisors, the SBA, and your bank.

4. *Where will we get the money to start?* You may need to borrow money, get a grant from a foundation, church, or business, or use your own funds from your treasury. Most businesses that get into trouble do so because they start with too little money to make the business work well at the beginning. Be sure you have enough money before you start.

5. *How much money will we get back? When will we get it? Can we wait that long?* Most for-profit businesses need to plow any profits back into the business for the first year or two, if there *are* any profits. If you need money quickly, you would probably be better off using your energies to start a different fundraiser that will give you income more quickly.

6. *Will this cause any conflict with our program goals?* If you open a pharmacy, you must be licensed by the state. Will this inhibit your running a bold campaign for better health care in your state?

7. *How can we prevent conflict of interest among our board members, the organization, and the people who run the business?* If your business will be spending money in your community, you have to decide how to control the problems of conflict of interest. The best way is to say that no one on your board can make money from your business. In fact, say that no one on your board can sell to your business, since some people *always* claim they are not making a profit from what they do. If a lawyer, accountant, insurance agent, or other business person wants the account, he or she can *either* sell to the business *or* serve on your board but *not* both at the same time. Of course, you should also make rules about not giving business to your own friends and family members. In a small town it

may not be possible to find people who are not friends or relatives, in which case you will need to set other rules.

8. *What will we personally do to make this venture succeed?* The board must commit itself and the organization to making this business work. Most of all the board members must invest their own time and energy as well as the resources and staff time of the organization. In 1981 I interviewed thirty-four nonprofits that had started for-profit businesses. The thirteen that made a profit in the first year were all started with funds from the organization's treasury, loans secured by the leaders, and funds raised by the staff and leaders through grass roots fundraising. The twenty-one businesses that were still losing money after the first two years (one had been a money drain for six years!) had all been started entirely with government or foundation grants. Although this is a limited sample, these organizations' experience mirrors the experience of successful for-profit entrepreneurs. If you personally have a stake in the success of the enterprise, it will have a much, much better chance of success than if it is funded entirely with outside money. As the experts say, "You can't sell something you won't buy." If you personally don't believe that this venture is worth supporting, why will anyone else? If the plan does not look good enough for your own money, then it is not good enough. Improve the plan or choose another type of money maker.

Getting Started

Once the board decides it wants to start a for-profit business, pull together an advisory board to help you for the first two years. Ask for the best people you can get. Tell them you are starting a for-profit business to produce revenue to support the work of your nonprofit organization. Ask experts to serve on your advisory board and give you advice as needed. Point out that the board of directors is still legally and morally responsible for the operation and finances of the nonprofit and the for-profit. The advisory board is there to give you advice. After the first two years, ask each person if he or she wants another two-year term. Replace the people who resign with new experts.

ADVISORY BOARD

Recruit the most successful small business people in your community, a lawyer and an accountant with experience with for-profits and nonprofits, an insurance agent, and a person from your bank with experience in helping new businesses get started. Depending on the type of business, you will also want to recruit experienced experts in marketing, advertising, public relations, retail, bookkeeping, selling, personnel, or other skills needed for your business. If you will use volunteer talent for part of your work force, be sure to ask for a leader who knows how to organize volunteers.

There is no need for all your advisors to meet as a group at the same time, though this can be helpful. But most likely the best business brains in your community are going to be very busy, so you will need to be available to meet with them at their convenience. The board of directors can appoint a subcommittee to plan the business and do the research. These people can make up a list of all the questions you need answered before you choose to start the business. Then assign committee members to interview the experts, write out their answers, and duplicate them for the committee. When you have completed all your research, present a summary of the advice, dos and don'ts to the complete board of directors.

First ask the financial people to give you advice on planning your finances and asking for the start-up money. Second, ask your lawyer and your CPA to check with the current Internal Revenue Service (IRS) regulations about unrelated business income. The federal government wants good nonprofits to accomplish charitable, educational, religious, or scientific work that will benefit the citizens. The work that your group does is called its *exempt function*.

If the IRS considers your organization a 501(c)(3) tax-exempt organization, then all the money you bring in to accomplish your exempt function is exempt from being taxed for corporate income taxes. However, if the IRS decides that the income from your for-profit business is not clearly related to your exempt function, then the IRS will consider that income just the same as any other for-profit income. In that case, you will have to pay taxes on the income at the same rate as a for-profit company. In 1982 this ranged from

16 percent of the first $25,000 net income up to 46 percent of the
net income that was more than $100,000.

Unfortunately, the law is vague and confusing, so you will need
the advice of an experienced lawyer and CPA (certified public accountant) before you set up your business so you are certain to collect and pay enough taxes on time. Be sure to get good advice before you start so you do not overestimate your profits or underestimate your taxes.

Ask your marketing and advertising experts to show you how to
do a feasibility study to find the best time and place to begin your
business. They can also help the finance people make up your
budget and cash flow plan for the first year.

Making It Work

Once you have a solid plan, and the board of directors has made
a commitment to the venture, you are ready to start. A business will
require at least one full-time paid staff person at the beginning,
with others added if the business grows. Even if you want most of
the labor to be volunteers to meet your program goals, you still need
one person who is responsible for making a profit. The business
manager must make a big sign to hang over his or her work area,
which says, "The purpose of this business is making a profit." If
possible, pay your business manager a salary plus commission so he
or she will benefit from the success of the business and have an extra
motivation to make it profitable as soon as possible. The nonfinan-
cial goals can be coordinated by a volunteer, but the business decisions must be guided by someone who is working full time with one
goal: making this business succeed. That person must get a written
job description from the board of directors and give the board a
written work plan each month. In between board meetings the
manager can meet with the president to review the work and get ap-
proval for any changes.

A business can be a dependable money maker if you set it up with
enough planning, enough money, ambitious staff, well-defined
goals, and the commitment of your board of directors. The White
Elephant thrift shop was started in 1921 to raise money to pay for
charity cases at Children's Memorial Hospital in Chicago. In 1981 it

operated with four full-time paid staff, eight part-time paid staff, and forty volunteers under the supervision of the Women's Board of twenty women. After paying all of its expenses and setting aside reserves for the next year's work, it gave more than $150,000 to the hospital. Of course, your business won't make that much money in the first year; neither did this thrift shop. But if you start this year, you can be making big money in the future.

See the bibliography, Chapter 14, for recommended reading on starting a business.

SELLING PRODUCTS

Katherine Hepburn once said, ". . . My first real, thrilling job was filling balloons with gas, then tying strings around them and making people buy them. They all said, 'VOTES FOR WOMEN'." Selling good products can provide a dependable source of income for the group as well as provide a satisfying form of involvement for your volunteers.

Some of the advantages of selling things are:

- You can work at your own pace. You can start small with an inventory of your own buttons and bumper stickers and work up to a wholesale business of cookbooks, calendars, how-to manuals, posters, and pamphlets.
- You can start with one or two people, then increase the committee as the sales increase.
- You can find the right job for every volunteer. One person can sell the products to the president of the largest department store, another can sell at meetings, and another can bill orders and keep the books in the office. There is a place for every personality in selling things.
- You have a means to reach beyond the membership for support. When you begin you can sell at every meeting and public activity to raise money from new people. When you get to be very big you will be filling mail orders for the whole country in response to ads in national media.
- Your members are learning valuable and marketable job skills.

Anyone who can sell anything, keep track of an inventory, manage the orders and billing, or do the promotion of a retail business will have skills to sell in the business world.

You can always start by selling membership materials to your own members. These might be buttons, bumper stickers, issue papers, or T-shirts. Unfortunately, for these your market is limited to your own members and collectors. Buttons and bumper stickers build morale and team spirit but return such a low profit per piece that they are not really considered money makers. In fact, most groups either lose track of their inventory or overorder so they become a promotional expense.

What you want to sell is something that will appeal to the public at large. It can still be issue-oriented but focus on the issue rather than the organization—for example, balloons that say "Votes for Women" instead of "The Chillicothe Suffragettes." In 1971 the Chicago public interest law firm Business and Professional People for the Public Interest was opposing Mayor Richard J. Daley's proposal to put an airport in Lake Michigan; it produced buttons and bumper stickers saying "Don't do it in the lake." They sold out and are now collector's items. When the Seattle-King County NOW chapter wanted a poster about job discrimination, it came up with a picture of Israel's Prime Minister, Golda Meir, captioned "But can she type?" It launched the group's retail business. Save Our Cumberland Mountains (SOCM) in Tennessee has marketed a postcard showing the "before" and "after" of strip mining.

What Should We Sell?

You can make more money with a product that is the only one of its kind—an original cookbook, a calendar, consumer guides. Consumer Advocates in San Francisco prepared books comparing prices of used car dealers and banks in California. CA cornered the market and raised more than $30,000 a year from the guides. The Traditional Mohawk Nation in New York sells posters, books, tapes, record albums, a calendar, and a newsletter, *Akwesasne Notes.* The revenue supports the nine staff members and the production of the *Notes,* the largest national and international journal of native affairs in the Western Hemisphere. Through its mail order business the Nation also encourages and supports local craftspeople to continue the native arts and crafts such as basketweaving and beadwork.

Ask two members of the board to interview local nonprofit organizations that sell products through their own stores, commercial stores, mail-order catalogs, convention booths, and personal contacts. Recruit the top retailers in your area to give you more advice. Ask your lawyer to help you copyright or trademark all your work before it goes on sale.

Also interview people who tried unsuccessfully to sell products to learn what will not work. Then turn that information around to choose what you will sell. For example, the Southern School is an alternative school for teenagers in Chicago's Uptown community, with a high population of Appalachian refugees. In 1979 and 1980 it lost approximately $15,000 from a Department of Vocational Rehabilitation demonstration grant on a plant store. When the grant ran out the store was closed. As Director Jerry Rothman says, *now* they all know what does *not* work. They had trouble selling their products such as glass terrariums filled with sand layered to make a landscape design because they were 1) fragile, mostly glass; 2) heavy, mostly sand and soil; 3) perishable, mostly living plants; and 4) faddish. If you turn these around, you see that successful products are (1) sturdy, (2) lightweight, (3) permanent or have a very long shelf life, and (4) offer repeat sales possibilities, such as food, greeting cards, or other consumable products. Having learned from its first failure, the Southern School is now planning to package and market tea through a local cooperative restaurant. Tea will meet all of the criteria for a successful product.

Opportunities

Start with a good product, sell to your own members, then expand to progressively larger markets. Here is a description of how the Seattle-King County NOW chapter did it:

> We started selling our products at our own meetings. With the money we made there we paid two members' expenses to sell at the National NOW convention. With some of those profits we began to

contact other NOW chapters, and we ran an ad in *Ms.* Magazine. And with that money we rented an office, installed a telephone, bought a mimeograph and typewriter, provided child care at our meetings, and generally support our budget! Step, walk, run.

WHAT TO AVOID

Don't sell somebody else's products. Many firms like to use organizations' members to sell their cleaning products, candy bars, fruitcake, trinkets, greeting cards, or Christmas cards. They pitch you on the "fundraising opportunities" when really they want to hire you as their short-term, low-paid, no-benefits salesforce. You never get as good a deal from an outsider as you can give yourself. Why sell somebody else's fruitcake and make 30 percent when you can run your own bake booth and make 100 percent?

The problem with selling someone else's products is that the majority of the money goes to the company that gives you this "fundraising opportunity." For example, a candle company sells you candles that retail for $6 each. You get to keep $2 each, and $4 goes back to the candle company. So you are only making 33 percent per transaction. Why not just ask your volunteers to ask the same people to give them the whole $6? Then you will make three times as much money in the same time, your members can spend more time on the mission of the organization instead of on selling trinkets, the chairperson can spend his or her time inspiring the volunteers to ask for money rather than struggling with boxes of inventory and order blanks, and the customer will get a terrific organization instead of an imported trinket! Say no to an outsider who wants to use your volunteers to sell for them instead of for you.

Selling: Retail and Wholesale

There are two kinds of selling: retail and wholesale. Retail means you are selling person to person a few items at a time. This can be done by any organization with enthusiastic volunteers who like to sell. Wholesale is selling your goods in volume for the buyer to resell to large numbers of people. If your merchandise has proven to be very popular, you can ask two or more people to begin wholesaling your products. Here is advice on retailing and wholesaling a cookbook from the volunteers who sell the most profitable cookbooks in the country.

You can adapt this advice to your opportunities. If you are selling good products, ask how you could get them out in your own community and then how you can reach beyond your own community to reach the general buying public in America. Be sure to ask the most successful for-profit businesses to give you more advice, too.

HOW TO RETAIL A COOKBOOK OR OTHER PRODUCT

All your members sell at retail. For retail selling you print enough books to saturate your own market — members of the parish and friends or residents of the town and visitors. Plan to do one edition and price the book one-and-a-half times its cost to you. If it costs you $8 per book, charge $12 per book.

Once you get the books, plan an introductory luncheon to launch the sales and introduce the book to the press. Do a midday meal so the working press will attend; they will not come to anything too early or too late. Give them a kit containing a selection of recipes, a copy of the cookbook, and a press release describing the book, the sponsor, the history of the book, and how to order it. Invite the food writers and editors as well as the feature writers and the reporters who ordinarily cover your work. Invite everyone who contributed to the book, praise their work, and send all your members home with at least ten copies to sell.

The marketing committee goes into full swing once the book is launched. They try for every possible column mention, "new ideas" column plug, and "good gifts" column plug. In October they send the book and press release again to all the column editors for the Christmas gift columns. They get on every talk show they can to promote it and take it to every fair and sale.

Most important, they have it sold commercially in the local department stores, the bookstores, and the specialty cooking stores. This means they make an appointment to see the buyer of books, in person, at his or her convenience. They take in the cookbooks and make arrangements to deliver more. Most stores buy books at a 40-

percent discount, but some will buy local organizations' cookbooks at a 30-percent discount, leaving you 70 percent.

The way to sell a lot of books is to get them into a lot of stores. The marketing committee should cover every possible store in your hometown, as well as every other store within reach. Anytime any committee member travels to another town, for business, shopping, or just vacation, he or she should take a copy of the book and a supply of order blanks to introduce the book to the buyers at the right stores. Once you have established your cookbook in several stores and have reorders, it is easier to get it into new stores on the strength of your record.

A buyer at a major big city department store explained what she looks for. She wants a professional look, an index, clarity and variety in the recipes, a simple layout, an interesting theme, and a good appearance throughout — clean type and nice illustrations. The store prefers local organizations' cookbooks since they sell best. Although there are 40,000 new books published every year, there is always a demand for new cookbooks. Many people buy cookbooks as gifts or as books to read, as well as for their practical value.

The marketing committee is also responsible for all the bookkeeping and mailing. It fills orders for the cookbooks, including gift cards, and does the shipping and billing. This can become a full-time job for the committee if the book is a success, but it produces a dependable source of income over the long run.

Since serving on a successful cookbook committee involves this drudgery, try to dream up some entertaining and glamorous events for the committee, too. One group threw together a gala spring housewalk. The ticket to see a special old home was a cookbook sold at the door. Then the guests were served May wine and tidbits made from the recipes, like the samples you get at the grocery store. Everyone was so impressed with the goodies that most people bought four or five more books when they left the house.

Another group had an old-fashioned box supper auction. Each cook made his or her special recipe from the book and prepared an appropriate setting for the dish. The pheasant mousse was served on heirloom china, and grandma's fried chicken came in a basket. An auctioneer read off the tempting menus and the noncooks bid on the privilege of sharing each dish with the cook. It was a super promotion, good for both cookbook sales and the cooks' egos.

How to Wholesale a Cookbook or other Product

If you have a high-quality cookbook, which can be determined impartially from the opinions of the food editors and store buyers, and if you sell out your first printing in less than six months, consider going to wholesale marketing. For wholesale marketing you have to figure out how you can sell your books by the thousands rather than ones, tens, or hundreds.

There are two major outlets for wholesale cookbook sales. First are department stores and bookstores, which buy all their books at 60 percent of the cover price. In other words, you sell in quantity to stores at a 40 percent discount. In order to make money, your cover price must be high enough that you can still make a profit when you sell the book at 60 percent of the cover price. This is done by going to larger printings, which reduces your cost per book, and selling thousands of books to stores. If your book is good enough to sell through regular store outlets, you can make more money selling 20,000 copies wholesale than you made selling the first 5,000 retail — and there is less work for the committee.

The second major wholesale outlet is mail order catalogs. Get a list of catalogs from a list dealer. Eliminate those that are obviously not for you. Some sell only imported or cheap goods, and others sell only luxury goods that cost more than $25. Choose the middle-range catalogs that sell good, medium-priced American products. Write to all of them, giving a description of your book and its sales history. Follow up with a phone call to determine if they are interested. You will have to negotiate a wholesale price with the catalog publishers. If you can get in both an East Coast and a West Coast catalog, the book will sell thousands. Although it takes a lot of work to get listed originally, once you get into a good catalog you can maintain a mutually profitable relationship for years.

You can also sell wholesale to other chapters of your national organization, either through the national newsletter or by displaying it at the national convention. Or consider buying a booth at the best trade show to sell your book to the buyers for all the national stores.

Banks are another outlet for bulk sales. Since every bank pays exactly the same rate of interest, they compete for accounts by offering premiums to attract new customers. Try to convince the bank's vice-president for marketing to buy the cookbook as the next premium. Explain that it has a double value, as a marketing tool and a public relations tool. The book is a tempting premium, and the bank's money will be going to a worthy civic organization rather than just another trinket peddler. Especially if you have the name of the town in the book's title, it is a natural for the town's bank to promote the town and the bank at the same time.

In addition to the larger profit you make by selling thousands of books wholesale, you will also expand your retail sales from the mail orders you receive from the order blanks in each book.

SELLING SERVICES

Services can make money when you run them like a business. You do it by selling your work instead of by selling things. Services can also pay off with positive publicity on your energy and creativity. Since all you need is lots of pep, service fundraisers are naturals for children and young adults or any low-income group.

Service fundraisers might include charging by the hour or by the job to:

- Walk dogs or wash dogs
- Baby-sit. Scout troops operate baby-sitting services at shopping malls in December
- Put on birthday parties
- Pick up newspapers for the recycling center
- Outside work: wash windows, rake leaves, mow lawns, shovel snow
- Errand service
- Wash or park or fix cars or bikes
- Address envelopes or Christmas cards
- Distribute samples

- Serve as a "typical consumer" for advertising agencies to test their ads, jingles, and commercials
- Take movies or photographs of kids or families
- Ask at your state employment agency for temporary jobs

Some groups run regular, year-round services as professional businesses. They let the members keep a percentage of the money they raise. Since it costs money to participate in any group, for car- fare, meals, phone calls, postage, and baby-sitting, this is a good way to recruit part-time paying work for your volunteers and raise money for the organization at the same time.

Talent Bank

Instead of running one service, like catering or deliveries, set up a talent bank. Ask the members to record on a card what work they can do, what they would like to do, and when they are available to work. Then publicize the "Metropolis Talent Bank." Make your reputation for having (or finding) the right person to do any odd jobs. Then if a club needs a speaker, or a family needs a Santa Claus, or a company needs its valentines addressed, they will learn to call you. You will need a variety of talents, from the strong and boring, like shoveling snow, to the exotic and entertaining, like tell- ing fortunes. This will allow you to find work for a larger number of volunteers.

Have a special division called the "Quitters' Relief Corps," con- sisting of all the members who are good with their hands. They relieve the folks who find they really can't build a color TV from a kit, or hook a rug with all the state flowers, or panel their den. The "Quitters' Relief Corps" allows them to save face and save their in- vestment. One group even saved a marriage after the man of the house had all the pieces for not one but *two* sailboats hopelessly mixed up in his basement. His wife needed the basement for a wed- ding reception, and either the boat pieces or the man had to go. The town talent bank built the boats (one went to the YMCA) and saved a happy home.

See the bibliography, Chapter 14, for recommended reading on how both adults and children can make money from services.

SELLING TRAINING

Just as you sell your speakers to the people who want to know more about your cause, you can sell training courses to people who want to learn about the way you work. The speakers bureau handles the retail business — the one-time sales. The training division can handle the year-round training sales. These will include both people who care about your issue and those who merely want to learn new skills.

What Can You Teach?

Ask yourselves what you are good at. If your organization is the first of its kind or the best of its kind, you will get requests for training. If you want to offer a variety of courses, you can find two people to chair the training committee, and they can sell your courses.

You can teach one subject such as first-aid, or you can teach people about both your purpose and how to accomplish it. For example, an environmental group could teach a course on air and water pollution as well as a course on how to do environmental research. A theatre could offer a course on George Bernard Shaw as well as a course on playwriting. Or, if you have a range of talents, you can offer a variety of courses. Francis W. Parker School raises its funds by asking parents to teach one to six night courses on what they know best. They offer courses such as Italian cooking, chair caning, starting a business, Shakespeare, conversational Spanish, volleyball, calligraphy, and public relations for community groups. Students pay $15 for a one-night course, $45 for a six-week course. The profits all go to the school. In the 1980–81 school year, they made $96,000 from 105 volunteer teachers; in the 1970–71 school year, they made $21,500. Their profits grow every year.

Wholesaling Training

If your organization has been selling training to people in your community, so you have skilled trainers and a good reputation, consider wholesaling your classes to corporations. The corporations can offer it as part of their job enrichment package, and their employees can learn what they want at their office or plant. Think about how your training can benefit the employees; then sell the company in terms of the benefits it will get. For example, a California battered women's shelter taught prevention techniques at a corporation. If they reduce the abuse of women, there will be less absenteeism and turnover among the female employees.

One successful training group in Chicago has found a way to wholesale training that your group can copy. Chimera Self-Defense for Women sells its training to businesses by pointing out that the women employees will feel safer, feel better about their jobs, *be* safer so they can work nights or in bad neighborhoods, and be absent less often. If you have skills you can teach other people, your organization can use this system.

Chimera ordinarily charges $25 for a six-week course offered at the YWCA, colleges, and women's centers. After four years it had enough good trainers and publicity that it wanted to offer its course to more women, make more money so some of its trainers could work full time at that job (they had been training part time after other jobs), and make more money so it could expand the organization.

Chimera decided to sell to corporations. Each student is still asked to pay her $25 so that she takes the training seriously, shows up on time, and attends all the classes. The company pays $50 per woman to have the training available to their employees at their office or factory. The company also supplies the place for the training, handles the money, and does the promotion and sign-up. In this way, Chimera *triples* its revenue from each class and cuts its overhead at the same time. It is also able to reach women in the daytime at their jobs who would never be able to come to evening classes because they have another job, school, or family responsibilities after work.

In the first year Chimera sold the program to five banks, five manufacturers, two large nonprofit agencies, two insurance companies, an accounting firm, and a department store. You will have different sales opportunities in your community, but you can certainly copy the sales system. Ask the students to pay so they respect the course and your trainer. Ask a business to underwrite the training because it benefits. You can double or triple your profits.

See the bibliography, Chapter 14, for recommended reading on making money by teaching adults.

7

How to Choose the Right Special Event

Special events or benefits are simply occasions that allow your members to ask other people for money. Many people prefer selling a ticket to a dinner or a dance to just asking someone for a donation. Special events give everyone a chance to get together doing something fun, they publicize the group, they bring in new members, and they give many people a chance to learn new skills. You get both money and a sense of accomplishment.

The ideal event is one that raises money, conveys a message about your program, and offers something for the spirit. The first goal, raising money, can be guaranteed through careful planning by the leaders of your organization.

The second goal is to get across a message about your program. When the Prison Reform Task Force sponsored the first major show of prisoners' art in New York City, it raised $10,000 in ten days. Just as important, it raised the public's awareness of problems in New York and New Jersey prisons. The show goers thought it was clever of the artists to include pieces of ticking, blankets, and pillow cases in their works. Then they learned the prisoners had to use their bedding because the prisons had insufficient art supplies. The publicity and pressure from the task force resulted in increasing supplies for most New York state prisons.

The third goal is to offer something for the spirit. Appeal to the best in the members. If you have a women's political organization, offer an interesting speaker rather than a fashion show. If you have a peace group, offer an international dinner highlighting the diversity of different cultures rather than a John Wayne film festival. If you have an ecology club, offer a garden walk rather than a car rally. If you are serious about improving the world, run events for intelligent, caring human beings. Never sell short the idealism of your own members just so you can sell tickets. In the long run, you will bankrupt their faith in the group, and that faith is the real currency you need to be successful.

What makes a special event special? The energy and imagination your leaders invest to make it special. Because it is going to take a lot of volunteer time to put on a special event, your planning committee wants to be sure that the event it chooses is worth the time and trouble. Like any other planning, the way you begin is to decide *exactly* what the organization wants to accomplish by doing a special event. Clear goals are essential.

If your *only* goal is to make money, it is probably a bad idea to hold a special event. Your committee members would be much better off simply asking the people they know to give money for the organization. Asking for money is always more profitable than having special events because it is quicker, it is 100-percent profit, and it is impossible to lose money. So, if your organization needs a certain amount of money quickly, the best way to get it is to divide the amount needed by the number of people on the board of directors to come up with individual quotas. Vote to ask for donations until each person has reached his or her quota. The president and other leaders will set an example by asking first, then help the others make their quotas. For example, if you need $3,000 and you have ten people on your board, each one needs to ask for donations until he or she gets $300. This could be from one church, three businesses, six wealthy individuals, or thirty members. It doesn't matter who they choose to ask, as long as they go out the next day to ask and keep asking until they get the money. This way the board can easily raise its goal in two weeks and have all of its time left to work on the other goals of the organization.

But let's say the organization already has a base of dues-paying members and major donors. Now the board decides it wants to find a way to make more money every year, recruit new members, give more people opportunities for leadership, get the group's name in the press in a positive, noncontroversial way, and have fun, too! This is the time to choose a special event. Just remember that special events are special: they will only account for a minority of your budget. They are too much work to expect your members to want to do them often, so you also need to develop some dependable, year-round money makers, especially dues and donations to pay the bills the organization has all year-round.

HOW DO WE CHOOSE THE RIGHT EVENT FOR OUR GROUP?

The right event is the one the leadership *wants* to hold. This is so obvious that it is easily overlooked. Some people think that some other group has a magical event that will be a no-risk, high-return, foolproof, every-time-a-bull's-eye benefit! Others use this and other fundraising books as a cookbook, leafing through until they find something that looks easy, or quick, or cheap, and say, "Let's do that!" But a benefit that worked for another group won't work for yours unless your own people believe it will work and say they want to do the work to make it work. The process of choosing the benefit guarantees its success more than any other factor.

To choose your first special event, the president can ask the board and other leaders to one planning meeting. Review the goals of the group, how much money you want, and how you plan to get it. Then see how much of that is projected to come from a special event. For example if your total budget is $40,000, and $20,000 comes from dues, $10,000 from major donors, and $5,000 from sales, then you need one or more special events to bring in $5,000. Special events always go into the planning last, after you have designed and established the renewable fundraisers. (Review Chapter 3, "Who Can Do It," if your group does not have an annual fundraising strategy.)

Discuss how much time the leaders want to spend on the event and how much time of the paid staff, if any, you want to assign to an event. Make a list of the other people in the organization who can work on an event. Then look at your calendar to see what are the worst times for your organization so you can plan for the best times. If your group lobbies, you will not want to plan an event during the legislative session. So a summertime fundraiser such as a fiesta, block party, or softball game would be good. On the other hand, if you are a student organization, the summer is a bad time so you could plan a fall back-to-school dance, winter carnival, or Ides of March toga party!

Once you have a rough idea of the dollar goal and the best time of year, ask the committee members to think about the fundraising events they have worked on for other organizations. Almost all adults who have the skills to rise to the top in your organization learned those skills somewhere else. If the group is all low-income people, they most likely know how to produce profitable special events from doing them for their churches. Get the group to talk about what they already know how to do, what they like to do, and how much profit is possible. Then see if that kind of event could be adapted to raise money for this organization.

Homegrown plans, like vegetables, are always the most popular, the most profitable, and hence the best. Dare to be different! If your own leaders have a good idea, try it. You may find everyone else copying *you* next year.

Loggers in rural Minnesota have used logging bees to make money. They cut down trees, sell the wood, and give the profits to their favorite organization. Although this seems like a busman's holiday, doing their regular work for free, it is what they do best, they know it will succeed, and there is no risk. They can net from $1,200 to $3,000. It is the best event for them. The Pilsen Neighbors Community Council in the Mexican-American community of Chicago sponsors a Fiesta del Sol each summer to "celebrate the multifaceted and many splendored nature of the Pilsen community." They prepare tacos, tortas, pollo en mole, and churros as well as cotton candy, hot dogs and hamburgers, melon and banana drinks, Mexican and American beers; they sell beautiful Mexican arts and crafts and offer continuous live entertainment with mariachis, dancers, salsa music, and rock and roll. Before the fiesta they sell ads in an ad book to raise money from the business community and politicians. In 1979 they netted $2,500; in 1980 they netted $3,000.

The Amnesty International (AI) adoption group in the Greenwich Village community of New York City sponsored an Argentine Concert Series in 1979. AI works to free prisoners of conscience and to stop torture and the death penalty throughout the world. Each local group "adopts" prisoners in one prison, then works to persuade the government in question to release the prisoners. The Greenwich village group had adopted prisoners and their families in Argentina, so they combined concerts featuring Argentine mimes and musicians with discussions about the issue. They did five concerts, reached the audience they wanted to reach, and netted about $1,200, every penny of which went to aid families of the "disappeared." Even farther away, the Amnesty International group in Sri Lanka (formerly Ceylon) sells tea it packages in AI boxes, the Australian group operates three thrift shops, and the Japanese group sells top-quality posters by leading artists. Each group chooses what it can do best, then uses those skills to raise money at the same time as they inform their community about its issues.

When you choose an event your own leadership has already done there is very little risk of failure. If another organization in your community has done that sort of event and makes a profit each year, it proves that your community *wants* that kind of event. You have smart leaders and a valuable program; do the same thing and you can't fail!

Some groups are afraid of copying other groups, even if they are successful, for fear that they will antagonize the first group or that the competition will make less money for everyone. Fortunately, competition makes more money for everyone, as long as you schedule your events at different times so the customers can enjoy all of them. For example, the Chicago chapter of the National Organization for Women (NOW) began a successful walkathon in 1978 (net $19,800). Several of the leaders and staff of Women Employed (WE) walked in the NOW walkathon, and decided to do the same

thing for WE in 1979. Chicago NOW does its fundraiser near
Women's Equality Day on August 26th; WE does its near National
Secretaries Day, the last Wednesday in April. Since the events are
always five months apart, many people can be walkers or sponsors
for both. The organizations share what they learn each time to
maximize their profits and have more fun. In 1981 Chicago NOW
netted $45,000 from its walkathon; WE netted $6,000.

What do you do if you do not already have any leaders with experience in fundraising? Some groups—organizations of youth, new
immigrants, or exoffenders, for example—do not have successful
veteran fundraisers in their groups due to the makeup of their
membership. In that case, before your board chooses a special event,
it needs to research what events other groups like yours have done.
You can track down other groups like your own through the state or
national networks, the community referral service, the United Way
or alternative payroll deduction group, foundations and religious
giving programs, reporters who cover your work, and the *Yellow
Pages*. If you can't find another group with members like yours, go
for the best advice you can get and adapt it to your own organization. See Chapter 13, Fundraising Forever," for suggestions on getting advice.

Once you find a leader from your community who has experience
in holding successful special events, is sympathetic with the goals of
the organization, and respects your members, ask him or her to
serve as your teacher. The only way to learn how to run profitable
special events is by *doing* so, so plan one as carefully as possible,
then plunge in. After the first one or two you will have enough
trained talent in your own group that your old teacher will be able
to come to your wonderful events as a guest!

PLANNING FOR PROFIT

The motto for every special event is "Plan your work and work
your plan!" Careful planning at the beginning will help your group
raise more money in less time and enjoy the experience more so
everyone will be eager to volunteer again next year.

Once you choose the event you want, pick out a date that would
be good for your group. Make sure there are no major conflicts with

this date for your membership, such as an important sports event, a religious holiday, or a family occasion such as a high school graduation. Get a big calendar and plan backward from the date of the event to the first planning meeting. Once the committee has made its timeline on the big calendar, make a one-page version for each member of the committee. Thus, each person will know the deadline for each step of the work. See the next chapter for an example of a detailed timeline for a rummage sale.

Once you know what you want to do and when you want to do it, make a list of all the tasks that need to be done. Then divide up the work. Some jobs, like publicity, can easily be handled by one person; others, like cleanup, are easier and much more fun with more people. Choose one person to be in charge of each major job, such as shopping, refreshments, decorations, entertainment, publicity, bookkeeping, and cleanup; then let those people recruit helpers.

After everyone has volunteered or accepted an invitation to work on a subcommittee, the chairperson of the event must make sure that each person knows exactly what needs to be done and when. *Never assume anything.* Make sure that Maria knows she is supposed to bring the extra chairs because she has a station wagon. Double-check that Fred will play the piano even if you know he has the music and can't wait. Not only is it dangerous to take anything for granted; it is also unpleasant to take any*one* for granted. Even if Harvey has run the ticket booth for the last twenty years, *ask* him *early* if he wants to do it again, and ask him how many people he wants to have help him.

All planning is most difficult the first year you hold a special event. After that you have trained leaders, experienced volunteers, and satisfied customers who make it all much easier the next time around. You can expect your profits to double the second year you repeat a special event if you keep clear records to pass on to next year's chairpersons. This year's chairperson can ask the subcommittee chairs to turn in a one-page report including the names of each person who worked on their committees (this will give you the talent pool for next year's chairs), what they tried that worked best, and what they tried that was too much work or too little profit to be worth repeating. Be sure to include all the good ideas you have the day *after* the event! Ask each person, "How can we improve this event next year?" Do this at an evaluation meeting/celebration a week after the first special event. As you can see from the samples in the next three chapters, your profits from special events will increase each year if you create an effective way to share this year's experience with next year's leaders.

Here is more advice from America's finest fundraisers to make your planning more profitable. Adapt these suggestions to fit your own people and your own opportunities. Following are ideas on how to estimate the costs of a special event, how to be a good shopper, how to estimate your income, how to price the tickets, how to use simple arithmetic to set quotas and pace your ticket sales, how to make a list of satisfied customers, how to sell through the mail, and how to write a good invitation. Remember that all of this will become easier, quicker, and more profitable every year your organization repeats this special event.

HOW TO ESTIMATE COSTS

If this is the first time your group has ever planned a fundraising event, assign one person to research the things you will need to buy. Other groups in your area can tell you what you will need for this benefit. By calling other groups first, you can learn what they already own, such as cash boxes, punch bowls, and costumes, and you can ask if you can borrow what you need.

Ask the groups who have already done this sort of event to answer these questions:

1. What will we need to buy or rent?
2. How much did it cost you last time?
3. Where is the best place to shop?
4. Who else should I ask?

For your early planning you will have to estimate your costs. For the final arithmetic, ask one person to get exact figures for each item you will need. Write down an exact budget, including every item and every cost. After the event compare this to what you really spent to learn how to improve your estimates next time. Especially if you assign your paid staff to work on a benefit, the cost of their time can add up to a lot more than you think in the beginning. Comparing your budget to actual money spent will help you hold down costs so you will increase your profit each time you repeat the same event.

If you are repeating an event from last year, be sure to recheck *every* cost. Everything goes up each year, but it never goes up by the same amount every year. For example, one year paper costs doubled, but the next year they went up only 10 percent. Also, you may not get last year's special price if the supplier is having a bad year, or you may get a *better* price if the supplier is having a good year. It never hurts to put the suppliers on your newsletter list either. If someone has been following your work for a year, he or she will appreciate what you have accomplished. This year that person may contribute more because he or she knows you and your work.

Professional Advice

In addition to the advice from veteran volunteers, be sure to ask for advice from expert professionals such as your insurance agent and your lawyer. You will probably need to buy extra liability insurance for any event in which you are entertaining the public in someone else's building such as a house tour and dramshop insurance for any event at which you are serving alcoholic beverages. If the organization does *not* purchase special insurance to cover the event, the members of the board of directors can be liable for the costs of any injury to a guest or damages to the location. The cost of additional insurance for special events is very low. Ask for advice from your insurance agent and your lawyer on how much coverage you need when you estimate the costs of holding a special event. If you decide that you cannot afford the insurance, either find a company to donate the insurance or choose a different event that will not require insurance. Since you as board members (*not* the paid staff) are liable if anything happens, doing without insurance is a false economy that is not worth the risk to yourselves.

Cost Research

Here are some general categories for your committee to consider when they estimate the costs of an event. Ask a local leader to give

you advice on what else you need to add for this type of event in
your area.

Location
Room rental (always get a written contract)
Janitor fee
On-site staff such as a projectionist

Printing
Tickets
Invitations
Posters
Program

Postage

Insurance

Entertainment
Band

Equipment
Sound system

Refreshments
Food
Beverages

Supplies
Consumable—decorations, prizes (anything you use only for this
    event)
Assets—lumber, extension cords (anything you can keep and use for
    future events)

Staff time
Total hours spent multiplied by hourly cost of staff

The Shopper

It is much more efficient and usually more economical to have
one person volunteer to be the shopper. His or her job is to get

everything needed for the event at the lowest possible price. The shopper finds out first exactly what the costs of the event will be.

The shopper is really a researcher and dispatcher. It must be someone who likes to talk on the telephone, has plenty of time, and will keep precise records. It is good for the shopper to be persuasive and great to be as miserly as Scrooge. The shopper may not have to actually buy or pick up all the supplies but must discover the best price available on each item and assign someone to pick it up.

The shopper answers these questions:

1. What does the group already have? For example, receipt books, ticket rolls, cash boxes. No reason to buy doubles.

2. Who can get what free? Record each donation and the name of the person who will arrange for it. For example, door prizes or a hall.

3. What can we borrow? For example, a raffle drum for the door prize drawing.

4. What should we rent? For example, a sound system.

5. What can we buy on consignment? This means you pay for more than you need, then return the balance for a refund. Many liquor stores sell this way, allowing you to return unopened bottles. This way you are sure you won't run out, but you won't have to keep or pay for unopened leftovers.

6. What will we have to buy for use only at this event? For example, ice, paper products, coffee.

7. What will we buy that we will keep after the event? If you can buy it and keep it to use again, it is an asset. For example, a coffee maker, trays, a flag, lumber, fabric, tools.

Obviously, the shopper needs to pay more attention to items in category 7 — things you will use over and over like a coffee maker — than items in category 6. There is very little difference in quality in plastic cups or paper napkins but a great deal in appliances.

BASIC RULES FOR THE SHOPPER

Always get at least three bids for any asset you buy or for any purchase over $25. Record other advantages besides price — guarantees, repair or maintenance service, delivery, or payment plans.

Sample Chart for Getting Supplies

Shopper's Name: E. Scrooge PHONE: 555-1000 EVENT: Christmas Party DATE: December 17, 1982

Item	Already Have	Store	Price	Advantages	Who Can Donate	Who Can Lend	Who Can Pick Up & Return
Receipts	500						Dr. Fujioka
Hall					American Legion		
Door Prize					J's Jewelry Store		Mr. Martinez
Raffle Drum						St. Bastion's	Sister Margaret
Sound System		S Sound	$15 Rent	will bill			Rev. Jackson
Liquor (all on consignment)		A	$40	will deliver			
		B	$45	free ice			Ms. Harrington
		C	$50	closest; open til 4 A.M.			Mr. O'Connell
Coffee Maker		D	$30				Mrs. Olsen
		E	$30	Repair in store			Mr. Valdez

Never guess.

Always assume it costs more today than it did the last time you bought one. Since the shopper's job is to get *accurate* prices and costs, he or she should always call and ask what is the price *now*.

Don't be shy. Always ask for special consideration. Your organization is doing important work that no one else in the community can do. Since the merchants will also benefit from your work, they ought to support you, too. Always ask for a contribution, then a discount, or a bulk rate, or deferred payment, or at the very least a door prize contribution.

Patronize local businesses. Especially if you are a neighborhood community group, they have the most to gain from your successes, so they have the best reason to give you a deal.

Thank everyone who gives you a contribution or a special deal. Be sure they are introduced if they attend the event. Send them copies of the program with their names in it. Be grateful and they will be glad to help you again next time.

HOW TO ESTIMATE INCOME

Although you can determine your costs accurately, you will have to estimate the income at the beginning. After you know the members' abilities, enthusiasm, and spending patterns, you will be able to predict the income very closely.

Write down all the ways you can get money from each event. To estimate your income before the event, multiply the number of workers by their quotas for each part: ticket sales, donations, etc. For income at the event, multiply the number of people there times their expected expenditure for each item. For example, if there are 200 people at the dance and half of them (100) buy a raffle chance for 50¢, you can estimate you will get $50.

Write down how much you anticipate earning from each part. Count on what you get in *before* the event and consider what you make *at* the event a bonus. You can never control the weather or flu epidemics or traffic jams, so don't depend on revenue from the party itself to pay your bills.

Obviously, this will be a lot easier the second time around. That
makes it especially important that you produce accurate and complete reports after the first event. In order to make the most helpful
report for the next time, you need to record what the income was
from each part of the event *this* time. Try to have separate cash
boxes for each thing you sell. (You can use shoe boxes or cigar boxes
if you don't have real cash boxes.) Write down how much change
was in each cash box when you started. After the event, add up all
the money in each box. Then subtract the amount you started with,
and you know the amount from each item. You now know that you
sold fifteen newsletter subscriptions but only four T-shirts, or fifty
sandwiches but only ten cakes. Next year you will know in advance
what your crowd wants, and you won't be stuck with leftovers.

How to Anticipate What the Income Will Be—Gross

Before the Event

People Working	Item	Price per Item	Quota/ Person	Gross/ Person	Total Gross
10	Tickets	$ 2.50	20 tickets	$ 50	$500
2	Patron Tickets	$25.00	5 tickets	$125	$250
5	Senior Tickets	$ 1.00	10 tickets	$ 10	$ 50
Total:17					$800

At the Event

People Attending	Item	Gross/ Item	Purchases per Person	Purchased by % of Crowd	Gross
200	Raffle	$ .50/ticket	1	½ = 100 people	$ 50
	Bar	$ .50/drink	2	100% = 200 people	$200
	Sand- wiches	$1.00	1	¼ = 50 people	$ 50
				Total:	$300

How to Estimate Income from Repeated Special Events

The first year you run a special event is really training for your leadership. Keep complete records, and the second year you can expect a 50- to 100-percent increase in your net profits. Every year after that you can expect the event profits to mirror the growth of the membership because you can give foolproof renewals to new people while your experienced salespeople sell to new customers. So, if your membership grows by 10 percent, your event profits should grow by 10 percent. When your membership is constant the event profits will remain about the same, going up only slightly as you raise prices to meet inflation. Otherwise the only time you can expect to see a big jump in your profits is if you get co-chairs who are especially ambitious and effective, if your membership is especially enthusiastic about the current program, or if the membership believes that this year is especially urgent. For example, many of the National Organization for Women's chapters showed record increases in profits from their August 26, 1981, walkathons because their members made an extra effort to raise money for the "last year" of the Equal Rights Amendment ratification battle.

How to Price the Tickets

One of the questions that always seems most perplexing for new benefit committees is how much to charge for tickets. After you have done a few benefits you will know which price range works best for your group. For your first time you have to combine common sense and luck.

There are eight things to consider when you price the tickets. Discuss all of these questions in your committee to get the best advice from everyone who will actually be selling the tickets.

1. *How much do we want to make on this event?* Let's say you are going to do a costume party dance at a church hall. All of your costs add up to $300. You would like to make $500. So you need to gross $800. Divide $800 by each possible price to find out how many tickets you need to sell to reach your goal. If you charge $10 you have to sell 80 tickets. If you charge $2 you have to sell 400 tickets. Then, if the members say $10 is too high but they can't sell 400

tickets, you may settle on $4, so you have to sell 200 tickets, which they can do.

Costs	$300
Profit	+ $500
Gross Income	$800 Goal for the event

Ticket price $4 × 200 ticket sales = $800 Goal (Gross)

2. *How much do others usually charge for this event?* If other groups usually charge $5 in your area for a party, and your members are used to paying $5, maybe you can charge $5, too. On the other hand, if no one ever charges more than $1.50 for an event in your area, you will have to do a super sales job, lower your profit goal, or add in other ways to make money besides the ticket price.

3. *What is the real cost to our members to attend?* If each couple has to buy two $4 tickets, that will cost them $8. If they also have to hire a baby-sitter, pay to park their car, and buy a couple of drinks, their total bill could be as high as $20! Be sure that your people will be willing to pay that much. It may be better and more profitable to have a daytime, free-parking, family event.

4. *What other income can we count on?* For example, if you run a cash bar for a hall full of people who like to drink, you can make $1 a person. For our dance example, this would mean that, if you have 200 thirsty people, you will make $200 on the bar. (Double-salt the popcorn.) Thus you now have to make only $600 on the tickets to cover costs and make your $500 profit goal. So you can price the tickets at $3 each. At first you have to guess what this income will be; later on you will be able to predict it fairly accurately.

Gross income goal	$800
Estimated bar receipts	− $200
Revised ticket goal	$600

$600-new ticket goal ÷ possible ticket sales 200 = $3 new ticket price

5. *Can we have more than one ticket price?* You can always have more than one ticket price to assure that everyone can attend and also to ensure that those most able to pay do so. For example, you

may have fifty members who are senior citizens on fixed incomes who would like to come to the dance. So set a senior citizen price at $1. You also know the local politicians will want to make an appearance and "say a few words." If you're lucky you will be in a district with several hotly contested races. Even if the politicians do not attend, they should buy tickets in advance. Charge the politicians and other people with more money than time a special "patron" price, say $25 a ticket. If you sell ten patron tickets, you get $250.

If you sell ten patron tickets and fifty senior citizen tickets, you will get $300. Now your 200 regular customers can pay only $2.50 to make the last $500.

10 patrons at $25 each		$250
50 seniors at $1 each	+	50
200 members at $2.50 each	+	500
	Goal	$800

See the section on theatre parties in Chapter 9 for more details on patron tickets.

6. *How will the price affect our image?* A lower price will make tickets easier to sell, so you will get a bigger crowd and reach people at all income levels. On the other hand, you may decide you want to give the impression of prosperity and success by sponsoring a classy, high-priced, downtown event. Consider how the price will affect everyone's impression of the group and the event.

7. *Do we want to give any tickets away for free?* This can be a useful public relations device. Many groups give free tickets to the press, clergy, or staff. Sometimes the sponsor gives tickets away to a good cause. For example, when BPI sponsored a concert with Antonia Brico conducting members of the Chicago Symphony Orchestra, all the tickets for seats behind pillars (which the theatre usually sells) were given to blind students. BPI also gave blocs of tickets to inner-city students who might otherwise never have a chance to hear the orchestra. The group also gave its copy of the movie *Antonia: A Portrait of the Woman* to the Chicago Public Library. All of which added to BPI's image as an organization concerned about quality of life for Chicagoans.

The other reason for giving away tickets is to create an illusion of popularity. Theatre people call this "papering the house." Especially for politicians, it is much better to give away lots of tickets and have a full house than to undersell and have empty seats. Of course the ideal is to sell every possible ticket, but if the night comes and you have to make a good impression, hand out all the unsold tickets as rewards for the workers to give their friends.

8. *What is the members' feeling about the importance of making money right now?* Enthusiasm is contagious, so a vigorous action campaign will spark a vigorous fundraising campaign. If the members feel they are in an exciting campaign, and they know they need the $500 to send forty members to the state capital for the key vote on crucial legislation next week, they will probably be eager to get out and sell tickets. A successful action campaign creates a feeling of camaraderie among the members. If victory is in sight, they will be willing to dig deep for a higher price than usual.

As long as the members feel that what they are doing is important and that they have a chance for success, they will work harder and contribute more to the group. If they have been inactive or think someone else is doing everything or that there is little hope for success, they may attend out of loyalty but will not make a special effort to sell or to give. Success breeds success. (Stitch this into your sampler under "People give to people.") You can charge more when you are winning than when you are in a holding pattern or have suffered a recent setback.

FINAL PREPARATIONS

Always number the tickets and keep track of who has which numbers. At the end of the sales each seller must turn in enough tickets and money to match the number of tickets he or she started with. For example, if you give Cliff twenty $4 tickets, he must return either twenty tickets or $80 dollars or some combination that adds up to $80. If he sells fifteen tickets, he turns in five tickets and $60. More than one fundraiser has turned into a fundloser because this simple step was *not* taken.

The last part of the committee's planning is to mentally walk through the event as though you were the customer. What would make you more comfortable, especially if you were new? There are several things you can do to make newcomers feel welcome. Use

name tags to help everyone learn names. Have several outgoing
people serve as hosts and hostesses to make sure each new person is
introduced to a veteran member. Put up a display of photographs
or recent clippings to serve as conversation starters. Station a few
pleasant young people to help the oldsters with stairs and coats.
Recruit an enthusiastic master of ceremonies to make frequent announcements and introductions. Print a simple program so everyone knows what happens when. Mark an area for lost and found. If
you are selling anything, be sure you have enough bags. Double-
check to make sure the washrooms are well stocked and clean. Anything you can do to make people feel wanted will make everyone
have a better time, spend more money, and guarantee that they all
will return next time.

If you want to provide child care at your special event, recruit
some dependable parents, grandparents, or baby-sitters to plan and
control the child care. See the Childcare Checklist developed for
special events at the end of this chapter.

MAKING A LIST—AND CHECKING IT TWICE

Remember that the best people to ask for money are people who
have already given you money. So always be sure to *get* a list of the
people attending an event and *keep* it so you can invite them next
time. You can give a receipt for every contribution; make a carbon
copy at the same time and keep the copy. If you are doing something with a lot of traffic and impatient people, offer a door prize.
Keep all the door prize slips with names and addresses. That will
become your invitation list next time or you can simply ask people
to sign a guest book when they come into the event.

A few people will ask you *not* to put them on your list; you must
always honor such requests. Mark their receipt or door prize slip
clearly "Do not mail" or "Do not include on invitation list." But
most people like to be notified of fun events, so they will be pleased
to give you their names.

Be very cautious about making a list from addresses on checks.
Some people do not want to receive personal mail at the office.
Many wives use checks printed with only the husband's name. If
Martha Washington gives you a donation, be sure you record her
name even if George's name is on the check. If someone doesn't

want a receipt, *ask* if you can put him or her on the mailing list and, if so, how the mail should be addressed.

After the event the committee can organize and analyze the list to make its job easier next time. Ask each person who sold tickets to bring the names and addresses of the people who bought tickets. By comparing the sign-in list with these lists you will learn who bought tickets but did not attend, who bought tickets in advance and did show up, and how many people bought tickets at the door. Thus if your records show that you sold 100 tickets in advance and ten people bought at the door, you can project that next year, if you presell 200 tickets, twenty people will buy at the door.

The last step of any special event is to prepare a donor card after the event for each person who attended the benefit or sent in money. See Chapter 13, "Fundraising Forever," for more advice on donor cards. A donor card will tell you the name and address of the donor, the amount of his or her donation, and their special interests. Every year it will get easier for you to sell your regular tickets and patron tickets because you will already have a record of who wants to give money to your organization.

SELLING THROUGH THE MAIL—INVITATIONS

After the committee has planned the event, signed a contract for the place for the date you want, and priced the tickets, you can decide how to sell the tickets. Person-to-person selling is always the quickest, easiest, and most profitable. Since personal sales can be traced, asking your leadership to sell tickets will also give you an accurate measure of who currently cares about the organization and which leader has a network of followers.

For large events, the committee may decide to sell tickets through the mail in addition to personal sales by the board of directors and active members. In that case, you want to make your written sales pitch—the invitation—as personal as possible. So recruit an addressing committee to hand-address the invitations and add personal notes. This is monotonous work, so it helps if there is an attraction like an interesting home, a tempting menu for the workers' meal, or a host that the workers want to meet.

Ask the secretary or chair of the membership committee to bring a copy of the organization mailing list. Ask each member of the committee to bring his or her address book, Christmas card list, or lists from other organizations that would be likely to support your organization or this event.

For your first special event, you will need to send about ten times as many invitations as the number of guests you want. If you want 150 guests, you'll have to send 1,500 invitations. As you become more experienced and refine your guest lists, you can reduce the ratio.

First go through the lists to eliminate duplicates. Then address the envelopes by hand. If it is a long list or a small committee, addressing may take more than one meeting. If you are in a hurry, you can begin addressing the envelopes before the invitations are ready, if you are *sure* they are the same size. It is better to plan ahead so there is plenty of time to do a good job. Also, ask your volunteer photographer to take a black-and-white photo of the committee at work for the next newsletter. Try to get the people who do the work behind the scenes out front in your newsletter at least once a year.

When you are finished addressing, make a copy of each list to keep with your own organization's lists. Give each list a letter code such as the following.

Code	List
OM	Our Members
OD	Our Donors
OS	Our Subscribers
MJ	Mary Jones's list
TS	Tom Smith's list
BW	Birdwatchers Club list
WF	Wildflower Society list
EM	Ecology Museum list
GC	Garden Club list

Write the code letters on the reply cards that go into the envelopes from that list. Then, as you get replies, keep a daily record of ticket sales and donations. At the same time, make a chart of how many contributions came from each list. After the event you will know which lists and what kind of lists will work best for your group next time.

Then deal out the envelopes so all the committee members get their own lists plus the names of anyone else they know from the

other lists. Now add a note on each invitation, like "Hope to see you
there," or "This will be Cecil Celebrity's only visit to Lexington this
year." The best note is a personal invitation such as "Can you sit at
my table?" or "I've got the company car on Tuesdays; can I give you
a ride?" Stuff, seal, stamp, and send the envelopes.

Follow up with phone calls if sales are slow. You must have an accurate reading of sales so you know how much to order. You also
need to know the number to set up the room so it will look full with
a small crowd or fit in the extras for an overflow crowd.

Invitations

Every invitation can include:
• The date, time, and place of the event.
• The price.
• The names of the chairpersons and committee members.
• A phone number for more information.
• A description of the program. (If you have booked a celebrity,
it is nice to include a photograph.)
• The exact name to write on checks, such as "Make checks pay-
able to FRIENDS OF THE FELINES."
• A description of how the profits from the event will be used to
accomplish the goals of the organization.

As an example of the last item, when Working Women, the national association of office workers, planned its 1980 premiere benefit for the film *9 to 5*, it chose an invitation that looked like a steno
pad with a cover photo of the stars Jane Fonda, Lily Tomlin, and
Dolly Parton pouring coffee for their "boss." Inside guests are invited to the premiere and a party with the stars afterward. The invitation says, "The proceeds from the premiere will go to help the
good work of WORKING WOMEN, a national association of office
workers. Acting as both a challenge and a conscience in behalf of
the millions of women office workers, Working Women and its
twelve local affiliates are beginning to show real gains in securing
pay equity, respect for work performed, enforcement of equal employment laws, improvements in cost-of-living raises, job posting,
job description, promotions, access to training programs, and
more, and much more to come." Never assume everyone knows
what your group does; tell them.

If the contribution is tax deductible, say so. If only part of the contribution is tax deductible, tell the donor the exact dollar amount that is deductible. Call the IRS and ask for "exempt organizations" if you want more help on this. The telephone number is listed in most telephone books under Internal Revenue Service and United States Government.

• A preaddressed envelope to make it easy for people to send you checks and the reply card. The replies may go to the home of one of the co-chairs or to the organization's office address.

• A simple card for people to order tickets or make a donation. Here is a sample of the card used by the Chicago Committee for Handgun Control for its second Lincoln Day Dinner in 1981. Its committee chose to take President Abraham Lincoln's birthday, February 12th, which traditionally had been a holiday in Illinois anyway, and make it "its own," since Lincoln was assassinated with a handgun. This way the committee could take a holiday that people were already used to celebrating and use it every year to make money for its cause. The first year the committee sold 220 tickets to the dinner; the second year it sold 500 tickets to the dinner; its goal the third year is to sell 1,000 tickets.

SAMPLE CARD*

COMMITTEE FOR HANDGUN CONTROL, INC.
109 North Dearborn Street, Chicago, Ill. 60602 (312) 641-5575
$15.00 per person. Sponsor, $200.00 for two tickets.

Please reserve_____ places for the Lincoln Day Dinner.

My check for $_____is enclosed.

Name_____

Address_____

Telephone (Day) _____ (Evening) _____

Reservation Deadline: February 9th.
Tickets will be held at the door.

☐ *I am unable to attend but enclose a contribution*
of $_____to help with your work.

THE LINCOLN DAY DINNER

---

* Reprinted with permission from Committee for Handgun Control, Inc.

QUESTIONS FOR THE PLANNING COMMITTEE
FOR A SPECIAL EVENT

Here are some useful questions to help your special event committee begin its planning. The chairpersons of the committee can revise this list to fit your own group. Then send out the list to everyone on the event committee and ask them to come to the next meeting with their own ideas and lists of names.

Planning Checklist—Questions to Ask First

What do we already have in the organization to make this fundraising project a success? What factors should we consider in choosing an event?

PEOPLE

1. What talents do our leaders have? What do we want to do? Is this the best use of our time right now? Would we be better off simply asking for money rather than planning and producing a special event? Can we use this event to help develop the skills of future leaders?

2. What talents do our members have? What do they want to do? What kinds of events have they held for other organizations?

3. How many members do we have who will *work* on this kind of event? List their names.

4. Who will we sell our tickets to? List the names of everyone to whom you personally can sell a ticket. Add the number of tickets you bought yourself. These are your sure sales. Then list the places and dates where and when you will try to sell additional tickets and how many you hope to sell at each location, such as "Wednesday night—choir practice—four tickets." Add up all the lists and you will know 80 to 90 percent of your ticket sales. The balance will come from sales by the members and friends. Unless your benefit features a recording, TV, or movie star whose name alone will draw a crowd, never depend on publicity for more than 2 percent of your sales. Publicity does not sell tickets; people sell tickets.

5. Are there any new people we can ask to work on this event? List their names.

6. Do we want any of our paid staff to work on this event? If so, who? What should they do? How much will their salaries add to our costs? Remember, volunteers are usually more effective and always free! If you do choose to pay an employee to work on a fundraising event, be sure two of your best volunteers serve as apprentices this year so they can do that job for free next year.

MONEY

1. How much seed money do we have to hold this event? Where will it come from — our treasury, a loan, or advance sales?

2. When will we have to spend the money? When will the money come in? What is our break-even point (income = expenses)?

3. Who will handle the money coming in? Who will control money going out?

4. Bank — will we need a separate account? Do we need any special arrangements to handle lots of cash?

TIME

1. How much time does the organization want to spend fundraising? Is there any way to shorten it?

2. Are there any major conflicts in the organization's calendar? the community calendar?

3. How much of our time do we want to allocate to this project?

4. If this event is to be repeated annually, is this the best time of the year for it?

5. What consideration should we make for bad weather (e.g., an alternative snow/rain date, inside location, or insurance)?

THINGS

1. What does the organization already own that we can use for this event?

2. What do our members own or have access to that they would like to use?

3. What do other friendly organizations have that they will let us use?

Planning Checklist for Goals—
What Do We Want to Achieve from This Project?

1. Amount of money, net; percent of annual budget.
2. Number of people involved; where and how.
3. Number of leadership roles possible.
4. Number of new members brought in.
5. Experience. Which new skills will be learned? What do we want to know for the next event and for this event next year?
6. Who will take the leadership positions?
7. How will it challenge the elected leaders?
8. What will be the publicity generated? How much, what kind, and where?
9. What will be the psychological effect of the event:
    a. within the organizations?
    b. outside the organization to people you want to join?
    c. to the adversaries, if any?
    d. to the staff?
10. Can it be repeated—in six months, one year? What is the probable increase next time?
11. Which new sources of renewable income will we reach?
    a. active members
    b. subscribers for the mailing list
    c. major donors
    d. local merchants, businesses, and professionals
    e. churches
    f. unions
12. Organizational advantages—morale, new people, new area, new style event.
13. Fun.

Basics for All Special Events

1. Notification of the police
2. Proper insurance
3. Cash boxes
4. Cash in proper denominations for each cash box
5. Receipts

   6. Literature on your organization
       Current newsletter or fact sheet
       Calendar of next month's meetings and events
       Membership applications
       Sale merchandise — buttons, cookbooks, research, etc.
   7. Sign-up list (Can be accomplished simply with door prize)
   8. Name tags for committee or everyone
   9. Emergency numbers for police, fire, and ambulance
  10. Cash for emergencies; coins for pay phone
  11. First aid kit
  12. Pens
  13. Tape
  14. Poster board and black markers
  15. Errand runner for emergencies and forgotten things
  16. Watch
  17. Aspirin
  18. Comfortable shoes
  19. All necessary phone numbers — band, host, speakers
  20. Name of paramedic, doctor, or nurse who will be present
  21. Sense of humor, tact, patience, and imagination

If location does not provide, also bring and know how to operate:
1. Fire extinguisher
2. Sound system

Child Care Checklist*

This checklist has been compiled by Bob Shurtleff, with the help of The Childcare Switchboard and The Toy Center in San Francisco. Veterans share their tested ideas for providing quality child care at special events.

CHOOSING A SITE

1. Is the site safe? Look for fire hazards, electrical hazards, open stairs, etc.

---

* Reprinted with permission from Bananas, Child Care Information and Referral.

2. Check for access to bathrooms and drinking water. Can children use them without disturbing the adults? Will adults using the bathrooms disturb the children?

3. Ideally, there should be separate spaces for different activities and ages of the children. For example, babies need a quiet space to sleep in, while older children may need an open space for more active play.

EQUIPMENT

1. Bring toys, paper, cloth, paint, crayons, scissors, play dough, balloons, books, and anything else that young people might enjoy.

2. Babies may need blankets, mattresses, and diapers.

3. FOOD! Always plan a snack. Children get hungry at different times, so it's a good idea to have apples, carrots, popcorn, and such for nibbling. A sitdown snack can also provide a quiet time for everyone. Don't forget—child care workers get hungry, too.

4. It's a good idea to have water or juice available in bottles with cups for drinks. This helps avoid quarrels at the drinking fountain.

5. Get a small first aid kit—Band-Aids, gauze, iodine, and such. If the parents are not going to be nearby, have them sign a medical release form so the child can get medical treatment in an emergency.

6. Bring name tags, sign-in sheets, pens and pencils, and masking tape to mark the things the children bring with them.

ADVANCE ARRANGEMENTS

1. Publicity for the event should include information on child care. "Child care provided" should mean that everything necessary for child care has been taken care of by those organizing the event. If child care is to be shared by the people who come to the event, advertise it as cooperative child care. If parents need to call in advance to get child care, say "Child care available by arrangement" and give a telephone number for people to call.

2. Have all the child care workers arrive well in advance. A preliminary meeting will usually be necessary with the coordinator and some of the workers.

3. Decide what the rules are. Child care works best when there are definite boundaries to the child care area. When and under what circumstances may children go in and out? Safety rules are important, too, like no running on the stairs. Rules may be necessary to protect the room you are using, such as no writing on the walls.

4. Have a structure ready for the children to come into. How will each child be greeted?

CHILD CARE WORKERS

1. Try to get an estimate of how many children there will be. Is it possible to have some of the parents sign up in advance? Plan for one adult for each five or six children.

2. Have a reserve force of child care providers, so there is someone who can help if there are more children than were expected. Plan for relief for the child care workers.

3. Try to have a balance of men and women doing child care.

4. Child care is work. Child care workers should be paid. If, as is sometimes the case, there is no money available, they should be paid in some other way—perhaps with admission to some other event.

ARRIVAL AND GREETING

1. One worker should greet the children as they come in. Have the parent fill in the sign-in sheet. You need to have the child's name, the parent's name, and any special problems, such as potty training or allergies.

2. Mark any toys, food, or supplies the child brings along, particularly baby bags—pen and masking tape work fine.

3. If there are any rules the children are expected to follow, tell them right away.

4. If a child is crying or fussing on arrival, the child care worker should take charge of the situation. Show confidence. Pick up the child and comfort him or her. Let the parents know that you are in control, so they can leave without feeling guilty.

PROGRAM

1. Plan as exciting and varied a program as possible. Can the child care be as exciting an event as what is planned for the adults?

2. Plan different activities for different age groups—quiet artwork and active games. Each activity needs to have a particular person planning and carrying it out.

3. If the main event is a concert or benefit, ask the musicians to come and perform for the children.

4. For short-time child care, one special activity can often be planned that will occupy most of the children—mask making, play dough, movies, a puppet show, rhythm band, face painting.

CLOSING TIME

1. Find out in advance when the event is scheduled to end, so everyone can be ready.

2. One worker should be in charge of signing each child out. Make sure the children leave with everything they brought. Make sure none of the children leaves without an adult.

3. Start cleanup well before closing time, so that the children have a chance to participate in cleaning up.

4. Have an evaluation meeting, either immediately or at some later time to talk about what went right and what might be done better next time. Ask the children and parents as they are leaving how they liked what went on.

Children are people. They deserve more than to be locked up together while the adults are off somewhere else. When they are upset or crying, they need loving attention. Child care workers should never be just a new kind of police. Children are entitled to freedom and self-determination. The freedom of a child should be bounded only by the necessity for safety and adequate group care.

The goal of good child care is to provide as exciting and fruitful an event for the young people as we plan for the adults. And it must reflect our politics and respect for children as people.

8

Benefits for Beginners

There are hundreds of special events you can hold to raise money. The next three chapters give you some examples of benefits that have worked well for grass roots organizations in recent years. There are five small events that need few workers and little seed money; five medium-sized events that need more time, money, and labor; and three biggies that need the largest investment of time, talent, and money.

Of course, you are not limited to these samples. Your local talent can always dream up something better using your own resources. A poor rural group in Kentucky invented the "Sorghum Stir-off" and raised $6,000 for its group. They planted four acres of sorghum cane for molasses, harvested it, refined it into 600 gallons of sorghum, bottled and sold it. An affluent urban group in Arizona ran a "Stock-a-rama" where people bought play money to "play" the stock market for a month. Forty volunteer stockbrokers kept track of each person's transactions. At the end of the month the person who hypothetically "made" the most money got a prize, and the person who "lost" the most got his money back. This group netted $4,000. Each event worked well because it was created by and for a specific group. You, too, can take a chance and pioneer a new event for your area.

The best way to collect new ideas is to ask your members what they would like to try. Check the section "Where to Get Advice" in Chapter 13 for more suggestions for getting fresh ideas. There are also several good books available on special events and how to run them best, listed in the bibliography, Chapter 14.

Here is advice from community leaders who have made a profit running simple, low-overhead special events. All of these are good for beginners. First is the rummage sale, which is a sale of used goods donated by your members and friends. This event gives you an example of the steps to take, from finding the first volunteers to writing the last thank-you notes. Even if your committee chooses to start with another kind of event, read through the schedule for a rummage sale to help organize your planning. It is easier to attract enthusiastic volunteers if they see you are serious about getting results.

The schedule will help you get the most accomplished because you can do first things first, divide the work in a way that is fair and fun for everyone, make sure everything is done and nothing is neglected, and show each volunteer how his or her work contributes to the final success of the event. Especially if this is your first special event, read through the rummage sale schedule to see how you can control your time and efforts.

Next are tested ideas on how to make money at house meetings, which are neighborhood get-togethers where your leaders talk about your goals and ask for contributions. Especially if your organization has a bold program, house meetings are an ideal way to raise money because you educate your community about your issues at the same time that you raise money and find new members. The house meeting is the most efficient and most profitable way to combine your organizing and fundraising in one series of special events.

The third example is the haunted house, a good fundraiser for any group that involves families with school-age children. This section includes many other ideas on using holidays for fun and profit.

Any group can sponsor the fourth example, potluck supper, any time of the year. A potluck supper makes an ideal emergency fundraiser since you need almost no seed money or lead time. We will also discuss the do-it-yourself cocktail party and other variations on the classic potluck dinner. This type of event is the best way to gain weight and make money at the same time. A foolproof fundraiser for churches for centuries, the potluck supper will work for any organization that likes to share good food and good times. In fact, one young comedian on the Johnny Carson show joked, "Well, you know Methodists. They believe you can get into heaven if you bring a covered dish." You may not get into heaven, but you will surely have many members who are already familiar with the potluck supper and be eager to do one for *your* organization.

Last is the raffle, a game of chance that is popular in almost every culture throughout the world. You sell tickets to your customers, then select a few winners who get a prize. Everyone gets a chance to support your organization and possibly win. Raffles make a good special event for novice fundraisers; so many people like to gamble that it is very easy to sell tickets. Once your salespeople have gained confidence from selling raffles, they can go back and sell memberships!

THE RUMMAGE SALE

A rummage sale is a sale of used goods donated by the members and friends of the organization. This event can be run by any organization for any purpose. All you need are volunteers who will donate and solicit used merchandise to sell at bargain rates to smart shoppers. Many churches run annual rummage sales at their spring fling or fall fair; some hospitals, schools, and women's clubs succeeded so well with their rummage sales that they turned them into full-time businesses and opened thrift shops!

Here is a detailed timetable for planning a rummage sale. The same kind of schedule can be used for any benefit. Especially if this is your first special event, read through this example, even if your benefit is something other than a sale, to get an idea of the steps to take from beginning to end. Use this as a sample only. If necessary, you could pull off a sale in three weeks instead of four or get more elaborate and stretch it out over two months.

Adapt this sample to your own membership and community. For example, People United for Responsible Energy (PURE) in Madison, Wisconsin, formulated one plan but held four sales. They designed one plan for publicity and preparation for their rummage sale but ran the same kind of sale four weeks in a row in the north,

south, east, and west parts of town. Their members got around to
see the other neighborhoods, and PURE made more money each
week by forwarding the leftover merchandise to next week's sale.

Groundwork

Ask two members to chair the rummage sale committee for the
next six weeks. It will take them a week to research the sale, four
weeks to prepare for the sale, and one week to do the follow-up.
Tell them you want them to spend all of their volunteer time to
make this event a success. It should be their first — and, ideally,
only — volunteer activity for the next month and a half.

Look for leaders who have already worked on this type of fundraiser in your community. You want people who will welcome new
people, inspire veteran volunteers to do even more, and help everyone have a good time. If your co-chairs are different types, such as a
veteran board member and an enthusiastic newcomer, a retiree and
a young business leader, or a homemaker and an office worker, they
will be able to reach more people. Their talents and skills should
complement each other.

The president should ask the pair, in person, to take on this responsibility. If this is the first time the group has done this kind of
fundraiser, the president and other leaders must also make it a priority and give lots of help. If the organization has done this sort of
event in the past, the president can introduce the new chairs to last
year's chairs (if necessary), and the secretary can give the new chairs
all of last year's files and records. The board already will have
planned the event into its calendar, allocated the necessary seed
money, and instructed the treasurer to write a check for advance
cash for the rummage sale's co-chairs.

Research Week

The co-chairs of the event will ask:

1. Which of our members have had experience with successful
rummage sales or garage sales?

2. Which community leaders have run successful sales-type
events and can give advice?

3. Which of our members are hardworking, dependable people who will be eager to help and contribute ideas for the first meeting?

Interview the sales veterans for advice on making the sale a success. Make yourselves a list of dos and don'ts.

Recruit the volunteers you want. Remember, you get what you ask for! Don't wait for people to volunteer; decide who you want on your committee; then go and ask them to join the committee. You will need to invite two or three times as many people as you need on the committee. Also encourage members of the board to come to the first meeting and bring potential volunteers. Ask each enthusiastic volunteer to bring a friend. Continue asking for volunteers throughout the planning weeks. *Never* turn down a volunteer! The job of the co-chairs is to find the right role for every member who wants to help.

Four Weeks Before Sale—First Planning Meeting

Introductions and background. The president of the organization begins the meeting by introducing himself or herself and welcoming all the volunteers to the meeting. Tell the group the purpose of the organization, what it has accomplished so far this year, and what its goals are for the rest of the year. Explain why the board planned to do a rummage sale at this time and how the money raised at the sale will help the organization accomplish its goals. This will help everyone understand the importance of making the sale a success.

Choose co-chairs. The president introduces the two people who have agreed to chair the committee and explains their qualifications. Most people are eager to work on well-organized events but reluctant to take responsibility for leadership, so they will be glad the chairs are ready to lead. After the introduction the co-chairs will take over chairing this and all future meetings. They will have planned what they want to accomplish at this meeting and divided the agenda between them.

Set goals. The committee can decide what it will accomplish through this event, such as 1) raise $1,000 net profit; 2) sell ten new memberships; 3) recruit and involve fifty volunteers; 4) get publicity in local weekly newspaper, metropolitan daily paper, two radio stations, and one TV station; and 4) have fun! Determine how much merchandise you will need to make your goal. The rummage sale veterans can give you a good estimate.

Set date. One day or weekend. Check to make sure there are no conflicting events or holidays.

Choose location. Large parking lot, school basement, adjoining garages.

Choose one person to handle publicity and hoopla.

Check to see if you need a permit or special insurance.

Ask each committee person to call his or her network to solicit merchandise. Donors need not be limited to members of organization. Act out how to ask for merchandise and how to ask for a contribution if someone does not have merchandise to donate. Establish collection point for merchandise.

Decide what you will sell—have an interesting item donated already that callers will be able to mention when they do their calls; such as a handmade quilt, TV, fur coat.

Set criteria for donations; clothing must be clean, marked for size and purchasable. You don't want garbage.

Decide whether you want to sell other things besides used goods; such as plants or baked goods. Decide whether you want to add other low-space, low-seed-money fundraising events: face painting, fortune telling, raffle for best piece of merchandise.

Choose a name for the sale. You can call it simply a rummage sale; name it after the location, such as a garage sale, barn sale, or bargain basement sale; or name it after your choice of merchandise. A preschool selling used children's clothes called its sale "The Kids Closet"; a health care group with a variety of merchandise called its sale "Trash and Treasures"; a church with quality merchandise including new items donated by wholesalers, called its sale "Collectibles."

Set next meeting in one week.

TWO DAYS AFTER FIRST MEETING—CHECK ON A QUICK START

Co-chairs divide list and call everyone on committee to see that they have started calls. They should have a positive report of their own to give committee members; e.g., "I've got four donations of merchandise and one cash contribution." The chairs record the results the other committee members have to report.

FOUR DAYS AFTER FIRST MEETING—DOUBLE-CHECK

Co-chairs call everyone on committee again. If there are people who have not gotten started yet, it is time to remind them that they will need to report in three days.

Three Weeks Before Sale—Second Meeting, First Reports

Get reports from everyone on the committee. If there is one person who is not working, recruit new people to strengthen the committee.

Approve press releases and fliers for neighborhood. Send releases to local newspapers and bulletin notices to local churches.

Begin collecting and sorting merchandise. Recruit volunteer to pick up donations that cannot be delivered.

Make arrangements with local charity or thrift shop to pick up any leftover merchandise.

Notify police of sale date. Make arrangements to get sawhorses and trash barrels from the appropriate politician. Notify neighbors of sale. Check with closest large public parking lot to okay use on sale day.

Recruit artist to make huge banner to hang on or over sale site the week before sale.

Buy any necessary city permits. For example, Toledo, Ohio, requires you to buy a $10 permit from the Department of Health if you serve food.

Get the members of the organization excited about your event. Create a gimmick to get everyone else to the sale. Add a coupon to the bottom of every agenda, every program, and every letter that other committees use during the next two weeks. Offer an attraction you know will get your members out: free baby-sitting, free ride on the fire truck, 20 percent off for all members with this coupon, or 30 percent off if you bring the coupon and a friend!

Two Weeks Before Sale—Third Meeting, Arrangements

Continue calls for merchandise and collection.

Go over prospect list to see if anyone was missed. Assign to your best caller any possible donor who has been skipped.

Make list of what equipment you will need to borrow, where you can get it, who will pick it up and *return* it.

Make a list of what you need to buy. Assign purchasing agent to buy it. (Of course, don't buy anything you can get free.)

Make a plan for the layout for sales day. Involved Citizens Against Crosstown on Chicago's Northwest Side held a garage sale using several garages on the same alley—one for clothing, one for household appliances and utensils, one for children's clothing and toys, one for books and plants, one with free coffee and baked goods for sale. If you anticipate a large turnout, you may also want to assign one area in which to check children, one area in which to check pets, and one area in which to leave "hold" merchandise.

Schedule your personnel: who will put up posters, who will sell, who will handle money, who will supervise coffee, who will arbitrate disputes.

Mail second press releases and calendar notices.

Week Before Sale—Final Preparations

Put up banner over sale site.

Place classified ads in papers. Distribute fliers around neighborhood.

Assign committee people to announce sale at local church and club meetings.

Sort and price all items. Test all appliances.

Collect clothing racks, cash boxes, coffee makers, mirrors, adding machine, any other equipment you need to borrow.

Mail final press releases and calendar notices.

DAY BEFORE—BRIEFING

Set up merchandise in garage(s).

Prepare clear signs for prices, hours, and parking, and hang them high enough for everyone to see.

Plan timetable and gimmicks; e.g., last two hours all merchandise is half price. Put arrow signs around neighborhood.

Call all workers to make sure they will show up or send a replacement.

Get cash and receipts.

Walk through the sale as though you were a customer. Be sure everything is clearly marked and you have enough bags.

Check security.

Brief all workers on potential problems. One common trick of garage sale shoppers is to remove price tag and try to bully salesperson into a lower price. Choose *one* person who is patient, firm, and tactful to be final arbitrator on all items discovered without prices. Be sure that everyone understands that your arbitrator has final decision-making authority — this is not the time for democracy.

Day of Sale

One hour before sale: all workers arrive. Chairs have already prepared coffee and doughnuts. Review sales procedures and be sure everyone knows who to send complaints or questions to — chairperson or arbitrator. Be sure everyone knows location of bathrooms, parking, and fire extinguishers. Thank everyone for helping at the sale.

Be sure you know how the electrical system works and where fuse boxes or circuit breakers are. Bring extra fuses.

Set up cash boxes and ledgers.

THE SALE

Start on time. If you've done your publicity thoroughly, you should have a line at the door.

Salespeople sell, advise, and keep an eye out for thieves.

One person has a table set up with organizational literature, written notice of the next meeting or event, membership applications, current issue of the newsletter, and organizational sales materials — buttons, T-shirts, cookbooks, research reports. He or she should pleasantly explain how the shopper can join or help the organization but should avoid all ideological disputes.

One person makes sure coffee is ready and coffee area is tidy.

Cashiers handle money. Give a receipt with carbon copy for all purchases over $5 by adults. This will produce a mailing list for the next event. Bagger next to cashier wraps and seals all purchases. Never leave too much cash out. Have one head cashier to approve all checks and large bills. Never cash a stranger's check.

Have a barker, or kids passing out handbills, or a teenager with a sandwich board to bring in more traffic off the street.

Chairpersons keep everyone calm and cheerful, find replacements for the no-shows, settle all disputes with the neighbors about parking or noise, and make sure that all jobs are getting done.

Photographer takes black-and-white photos for next newsletter.

Close on time.

AFTER THE SALE—CELEBRATION

Have small party or special refreshments for workers. Share funny stories. Chairpersons personally thank each person for a job well done.

All cash is accounted for and deposited at bank. All merchandise not sold is picked up by charity the group has chosen.

DAY AFTER SALE—WRAP-UP

All borrowed equipment is cleaned and returned.

Garage is completely cleaned up and contents replaced.

Modest but imaginative gift given to host/hostess.

Thank-you notes sent to: workers, people, and organizations who lent equipment; police and politicians who provided services; anyone who gave you a plug in a publication or at a meeting.

Apologies are sent to any neighbors or anyone else who complained.

Take down signs and pick up any litter.

Press release sent to local media reporting success of event with photo of chairperson or clever news item: mayor buys antique gavel; local celebrity buys "X" for her famous "Xs" collection, etc. This is good reinforcement for the people who worked hard and will improve attendance for the next event. Done correctly, you can establish that your organization's events are *the* place to see and be seen.

President calls to praise co-chairs.

Week After Sale—Reports and Payments

Sale chairpersons prepare report for meeting. Record the gross, expenses, net, number of customers, problems, and suggestions for next year. Include list with names and telephone numbers of all workers. Give bills, receipts, and any balance of cash advance to treasurer.

Treasurer pays all bills.

Membership chairperson and sale chairperson prepare list from receipts of customers. Check against list of current supporters.

Send thank-you note and membership application to big purchasers not currently on your supporters list.

Prepare card on all new donors, recording money spent, date, name, and address.

Clearly mark and store receipts.

Send report on sale to everyone who donated merchandise or money and thank them for their help.

Prepare story for next organizational newsletter, including names of all workers. Choose and caption flattering photos of the workers. Double-check the spelling of names. Be very positive and highlight both the fun and the profit. This will make it easier to get volunteers next time.

ORGANIZATIONAL MEETING AFTER SALE

Board puts sale report at the beginning of the agenda.

Co-chairs announce profit and number of new members, share what they learned running the sale, and praise their volunteers. Circulate clippings of "before" and "after" stories in press. Play tapes of good radio and TV coverage. Show slides of the preparation, sale, and cleanup if you have a volunteer photographer/historian.

President praises the sale co-chairs and recognizes all workers at the meeting. Show how the garage sale profits and new members fit into this year's plan. Point out how this money will help the organization achieve its goals.

Rummage Sale Repeatability

It is almost impossible to lose money on a rummage sale since all of your merchandise is donated. If you can also get a supporter to donate the printing for your posters and fliers, the postage for your press releases, and the coffee for your workers, then you will have 100-percent profit!

If you repeat your sale each year, you can make more money each year because you will know which things sell best in your community, how much to price items, which publicity outlets produce the most shoppers, and which weekends are the best. Most groups find the best sellers are children's clothing, knickknacks, and useful appliances like toasters and irons. You can research prices by shopping at the local thrift shops. See how much they are charging and charge half of that. Since your sale is only one or two days long, your goal is to sell out!

Ask garage sale veterans for advice on the best weekend or simply test different weekends the first few years you do a rummage sale. Some groups like to tie in with a larger event that is being sponsored by another group in their community. Public relations professionals call this "taking a ride" on someone else's publicity. They do the work to draw a crowd; you get the profits. For example, some citizens' groups sponsor neighborhood fairs; some block clubs sponsor block parties, garden walks, and antiques sales; some merchants' associations sponsor sidewalk sales, craft sales, and art shows; most counties sponsor county fairs. If you schedule your sale the same weekend, you can get more customers with no more time or money spent for publicity. For example, the Amnesty International group in Toledo, Ohio, does a garage sale each year in conjunction with the historical district festival put on by the Women of the Old West End (WOWE). As they report, "We all bring our junk collections of the preceding year and sell same. Because we are sitting in the middle of a huge Historic District Festival, which is alive with music, singing, dancing, and intoxicating beverages, we experience almost

no difficulty selling everything we can get our hands on for out-
rageous prices."

On the other hand, some groups find their members would
rather attend the big event, then volunteer to work at the sale on a
different weekend. Ask your volunteers what they want or test it
both ways to see which works best.

The biggest advantage to repeating a rummage sale every year is
that you can collect merchandise all year-round. Put a reminder in
the newsletter every month that you want members and friends to
donate rummage for your sale in June. Organize a committee of
drivers with vans, trucks, or station wagons to pick up the merchandise and take it to a storage place. About two months before the
sale, add a written reminder to every agenda and give the co-chairs
of this year's sale an opportunity early in the agenda to recruit
volunteers and ask for contributions. With more merchandise and
more volunteers you can't fail to make more money!

Variation for Coalitions

Some coalitions combine all their rummage sales into one
megasale. In the city you can ask a large public parking garage,
such as a hospital or department store garage, to let you use its
building. In the suburbs or small towns you can ask for a school
parking lot or gym or a large church hall. Each group in the coalition gets a space to sell whatever it wants. Other organizations,
craftspeople, and merchants can also buy space to sell their products. It is easy to attract more customers because you offer variety
and one-stop shopping, like a shopping mall.

Under this system, a coalition of neighborhood groups can sponsor a giant rummage sale. The umbrella group will organize the
event; handle publicity; sell space to smaller groups, individuals,
and merchants; provide security and cleanup; and run the gate.
Each group decides what it wants to sell in addition to memberships
and its own issue materials like books, T-shirts, and bumber
stickers. The choral group can sell used records and music; the
friends of the library can sell used books; the day care center can
sell used children's clothes and games; the battered women's center

can sell women's clothes and housewares; the garden club can sell
garden tools, seeds, and plants; the artists' cooperative gallery can
sell artwork and crafts; the softball team can sell beer and hot dogs;
the high school band members can sell ice cream; and the senior
citizens club can sell baked goods and coffee. Local residents can
buy space to run their own garage sales, and local merchants can
buy space to sell their end-of-season inventory. Everyone will make
more money and have more fun when they all work together every
year. (Also see "Bazaar" in Chapter 9 for more ideas on food,
games, and merchandise for a coalition sale event.)

THE HOUSE MEETING

A house meeting is simply an occasion to get neighbors together
in someone's home, tell them about your program, and ask them
for money. This event works especially well for any organization
that has a clearly defined geographic area. For example, a political
candidate can attend house meetings in each precinct, a church
fundraising campaign can hold house meetings in all parts of the
parish, and a community organization can sponsor house meetings
wherever it has members. If the people you want to reach do not all
live in the same area, you can offer the same format in any location
where you can get your people together, such as a downtown restaurant for office workers, a park for environmentalists, or a clinic
for health care consumers. Each meeting can be planned to produce both immediate donations and future meetings.

Volunteers

The president will ask two volunteers to serve as the co-chairs of
the house meetings. It is the responsibility of the co-chairs to
prepare all written materials, recruit people to host meetings, help
each host get guests to his or her meeting, recruit and train others to
ask for money at the meetings, and coordinate the schedule for the
meetings. The co-chairs serve as "mission control" to keep everything running smoothly during the meetings.

Each successful meeting needs three volunteers: 1) the host, who
supplies refreshments, invites neighbors, and cleans up; 2) an of-

ficer of the organization, who explains why you want the money (for political campaigns this person is the candidate); 3) someone to ask for and get money from the guests at the party. The co-chairs should host the first two house meetings so they understand what is involved. After the first two meetings the co-chairs recruit new hosts; since the hosts do not have to ask for money, it is not difficult to find volunteers. The co-chairs can be the ones to ask for the money at meetings, or they can train a team of irresistible salespeople to ask for the money at the meetings.

Preparation

The co-chairs will ask someone to be the host or hostess for the meeting. Choose a date two to three weeks away. Print up invitations with the date, time, and place. The host or hostess can distribute them in the neighborhood, at the club or church, and mail a few to other friends farther away. The written invitations should be distributed about one week before the house meeting and then followed up with as many phone calls as possible. You can expect about a 10-percent turnout from strangers and about 30 percent from people you know. Thus, if you are the host for a meeting in your precinct for a political candidate and you have invited 200 people in the precinct, expect 20 to show up. If you are the hostess for a meeting to discuss the pledges and program for your church and invite 90 people from your church, expect about 30 to show up.

The host or hostess prepares simple refreshments. Coffee is most popular, but you could serve lemonade or iced tea in the summer or hot cider or hot chocolate in the winter, plus cookies or snacks. Feel free to use paper cups. If you are holding a series of house meetings and want to get more volunteer hosts, simple refreshments will make it easier to recruit new people. Do not serve alcoholic beverages.

At the Meeting

Use name tags so people get to know each other. One reason people like these meetings, especially in big cities, is that they give everyone a chance to meet some neighbors. The host should make

sure everyone is introduced and that everyone understands the purpose of the event. Be sure to have plenty of literature on the group
available for the newcomers.

THE SPEAKER

The first choice for a speaker is an officer of the group, or the
candidate at a political meeting, or the pastor at a church gather-
ing. The speaker explains what the group is doing, how it affects
the people in the room, and exactly why the group needs money.
For example, the president of a block club could outline the history
and goals of the block club, explain that it has received permission
from the city to make the adjacent vacant lot a playground, and
that $2,000 is needed for equipment. The speaker then asks for
questions and answers them briefly. Keep everyone on the topic. If
someone asks why the block club hasn't done anything yet about the
parking problem, agree that it is a serious issue, refer the questioner
to the head of that committee, and return to the playground discussion.

THE STING

Someone besides the speaker or the host should actually ask for
the money. Since the speaker is your president or candidate, he or
she must keep open communications with the whole community.
It's poor etiquette for the host to ask his guests for money. Expecting the host to ask for money would also make it much more difficult to get future hosts. So choose another person who is poised,
convincing, and persuasive to ask for the money. This can be one of
the house meeting co-chairs or someone they trained.

The asker can pass out preprinted pledge cards, which have
spaces for the donor's name, address, and phone numbers, plus
boxes to check for the amount he or she wishes to contribute. For
example, you could have boxes marked $25, $10, $5, and "other."
Indicate on the card how to make out checks. The chairperson explains exactly what the money will go for: $200 for bulldozing, $300
for swing sets, $300 for benches, $500 for fencing, $500 for land-

scaping, and $200 for signs. Then the chairperson asks for a specific amount with a reason why that amount was chosen. "There are 200 families who signed the petition for this playground. If each one gives $10, we can get the work done and have the park ready before school gets out." The chairperson makes the need urgent and adds a specific time limit, like "before school gets out." This helps prevent people from saying, "I can't give now. I'll send something in." The chairperson should also honestly say, "I think this is long overdue in our neighborhood, and I have given my $10 already." Do not ask for questions—they have already been asked, and they have been answered by the speaker. Ask people to fill out their pledge cards or their checks now, and say you will collect their cards and the money.

Now comes the hardest moment. Stop talking and smile. The chairperson has to keep quiet and just wait. This will induce the audience to fill out the cards or write checks. Since the American school system is designed to make people acquiescent about filling out forms, they will do it when everyone else does. After they feel awkward long enough in the silence they will write out the check.

PRIMING THE PUMP

Be sure you know a few people who are coming and ask them in advance to give so they will get things moving. They have their check or cash ready and say at once they want to give. After they hand in their cards and checks, encourage the others to follow suit. They also help during the discussion if anyone in the audience has an ax to grind or wants to tell a long story about hating playgrounds because he or she fell off the swings at the age of seven. The givers make sure the discussion always gets back to the playground, why it is a good idea, and why money is needed *now*.

COLLECTING THE CARDS

You can apply fundraising "triage" to the group. *Triage* is a battlefield term for dividing the wounded into those who will live without any care, those who will die no matter what the doctors do, and those who will live only with immediate care. The doctors work on the last group. In the same way, you can divide any fundraising audience into groups for the best return on your efforts.

There will be some who will give no matter what. Even if the speaker is late, the coffee is terrible, and they don't get a seat, they are going to give because they have already decided the playground is a good idea and their kids will love it.

Then there are those who will never give. They come only for the refreshments and to be seen looking concerned about the community. They won't give to you, and they probably don't give to anyone else, either. After a while you will get to know the deadbeats and just send them to the cookies. You need to be careful not to waste your time trying to get money out of a hopeless case while missing someone who would like to give.

This is the middle category and the focus for the chairperson. These are people who have not made up their minds and want more information. Take the time to explain any details they want to know — insurance, security, or supervision. The chairperson's job is to get their donations *now*. If they say they want to think about it, or have to ask the wife or husband, or that they will mail it in, try to convince them to decide right away. If you don't get the money that night, you will most likely never get it. Less than 2 percent of the people who say they will put it in the mail really do.

WRAP-UP

The house meeting chairperson will ask for as many donations as he or she can. Plan a system with the treasurer and membership chairperson to turn in the money and new names coming in at each meeting. Also ask enthusiastic guests if they would like to host a coffee in their home. Even if it is on the same block, you can schedule another house meeting there in four weeks. Choose a different day of the week, and you will be able to reach people who missed this meeting.

Compliment the host on what a fine job he or she did. The co-chair must send a written thank-you note to the host the next day. You can address the envelopes ahead of time and even write the notes ahead if you are busy; then add a "P.S." after the meeting.

The officer who spoke at the meeting can call the host the next day to thank him or her for the hospitality and good work for the organization.

Repeatability

House meetings can be repeated as often as you want. Intense political campaigns will run three meetings a night in three different precincts. Church stewardship campaigns will schedule four to eight house meetings each year. In fact, some people have been known to give to a good cause more than once just so they could go to another house, meet new people, and hear the inspiring speakers!

Note: This example describes using the house meeting to get a one-time donation. You can also use house meetings to ask people to buy memberships or to make pledges to support your group. See Chapter 4 for more advice on dues and pledges.

THE HAUNTED HOUSE AND OTHER HOLIDAY FAVORITES

The haunted house is an example of a holiday fundraiser. It is really amateur theatrics, used to entertain and to deliver shoppers to your fall bazaar. The whole thing is tied to Halloween, October 31. Other holiday examples are listed at the end of this section.

Preparation

The first thing you need for a haunted house is an old spooky-looking house. An ideal house has a scary exterior, lots of rooms inside, and a floor plan that will allow you to run people in one door and out another. Old homes often have front and back staircases, so this will work nicely. The house must be structurally sound; you cannot use anything dangerously dilapidated.

Although a house is preferable, you can also haunt a smaller area. Scout groups and 4-H clubs have run the haunted basement, the haunted attic, the haunted schoolroom, and even the haunted barn. Church groups have run the haunted tent and the haunted choir loft.

An ideal setup would be an old parsonage next to a church where you can also run a small sale and serve refreshments. Since many old parsonages qualify as haunted house architecture, this makes a good fundraiser for church groups.

Arrange to use the house the weekend before Halloween or two weekends before. If a family is living in the house, you will have to close off certain rooms and offer them another place to live while their house is being haunted.

INSURANCE

You must have adequate insurance for crowds going through a house. If you are using a parsonage, it may already be covered on the church policy. Otherwise, you will have to get special short-term liability coverage to cover any accidents or any damage to the house. Ask your insurance agent and lawyer for advice on necessary insurance.

DECORATION AND SCENARIO

Get a committee to decorate the house. Set skeletons and black cats all around the house and tape a huge King Kong face over a second story window. Find someone who is good with electricity to rig up scary lighting and sound effects. Plan a theme for each room: catacombs, mad scientist's lab, vampire's crypt, wolfman's lair, witches' kitchen, Dracula's den, or outer space *2001* science fiction room. Ask for volunteers to play Halloween roles in each room: witches in the kitchen brewing up some fiendish broth, a vampire to sit up in the coffin when the tour comes by, a pair of mad scientists building Frankenstein's monster, a cuckoo astronaut for the outer space room. Each character is responsible for his or her own costume and props. Have the characters in each room work out a little business to do when the tour comes by.

The Tour

Have a few people who are good with children serve as the tour guides. They lead the kids in groups of five or six through the house and introduce each act. For example, when the group approaches the vampire's crypt the guide tells the kids they have to be very quiet since it is daytime and the vampire is sleeping in his coffin. Then the guide opens the door to a sinister room with a coffin in it. The vampire sits up and says something scary to the kids.

CHARGES

Charge each kid a quarter (25¢) and each adult a dollar ($1) to go through the house. Many kids will go through more than once, especially if you run a good show and are open more than one day, and adults will love to go through just to see their friends perform. If you are open from 10:00 A.M. to 5:00 P.M., you can run several hundred people through the house.

PROFIT FORMULA

Your profit is all the tickets you sell minus the cost for the insurance. If you get the insurance donated, it is all profit. You can also set out a plastic pumpkin for donations so adults can put in more money when they leave.

The profits from the haunted house are relatively low, but the people involved will have a ball. There are almost no costs involved, and you will be providing a service to the community by offering good safe recreation for the kids.

The way to make more money is to take the kids and their parents through the house and into the church basement for a small harvest bazaar. Set up the foolproof bake sale featuring autumn favorites like pumpkin pie and homemade preserves. Especially if you are in a big city, dried fall flowers and vegetables like gourds, pumpkins, dried weeds, cattails, and Indian corn are great money makers. Ask someone with a station wagon to make a trip to the country to collect the produce. Mark it at one-half what the florists are charging, and you will easily sell out. Sell apple cider and doughnuts and run a small rummage booth. You can also run a raffle for favorite fall prizes like tickets to an important football game, a turkey with all the trimmings, or a turkey dinner for four at a good restaurant.

ANOTHER SPIN-OFF

Sponsor a Halloween costume party for the adults in the evening. Characters from the haunted house can do their bits for extra entertainment during the band's breaks. Call it "The Monster Mash" and ask everyone to come as a monster. You can have a "Harvest Home" barn dance with square dancing or a "School Daze" sock hop with '50s and '60s records. In an election year you can ask people to come as their most or least favorite politicians and sell candidates ads in your ad book.

Holidays

Other holidays that lend themselves to fundraisers include:

NEW YEAR'S EVE (DECEMBER 31)

Have a dress-up party or dance. It is possible to run your regular event with extra prizes and razzle-dazzle. One organization in Buffalo, New York, runs its bingo game on New Year's Eve. They make more than $1,000 because they make it *the* place to be on New Year's Eve. After bingo the members and workers go out to celebrate another great year.

TWELFTH NIGHT—JANUARY 6 (THE TWELFTH DAY OF CHRISTMAS)

Sponsor a night of Elizabethan revelry, complete with Renaissance costumes, a feast, dances, jugglers, and fools. In the Middle Ages the serfs got the twelve days of Christmas off from their drudgery at the manor, so they really whooped it up on the last night. Ask the library for a book with costume and menu ideas.

LINCOLN'S BIRTHDAY (FEBRUARY 12)
OR WASHINGTON'S BIRTHDAY (FEBRUARY 22)

Have a patriotic birthday party with American foods and revolutionary costumes. If you saved all your bicentennial handouts you should also have good colonial recipes and games to use; the library can supply more ideas.

VALENTINE'S DAY (FEBRUARY 14)

Good for a dance or a ladies' luncheon. Natural opportunity for a press event to expose the current "sweetheart deal" between local politicians and road/dam/development builders.

ST. PATRICK'S DAY (MARCH 17)

Perfect for a corned beef and cabbage dinner or a beer blast. You can also join or start your local parade. Casey Kelly, publicity chair and Grand Colleen for Chicago NOW, organized a delegation to march in the St. Patrick's Day parade as the "Chicago Irish Feminists for ERA."

APRIL FOOL'S DAY (APRIL 1)

Connecticut ACLU organized forty-eight "April No-Fools Day Parties" across the state. They mailed an invitation that read:

On the eve of a traditionally humorous date, at parties statewide, we will seriously dramatize our determination to REFUSE TO BE FOOLED by government — to protect our civil liberties — and to raise funds to carry out the heaviest legal commitment ever.

They asked for a minimum of $5 and raised a total of $7,600.

MAY DAY (MAY 1)

Celebrate the coming of spring with spring revels, May baskets and a maypole dance. This is also Law Day, by presidential proclamation, and Solidarity Day for unionists and socialists.

Business and Professional People for the Public Interest (BPI), a Chicago public interest law firm, chose May 1st "Law Day" to celebrate that we live in a nation under laws and to raise money for the highly successful law firm. They organize a day-long series of events including mock trials by high school "street law" students, free movies, a luncheon for lawyers, and a dinner featuring a major speaker such as Nicholas Von Hoffman or I. F. Stone. In 1979, they made a net profit of $49,500; in 1980, a net of $55,000; and in 1981, a net of $75,000 from contributions from individuals, businesses, law firms, and other professionals.

INDEPENDENCE DAY (JULY 4)

Perfect for parades, sack races, barbecues, picnics, ice cream socials, and any other All-American festivities.

HALLOWEEN (OCTOBER 31)

Costume parties, haunted houses, and fall bazaars.

SEASONS

Christmas Season: Now commercially defined as the day after Thanksgiving (fourth Thursday in November) until Christmas, December 25. Time for Christmas craft sales, caroling, dinners, and bake sales.

Spring: Spring bazaars, plant sales, garden walks.

Summer: Any kind of outdoor sports or contests, picnics, barbecues, and fiestas, walkathons and marathons. Celebrate Midsummer Night's Eve, with some Midnight Madness.

Fall: Fall bazaars, harvest celebrations, hayrides.

Winter: Winter sports like ice-skating, sledding, and tobogganing, Christmas or Hanukkah food and craft sales, indoor events like speakers and movies.

DATES TO AVOID

Mother's Day, Father's Day, Thanksgiving, and Christmas are reserved for family affairs. Memorial Day and Labor Day are often used by labor unions or corporations for picnics or sports. Check your calendar to avoid Ash Wednesday, Good Friday, Easter, Passover, Rosh Hashanah, Yom Kippur, and Hanukkah, which change dates each year.

OTHER HOLIDAYS

Friday the 13th. Have a "Festival of Fate" party starting at 8:13 P.M. Book a fortune teller and a palm reader to tell people's fortunes. Serve Chinese fortune cookies. Sell tickets for $13.13. Put on a skit about the good luck the organization will have next year.

Sadie Hawkins Day. Officially February 29, but you can do it any time in leap year. Next leap year is 1988. Leap Years are the same as Presidential election years and Olympic Games years. Tradition holds that women can ask men to marry them in a leap year. Sadie Hawkins Day is the chance for the women to invite the men to a dance or party.

Make up your own holiday. Celebrate founder's day, the birthday of the organization, the day you get your tax exemption, the president's birthday, installation of officers, and, of course, *all* your victories! You can also celebrate the holidays that are important to your own members, such as Dr. Martin Luther King, Jr.'s birthday (January 15) for a black leaders' award luncheon, Susan B. Anthony's birthday (February 15) for a "Failure Is Impossible" feminist fête, St. Joseph's Day (March 19) for an Italian dinner, Cinco de Mayo (May 5) for a Mexican fiesta, Bastille Day (July 14) for a French wine and cheese party, or Margaret Sanger's birthday (September 14) for a family planning group's family potluck.

See the bibliography, Chapter 14, for recommended reading on holiday fundraisers.

THE POTLUCK SUPPER

The potluck supper is a delightfully high-calorie low-cost fundraiser. Each person or family brings a dish that will serve ten or more and pays a small amount for admission. It is a great way to get families together and an excellent way to introduce small groups in a new coalition to each other.

This is an especially good fundraiser for low-income organizations because it allows you to have a festive meal together without paying the high price for a restaurant or hotel. And your own members get all the compliments for the food! Many low-income groups face the problem of a limit on how much they can tax their own members versus a desire to make more money. You can solve this problem by combining a potluck dinner with another more profitable fundraiser such as an ad book. Your members make money by selling ads to people who have more money, such as politicians, churches, merchants, and corporations. Then distribute the ad book at a potluck dinner that all of your members can afford to attend and make a contribution of their time and talent in the dish they bring.

Preparation

Select two people to serve as co-chairs for the potluck supper. They will recruit a committee of volunteers who choose a date and place for the potluck. Look for a large free room with enough tables and chairs, running water, and electricity. A church or school hall is fine. If you can get access to a big kitchen, too, that is even better. Ask the pastor, principal, or janitor to show you how to light the stoves and the location of the washrooms, garbage cans, fuse box or circuit breakers, and fire extinguishers. Ask if there are any special hints about using the space, such as which outlets to use for the large coffee makers so you don't blow the fuses.

Count the number of tables, chairs, plates, cups, glasses, salt and pepper shakers, cream pitchers and sugar bowls, trays, knives, forks, and spoons. Make arrangements to borrow extras of anything you will need for the size of your group. Ask your shopper to buy coffee, tea, milk, cream, sugar, napkins, and place mats. For a festive occasion, ask a local liquor store or wine shop to donate wine for the potluck.

Make up a flier telling your members and friends the theme for the potluck and what they should bring, such as "a dish to serve ten people." Explain any restrictions, such as no meat or desserts for a Lenten potluck. Sell numbered tickets in advance so people make a commitment to attend and you know how many places to set. If someone says he can't cook, suggest he bring fresh fruit or cheese and sell him a ticket anyway.

BEFORE THE DINNER

Have a committee come in early to make sure the room is clean, the tables and chairs are set up, and the coffee is made. Set the tables with place mats, napkins, silverware, salt and pepper shakers, cream and sugar, and bread and butter. You can add simple centerpieces from the members' gardens or have the kids make holiday place mats for Valentine's Day or Christmas.

The committee makes up a buffet table on which to put all the food and makes sure there are enough large spoons and forks to serve everything. It usually works well if you can put long tables in the middle of the room so the diners can serve themselves in two rows from either side of the table.

At the Dinner

Have two people be the hosts — responsible for getting all the food out, keeping early dishes warm, and making everyone feel welcome. They say nice things about *every* dish. In addition, they recruit a team of waiters and waitresses to pour coffee, clean up spills, and help serve anyone who needs help at the buffet.

Set up a ticket table by the door. Most groups charge about $2 for adults and $1 for senior citizens and children.

If anyone comes without a dish, he or she can pay double, $4 for adults and $2 for seniors and children. Or let the noncooks do the cleanup.

PROGRAM

You can have a simple program consisting of the president welcoming everyone and talking a little about what the group is doing now. If there is a piano in the room you can always have a sing-along with dessert. Keep the program short, since most people really come to eat and talk with their neighbors.

Afterward

If you are using the school's dishes, you need a team to wash up and put everything away. Put all the tables and chairs back the way you found them. Be sure people take their empty dishes home or that one person takes all the empty dishes to a central location to be picked up. Be sure to thank the principal or other individual for the use of the room. Turn off all the lights and stoves and lock the room after the last person leaves.

MIXER

Potlucks are a good way to get a couple of small groups to meet each other. Be sure you have a host or hostess who introduces the guests to each other. Use name tags and try to mix up the seating so everyone gets to meet someone new. One gimmick that works well at rearranging people is to set up twelve tables and mark them with zodiac signs and dates; e.g., Gemini, May 21–June 20, or Aquarius, January 20–February 18. People will pick up their food and sit at the table for their sign. Clip the horoscope from that day's paper and mount it on the sign to make a dandy conversation starter.

The zodiac mixer works best with all-adult groups. It does not work if there are many families so that adults must sit near small children. For groups with lots of kids, you can mix them up by school, neighborhood, or parish or simply in order of arrival. If there are a lot of children, it is good to have another large room nearby in which the kids can play, since they usually finish first.

PROFIT FORMULA

Your profit is all the ticket sales minus your costs. The costs should be no more than paper products like place mats and beverages.

Repeatability

You can repeat a popular potluck each year on the same holiday. Some rural groups that ask their members to travel long distances to attend board meetings run monthly or quarterly potlucks before the business meetings. Members get better food at a lower cost than if they had to eat in a restaurant. The groups use the profits to pay for their meeting costs and to offer subsidies to equalize the leaders' travel expenses. Some groups with busy schedules and intense working conditions schedule monthly potlucks so the leaders and staff can share what they are all doing.

Variations

You can also run a potluck as a picnic. It is easiest to have everyone bring cold dishes like fried chicken or meat loaf rather than trying to grill hot dogs. You can add softball games or Frisbee contests.

Have a theme. For the Fourth of July you can have all American or regional dishes. For Christmas or Hanukkah you can have holiday specialties. Or you can have an ethnic dinner in which everyone brings an ethnic dish like sauerkraut, tamales, lasagna, or borscht. This works well in big cities where there are lots of ethnic groups. Tell your people to bring grandma's best dish.

Use a potluck to launch the sales drive for your group cookbook. If you have put together a cookbook of the members' best recipes, ask each person to bring the dish he or she submitted. Then people can have personal recommendations to make when they sell the book, like "Try the 'Rice That Stands Alone' on page 27 or 'Grandmother's Snickerdoodles' on page 104." Invite the food editors and feature writers of the local paper to the picnic to sample the fare. Give them cookbooks and press releases and encourage them to do stories on the cookbook.

Some groups use a potluck as one of the rewards for the end of a successful fundraising campaign. The top sellers get to come as guests without bringing a dish, and the people who sold the least are responsible for cleanup in addition to a dish.

INTERNATIONAL FOOD FEAST

The International Food Feast is a large-scale, dressed-up potluck dinner. Whereas the potluck has just random donation from the group's cooks, the International Food Fest has well-organized donations from each ethnic group represented in the membership. Besides highlighting the cuisine of each ethnic group, the feast can also present an entire program of entertainment, costumes, and decorations to portray each group's customs.

This is a natural event for organizations with great ethnic variety in their membership—urban parishes, metropolitan community organizations, senior citizens' coalitions. It also makes a great fundraiser for regional get-togethers of youth groups, women's clubs, or civic organizations. It works perfectly for organizations that promote international understanding like the American Field Service, urban visitors' centers, or university international programs.

THE TASTE AND TELL

For smaller groups, a delightful variation on the International Food Feast is the "Taste and Tell." This can be done at a luncheon or coffee hour or as an addition to a monthly meeting.

Recruit about twenty people to make their special family dessert recipe and bring it to the Taste and Tell. They tell the history of the recipe and its creator and may have stories to tell about the unusual equipment they use to make the dessert, like a krumkake iron or the old family bundt pan. This is a grown-up "show and tell" where everyone else walks around and samples your goodies.

The Taste and Tell works especially well at Christmas time. Some churches have each ethnic group decorate a small Christmas tree in the style of its homeland. Others display cherished Christmas decorations like handmade ornaments or creche sets. Each person tells the story of the decorations and serves the national dessert. It is an honor for the tellers and a joy for the tasters.

You can either charge a flat price for the Taste and Tell or put baskets near each table for donations, with a suggested price per sample. You will probably make more charging 50¢ per sample since most people lose all self-control at the sight of homemade German chocolate cake, English trifle, Italian cannoli, Greek baklava, French pastries, or Mexican churros.

THE DO-IT-YOURSELF COCKTAIL PARTY

A cocktail party variation on the potluck makes a super emergency fundraiser. This is for your own members, to raise money on the spur of the moment or to celebrate a victory and raise money at the same time. Instead of bringing a cooked dish they bring liquor.

One member with a large home is the host, who sets up a bar with glasses, mixers, and ice. A few people volunteer to bring snacks and dips. Each person brings a bottle and puts it on the bar. Then each time they make themselves a drink they charge themselves a dollar. Teetotalers can charge themselves 50¢ per soft drink.

This can raise $50 to $100 an evening. Many people figure they are going to go out on a Saturday night anyway. This way they party together and donate the money they would have spent at Joe's Bar to the organization. And they all get a chance to get to know each other better.

THE RAFFLE

A raffle is a game of chance. You sell chances to win prizes. All of your customers support your program and hope to win a prize.

Raffles have been popular in America since colonial days. Boston ran a raffle in the 1660s to help Harvard University. In 1981 fifteen states ran raffles called lotteries. Illinois's lottery grossed more than $98 million in 1980. Of this, 47 percent went for prizes and 17 percent for operating the lottery, leaving a net profit of 36 percent for the state to spend on education, tax relief, and human services. If your organization is in a state that runs a lottery, your members are probably already familiar with raffles.

Advantages

The price is low. Most groups price tickets at $1 each or six for $5. Anyone can afford a raffle ticket.

It gets everyone involved. Because of the low ticket price, *everyone* can sell them. A raffle allows you to include your lowest-income members, children, students, and senior citizens in your fundraising program.

You are selling people something they want to buy anyway. Customers do not have to be crusading consumers or ardent environmentalists. Everyone loves a chance to win.

You can increase attendance at your meeting or party by scheduling the drawing there.

Sales are traceable. You find out who your best leadership is, who has networks, and who produces.

A raffle can be combined with any other event—dinner, meeting, pet show, theatre party, or dance.

It's fun.

You can use a raffle to turn a valuable but useless merchandise gift into usable cash. Mother Teresa, the nun who won the 1979 Nobel Peace Prize for her work among the poor in India, used this technique. Pope Paul VI gave her a Lincoln limousine that someone else had given him. As a car it was useless to her work. As a raffle prize it brought in some $100,000 to help feed and clothe poor people.

Closer to home, many groups use a raffle as a spin-off from an ad book campaign. As the members solicit the business community for ads, they always find five to ten merchants who insist they have no money to give but will give merchandise or gift certificates. Save the merchandise and certificates and use it to run a raffle, either separately or during the event at which you distribute the ad book.

Raffles make good emergency fundraisers because you can raise money quickly and easily. In 1981, Mrs. Alice Ballance raised $30 for the Kiddie World Day Care Center in Windsor, North Carolina, by raffling off a stuffed bird made by the children. She accomplished the raffle in *fifteen minutes* during the lunch break of a fundraising workshop held at the center!

Disadvantage: Number of Transactions

Raffles require a very large number of transactions for success. It takes lots and lots of $1 sales to make a decent profit. Evaluate how you want to invest your members' time. Is it better for them to sell a hundred $1 raffles, ten $10 dance tickets, or one $100 page in an ad book?

Preparation

Ask the board members to discuss how they feel about using a raffle to make money. Most people think it is all right because they like to gamble. However, some people object to raffles and other forms of gambling since the vast majority of people lose money. If more than a third of your board of directors are opposed to doing a raffle, choose a different fundraiser to make money for your group.

If the board *does* want to do a raffle, ask one person to find out if your organization needs to buy a city or state license. Call the city Department of Finance or the State Department of Regulations and Licensing, and ask for an application. The license is usually good for one year. In 1981 a raffle license cost from $100 in Chicago to $5 in Wisconsin. Not all cities or states require a license, but if yours does, be sure to read the regulations before you plan your raffle and follow them exactly when you run the event.

Make or buy chance tickets — printed with the name of your organization, date and place of the drawing, list of prizes, price, and a number. Add "Winner need not be present" if true. Each ticket has a detachable stub with the same number and spaces for name, address, and phone.

Chances can simply be mimeographed, cut up, and collated. Or they can be printed by a commercial printer. The printer may try to sell you a "cover" for a book of five or ten chances. A cover is just heavier paper sandwiching the chances. It is just an extra expense for something you will throw away. Order your chances without covers. If you plan to sell chances to labor unions or union members, use a union printer. Ask him or her to print the union "bug" on your tickets.

Choose the prizes. Everyone's favorite is cash. Other attractive prizes are appliances, trips, and gift certificates. A team of members should try to get prizes donated by local merchants. Remember: the less you have to spend on prizes, the higher your profit will be. Your leaders will know what the community wants.

Rural groups have raffled off sides of beef, rifles, and quilts. City groups have raffled off tickets to Broadway musicals, dinners at expensive restaurants, and gift certificates to jewelry stores.

One advantage of cash prizes is that the jubilant winner can donate part of the prize back to the organization. Especially in a low-income community, a large cash prize gives the winner a chance to make a major gift to the organization that he or she could never make otherwise. If the winner asks how much would be right, suggest that other winners have contributed 20 percent. So, if the prize is $5,000, you may get $1,000 back; if the prize is $100, you may get $20 back. This is not mandatory, of course, simply a nice tradition to encourage.

In fact, some groups get even more back. Carol Mohawk said the winner of the Akwesasne Freedom School's 1981 raffle gave the entire $1,000 prize back to the school! Because his own daughter went to the school, he knew how good it was and how well it would use the money. The 1980 winner was a mechanic who did not return the prize but now feels so good about the work of the Traditional Mohawk Nation that he fixes its ambulance and helps in other ways. Carol points out that the raffle gives them more money and more cooperation at the same time!

For bookkeeping purposes you should pay out cash prizes with a check. Record the winner's name and social security number for your tax reports. For any cash prize larger than $600 it is the organization's responsibility to make out a Form 1099 for miscellaneous income. One copy goes to the winner, one to the IRS, and one to the organization's files. Get Form 1099s free from your IRS office.

It is the winners' responsibility to report cash prizes on their income tax forms. Some people think if they win money from a tax-exempt group they don't need to pay taxes on it. Alas, Uncle Sam says income is income.

How to Boost Sales

Be sure everyone has tickets all the time. If each member carries a few books in a purse or pocket, chances can be sold to everyone the members meet.

Set an ambitious goal. Have frequent money turn-ins so you know how you're doing. Build in some friendly competition between your committees or regions.

Use incentives. Reward the top salespeople. Have each seller put his or her name on the back of each stub. Whoever sold the ticket to the first-prize winner also gets a prize.

Work systematically. Learn where and how you can sell. Set up a table outside a supermarket on Saturday or a church on Sunday, after getting permission from the manager or pastor. A team of two people can sell $100 worth of tickets in about three hours this way.

Try going door to door. Selling chances to your neighbors gives you an opportunity to identify potential new members.

Kids love to sell chances, especially those in the ten-to-twelve age group. Offer a modest commission or a party at the end of the afternoon, and you'll be amazed at the results.

Ask business people to buy more chances to support your group. They can easily buy $10 to $100 worth.

Ask *everyone* to buy a chance. Remind them of your victories and how these results have helped them personally. A national survey showed that only 4 percent of those interviewed had contributed to political campaigns. However, 89 percent said they would contribute *if asked*. Raising money proves you are serious about your goals. Everyone should support your important work—*ask them*.

Keep in touch with your sales team leaders daily and keep up the pep talk.

Mechanics

Number all tickets. Keep track of who has which tickets and what money is due in.

Be sure you get all the stubs in *before* the drawing.

Democratically select an impartial person to do the drawing. If a small child does the drawing, even the most cynical gambler won't complain of a fix.

Decide whether or not you want the paid staff members to be able to enter the raffle. It makes for very poor public relations if staff members win the prizes. Since some people are skeptical about the honesty of all forms of gambling anyway, it is much better to simply make a rule forbidding the staff to enter the raffle. Even if they say they never win anything, the only way to guarantee they don't win is to make sure they don't enter.

Keep all your stubs to use as a base for the list to mail notices of the next raffle or other fundraiser.

Repeatability

Once you establish your sales networks, it is easy to repeat a raffle. State lotteries run weekly drawings, and some community organizations run monthly raffles.

THE RAFFLE AS AN ONGOING FUNDRAISER

Fifty-Fifty Monthly Raffle. A small-town civic group runs a fifty-fifty monthly raffle. It gives away half of the money collected and keeps half. Since it sells about $500 worth of tickets a month, it regularly nets about $250.

The tickets are distributed through the chamber of commerce and the tavern association. Some of the businesses resell the tickets. Others just consider it a regular contribution and "eat" the tickets. Members of the civic group also sell tickets. One bartender, whose wife is on the group's board, makes customers buy a ticket before they can buy a drink.

The drawing is held every month at the group's regular meeting, which boosts attendance and adds some fun to an ordinary business meeting. A monthly raffle like this produces dependable income from the business community, members, and nonmembers.

9

Intermediate Special Events

Here is tested advice on five medium-sized special events. These are all good for groups that have a team of experienced fundraisers and from $50 to $500 in seed money. Although these events require more work than the beginner benefits, they will enable you to involve a lot more volunteers and attract a lot more guests. An industrious publicity chair can use these events to put your organization's name in your local newspapers and the state and national network newsletters. Best of all, these are loads of fun, so it is easy to recruit volunteers after the first year. Once your members see what they get to do (and your leaders learn what *not* to do), your organization will have more fun and make more money each year. All of the events can be repeated once a year.

The first example is the auction, a flashy way to get big spenders to spend a lot of money on you. They do not need to be enthusiastic about the purpose of your organization; they only need to want to get a bargain and get to show off in front of their friends at the same time.

The second example is the bazaar, a collection of several small fundraising activities in one location. You make money by selling games, food, and handmade or bargain merchandise. The bazaar has been the backbone of church and school special events for decades. Your organization probably has people who have worked on a few bazaars and shopped at dozens of them. Your group can do it, too, and have the same dependable success year after year.

The third example is the dance, which is the most flexible of the medium-sized fundraisers. A creative committee can do the same work but change the theme each year. Thus it *seems* like a new event, but you are guaranteed success because you are repeating an event that works. Especially if your community offers few opportunities for people to dance, this is a surefire money maker for your group.

The fourth example is the house tour, which is simply a tour through the homes of a few of your members or friends. Since the homes are already there, your only costs are printing, flowers, and insurance. Get these donated, and you can make 100-percent profit on a house tour. It is easy to start small with one or two homes, then build up to six or eight per year. This event is especially good for organizations in historic districts or attractive suburbs.

The last example is a theatre party, where the theatre does all the production work so all your volunteers need to do is to sell tickets. This is the easiest of all of the medium-sized benefits, so you can choose a theatre party even more than once a year. The theatre party example includes a discussion of patron tickets, which are higher-priced tickets to the same event. You can sell patron tickets anytime you want to make more money from your major donors, politicians, and local merchants.

THE AUCTION

An auction is simply an entertaining sale. You make money because the auction items are all donated. Extra excitement comes from celebrity auctioneers, unusual donations, and friendly competition.

Preparation

The major part of the work for an auction takes place before the auction itself: soliciting the donation of goods and services to auction off. There are three ways to do this. This wrong way is to go out and buy the art and other items you want to auction off, then auction them and try to make more than you spent. This will produce a fundloser or, at best, a very small profit and very large worries. The second way is to ask several artists to donate works for you to auction on commission. Then you get part and the artists get part of each sale. This limits the variety of your auction items — and your profits.

The right way to do an auction is to have everything donated. Rural groups have asked farmers for hay, farm equipment, sides of beef, and even cattle to auction. City groups can ask artists to donate works for the publicity involved. Everyone can ask stores to give you merchandise. Best of all, ask people to donate their services and talents. Dinners, lessons, and recreation donated by interesting people make the best auction items since they bring in high bids but cost you nothing.

SAMPLE AUCTION ITEMS

Art—paintings, photographs, sculptures, prints.

Crafts—jewelry, pottery, weaving, carpentry.

Cartoon originals—especially political cartoons. Write the artist in care of the newspaper.

Autographed books or records.

Contributions of services by people:

Recreation: Offer the chance to ride on a sailboat at a lake, ride on horses at a ranch, drive a race car, have a wine tasting at a vineyard, or drive a snowmobile at a farm.

Inside tour: Tour backstage at the opera, aquarium, museum, guided by the director.

Meals: Donors offer to prepare and serve, in your home or theirs, their famous curry dinner for twelve, or fondue for four, or the ultimate romantic dinner for two.

Lessons: Professional, teacher, or prize-winning amateur can donate lessons in belly dancing, scuba diving, speed reading, woodworking, self-defense, bowling, auto repair, Chinese cooking, knitting, etc.

PARTICIPATION

Arrange with the sponsoring agency for the highest bidder to get to: play in the symphony, sing in the chorus, be a batboy/girl for the professional baseball team for a week, be a Senate page, be an extra in a movie, carry a spear in the opera, do the weather on the TV news, or sit on the bench with the hockey, football, or basketball team.

TALENT

For the high bid, you get an artist to design your stationery, an interior decorator to design one room in your house, a plant doctor to perk up your plants, a professional to help your swing/serve/ punt/swan dive or whatever, a mechanic to tune up your car or motorcycle, a barber/hairdresser to cut/style your hair, veteran parents (or grandparents) to put on a birthday party for your kids and guests, a jolly person to play Santa Claus for your family or group, a seamstress to replace all missing buttons, a handyman to fix all the odds and ends that need repair in your house, a carpenter to build anything wooden of your own design from a birdhouse to a rolltop desk, a Santa's helper to address and mail all your Christmas cards or to wrap all your presents, a veteran host/hostess to supply you with hors d'oeuvres for fifty for your next party, a healthy teenager to mow lawn/rake leaves/shovel snow for a season, a responsible baby-sitter to watch your kids for a whole weekend, including a trip to the zoo, or a person with car to be your driver for a day.

As you can see, the possibilities are almost endless. The beauty of an auction is that you can sell anything that one person will donate and someone else will want to buy. Some of the most unusual auction items make the most money and get the best publicity. For example, the Massachusetts ACLU auctioned off the chance to have your name in Kurt Vonnegut's next book—and got $550. The Chicago ACLU auctioned off the chance to have your name in lights—on the marquee of the famous Biograph movie theatre. The Biograph is the place where the FBI gunned down John Dillinger in 1934. After much spirited bidding, a politician bought the privilege for $127.50. The bidding was so much fun that the theatre owner, who was at the auction, gave them the marquee again, which they promptly sold for $125.

SOLICITING CONTRIBUTIONS

As you collect your contributions, catalog each item very carefully so you know who gave it, the value, the recommended starting price. With the advice of an experienced auction producer or auctioneer, arrange the contributions in order so you have a variety of price and interest.

Next ask celebrities to serve as guest auctioneers and schedule them at intervals through the evening. They can auction off their own contributions or else just serve as auctioneers for a few items. Some possibilities are sports figures auctioning off lessons or autographed equipment, TV or radio stars auctioning off autographed scripts or clothing, and politicians auctioning off a service (like dinner in the governor's mansion — not ticket fixing). These can also be great publicity getters.

PROGRAM

Design and print an attractive program describing each item, the amount of the starting bid, and the name of the donor. Mail this out two weeks before the auction to everyone who has already bought a ticket. Give a program to everyone who buys a ticket during the last two weeks. This will get them thinking about what they want to buy. Also mail the program to everyone on your major donor list. Allow people to mail in sealed bids on items in the program if they are unable to attend the auction. One of the auction committee members places the mailed bids for the absentee supporters. Any auction items you receive during the last two weeks can be added on a mimeographed sheet inserted into the programs on the day of the auction. Be sure to have enough programs at the door for everyone who comes to the auction. Do not expect your guests to remember to bring along the program you mailed to them. See the sample at the end of this section.

AUDIENCE

For the auction to be a success you need an audience of people who will buy the merchandise. The more money the people have and the more likely they are to spend it, the more money you will make. While your own members may dig deep to make contributions, and others may spend foolishly to fulfill their fantasies, you still have to consider how to get people with bigger budgets to the auction.

There can be a problem if there is a big difference between the average income of the membership and the average income of the auction audience. On the one hand the members may complain, "Everything was too expensive—I didn't get to buy anything." On the other hand, if you don't have the rich people, you will not make enough money or have enough bidders to make it fun. One compromise is to auction a wide variety of items so everyone can at least bid on something. Or make each ticket a door prize ticket. Stop every five or six items to draw one or two door prize tickets and just give away some low-priced items or any item you have in quantity. Or you can take all of the lower-priced items, like crafts, prints, or plants, and set up a sale where you just mark things with a price and sell them. This eliminates the least profitable items from the auction itself. You will still sell all the crafts and plants, and you leave more time to raise the bids on your more exciting donations. This way everybody can go home with something and the organization will end up with the highest possible profit.

LISTS

Try to get lists of people who would be likely buyers for your art and services. This would include the lists of guests from any other auction held in town in the past year, lists of museum members (for an art auction), lists of wealthy supporters of the local politicians, plus names from every person on the committee. Just ask everybody to suggest all the people they can possibly think of and send them invitations. (Of course, be sure to make a list at the auction for the next time.)

Send invitations and try to presell as many tickets as possible. The ticket price should cover the room, printing, a professional auctioneer if you have one, and refreshments. Get a tempting door prize and list it on each ticket with "Winner must be present" to encourage people to attend.

Do lots of advance publicity, with photos, to inform the public of your exciting and unusual bargains. An auction is one fundraiser to which people will come as a result of publicity and will buy even if their feelings about your group are neutral. There are people who love the thrill of bidding and the chance to get a bargain. They watch for notices of an auction.

Your own members should sell as many tickets as possible in advance. You should promote the auction in the newsletter and do a mailing to your own contributor list. Give everyone who donates auction items four tickets, too.

At the Auction

AUCTIONEER

Hire a professional auctioneer unless you are very confident about an amateur whom you have seen work. Use your celebrities for variety and to attract the audience, but you have to depend on your auctioneer to keep the auction moving, keep people bidding, and get the totals up in a fun way. The auctioneer's most important skill is controlling the tempo so people don't get bored and start to chatter or wander away. The auctioneer also has to know how to work several bidders against each other so they spend a lot of money but still feel good.

Be sure to observe an auctioneer's style before you hire him or her, since some professonals are used to working high-priced, high-powered shows and may overpower your crowd. You need someone who understands that the purpose of the auction is both to raise money and to impress the audience with the organization.

VOLUNTEERS

Line up volunteers to work the door, serve refreshments, carry and display the auction items, accept payments and give receipts, pass out numbers for the bidders, help the auctioneer identify bidders, and make sure everyone goes home with the right thing. Make a complete record of who bought what. Artists especially need to know who has bought their work in case they ever need to borrow it for a show. It's also nice to include the information with your thank-yous so the donors know how much they have helped the group.

THE KEY TO SUCCESS — TEMPO

You need to keep people interested, keep them buying, and simply keep them in the room. It helps if you start early (7:30 P.M. on a week night; early afternoon on weekends) and have people circulate with coffee and snacks. Have each auction item on display with a tempting description and the starting price so people can decide what they want. Intersperse celebrity auctioneers to add excitement and vary the merchandise to increase bidding. Another gimmick is to have your "winner must be present" door prize drawing at the end of the evening. Since the people have already bought their tickets and want your door prize, they will stay to see if they won. Limit the auction to about two hours.

Be sure to test the room's sound system in advance. If it is not strong enough to make your auctioneer heard easily over normal crowd noise, rent or borrow a better system and use it for your auction.

One problem is created by people who get bored easily or early and want to talk in the back of the room. They distract the rest of the crowd. Have several ushers who will shoo the talkers into another room, explaining that they will be notified when the item they want comes up.

PROFIT FORMULA

The profit on the auction is your sales total minus the cost of invitations, tickets, and the auctioneer. If you auction art work on commission, it is your percentage of the sales minus the costs.

Variations

There are three variations on the auction that are less profitable but also less work:

THE AUCTIONEER'S AUCTION

There are auctioneers who will deliver a whole package auction to your audience. They bring the art, the carriers, the auctioneer, the prices, the bookkeeper—the whole show. All you have to do is deliver an audience that wants to buy the art. This works best for upper-income groups that have spenders who will buy the art. Your profit is the percentage you get from the total sales.

THE DUTCH AUCTION

This can be tied onto any dinner, meeting, or rally if you have a group of fifty or fewer. Each guest brings an item to auction off, either an unusual artifact, homemade baked goods, handicrafts, or a gift-wrapped mystery item. A peppy, funny auctioneer convinces the crowd to buy one another's treasures.

THE MEMORABILIA AUCTION

This is good for a quick fundraiser for a group that has been around more than two years. Get together in someone's home or at your regular meeting place and auction off organizational mementos with special historical significance or sentimental value. You can auction off the first button; the original art for the first logo; early bumper stickers; the first convention program autographed by the first slate of officers; the first T-shirt; autographed copies of the first legislation you had passed; signed letters from the president, governor, senator, or mayor; secret corporation memos telling their employees to have nothing to do with you; or the original draft of the organization song.

Here is a sample of a page from the program of the Resurrection Pre-School auction of 1980. They made $11,000 in 1980 and $11,300 in 1981 for scholarship funds. Auction Chairperson Maree Bullock stressed the importance of setting an ambitious goal. Earlier benefits had made between $4,000 and $5,000. Her committee set a goal of $10,000, organized the 52 parents of the students (50% get scholarships), then made their goal and more!

Sample Page from 1980 Auction Program
Resurrection Pre-School

33. WOMEN'S TIMEX DIGITAL WATCH
         Donor: First Federal Savings of Chicago
         Value: $31.95 (Sold for $34)

34. FRAMED COLOR PHOTO OF THE JANUARY 1980 ISSUE OF
     THE CHICAGO MAGAZINE COVER - SIGNED
         Donor: Judy Shafer
         Value: $75.00   (Sold for $100)

35. FRESH FLOWER CENTERPIECE DELIVERED TO YOUR
     HOME WHENEVER YOU ORDER
         Donor: Potpourri Flower Shop
         Value: $20.00   (Sold for $37)

36. STANDARD SIMPLE WILL FOR HUSBAND AND WIFE
         Donor: Andrew A. Golko, Attorney at Law
         Value: $100   (Sold for $66)

37. HOME CANNING SESSION - WILL TEACH YOU HOW TO
     CAN EITHER TOMATOES, PEACHES, PEARS, APPLES,
     JELLIES OR JAMES - INCLUDES ITEM TO BE CANNED
     AND JARS
         Donor: Moria Epperson
         Value: $30.00   (Sold for $43)

38. SLUMBER PARTY WITH DEBBIE BOILEVE - TWO PRE-SCHOOL
     FRIENDS ARE INVITED TO COME TO DEBBIE'S AT 4:00 p.m.
     ON A FRIDAY AND STAY UNTIL 12:00 NOON ON SATURDAY
     They will help make dinner, play with a special
     private supply of teacher toys and crafts
     (including 2 live cats), look at and listen to a
     library of children's books and story records --
     PLUS -- share secrets, giggle, and do all the
     things people do at slumber parties - Pre-School
     style.
         Donor: Debbie Boileve
         Value: $40.00 (Sold for $102)

THE BAZAAR

The bazaar is a modern-day version of the medieval fair, offering novelties, bargains, food, drinks, and entertainment at the same place. In the middle ages, itinerant merchants would set up their wares in the marketplace at holiday time, offering shoppers new and varied merchandise. Today the shoppers come to you, but they are still looking for bargains, novelty, and entertainment.

The key to success is plenty of advance planning to produce as much variety as possible, because the way you make money at a bazaar is by seducing your customers into making a lot of small purchases. Although a customer may not buy the $25 silver candlesticks in the flea market, they will drop $1 on the pony ride, $2.50 at the bake booth, 50¢ at the raffle, $1 for bayberry candles, $1 for handmade Christmas ornaments, 50¢ for a handmade catnip toy, and $3.50 for a cookbook. They have now spent $10 and still have to get their lemonade. The more you offer, the more they will spend.

Preparation

Choose a day or a weekend, preferably in the spring or the fall. Fall works best because people are shopping for Christmas decorations and gifts. You can also reap a lot of good things for the flea market and old clothes sale from the members' fall cleaning. You can run the bazaar on Saturday from 10 A.M. to dusk, or Saturday and Sunday, or Friday night and Saturday.

Choose a large space. You can set up indoors or outdoors or both. It is easier to set up indoors, because you can get ready ahead of time. If you have the room, you can sell all your merchandise inside, while you run games and sell food outside. Try to get a prominent location on a busy street with plenty of parking. A church or school hall with adjoining parking lot is excellent.

MERCHANDISE

The attractions of the bazaar can be divided into three categories: things to buy (merchandise), things to eat and drink, and things to do—games and entertainments. The more you have of each, the more money you will make. To get a lot of each, you must plan ahead to get your committees working several months in advance.

When you have chosen your location, make up a sample floor plan, dividing the area into booths or tables for each thing you will sell or game you will play. When you know how much space you have and what kinds of booths you want, you need to recruit a committee to get the merchandise, to price and mark it, and to serve as salespeople on the day of the bazaar. From some booths, like the lemonade stand, you will need a crew to make and sell the lemonade just for that day. For the handicraft booth, you will need to sign people up several months in advance to give them the time to produce the goods.

HANDICRAFTS

Handicrafts include anything made by hand. These are usually great sellers because they are attractive, they are one-of-a-kind pieces you cannot buy in a store, and they make special gifts. You can ask people to donate completed items to the booth. If you can get quantities of material free, you can give the workers the materials for their project. They contribute the labor and the talent. If any members complain they are not talented, have some simple, foolproof projects ready to suggest for the beginners, like fringed place mats or catnip mice. If you will all be working on the projects for several months, you can get together one night a week, with simple refreshments, to work on your handicrafts. Some people may decide to contribute something just to get in on the weekly "sewing circle."

Encourage people to make simple, colorful, salable, completable projects. It will take as long to make one embroidered tablecloth as it will to make fifty animal bean bags, but it is a lot easier to sell fifty $1 bean bags than it is to sell a $50 tablecloth. If you get something really special like a quilt, you might consider putting it in as a raffle prize or using it for a silent auction, as explained later in this section.

Some sample merchandise for the handicraft booth could include afghans, pillows, place mats, napkins, aprons, eyeglass cases, bookmarks, potholders, hats, shawls, ponchos, mittens, scarves, baby things, tote bags, covered hangers, pet toys, baby blankets, candles, picture frames, dried flower arrangements, and paperweights. Also handmade renditions of the current fad, like the pet rock.

Christmas Booth. A subdivision of the handicrafts booth is the booth for all the handmade things that are Christmasy. These include tree ornaments, house decorations, wreaths, card holders, bayberry candles, and Christmas cards if you have your own design to sell. (Avoid selling other people's Christmas cards because you do not make enough profit.)

HERB BOOTH

The old herb cottage can sell herbed vinegars, potpourri sachets (made from your dried rose petals), dried herbs from your garden, small potted herb plants like chives, plus the ever popular catnip toys. You can also sell here all your bottled or canned foods—jams, jellies, preserves, pickles, relishes, chili sauce, spaghetti sauce, brandied fruit.

USED GOODS

Divide your used goods into wearable and nonwearable items. Put the clothes into the "Boutique" and put everything else into the "Flea Market."

Boutique. Used clothes. Presort all the clothes and throw out everything that is dirty. (Ask donors to contribute clean items only.) Hang everything on a hanger. Sort by men's and women's, boys' and girls' wear. If you have the space, put men's things in one room, women's things in another, and kids' clothes in a third. Mark each item, pricing everything very low, because you need to sell it in one day. Have enough room for people to look at the clothes and, if you have the space, make a fitting room, too. Borrow some full-length mirrors. You also can sell accessories like purses, wallets, hats, and jewelry. Don't bother with shoes and boots unless you can get almost-new kids' shoes or specialty items like imported sandals, beach clogs, or ski boots.

Flea Market. The flea market is where you sell everything else that is secondhand—dishes, glasses, ashtrays, trays, planters, books, records, candlesticks, appliances that work, knickknacks, pictures, bottles, etc. The biggest job of the flea market committee is getting everything out attractively and putting a price on each item. Again, price everything low so it will sell.

Whereas the attraction of the handicrafts booth and the herb cottage is the variety and quality of handmade goods, the attraction of the boutique and the flea market is the variety and *quantity* of secondhand goods, especially the bargains. If your prices are low enough, bargain hunters will load up, go home for more money, and come back again. If you have collected all the members' white elephants over the past few months you should have more than enough merchandise. Of course, your members always can ask their neighbors for their castoffs too.

THE BAKE BOOTH

The bake booth is a real gold mine that can be run as an independent fundraiser or added to almost any daytime event. You need an energetic chairperson who will recruit literally everyone in the group to make something for the bake booth. Don't take no for an answer. Anyone can bake. If they never did before, it is high time they learned. At least ask them to buy two boxes of brownie mix for someone else to bake. The bake booth needs two kinds of goodies. First, you want small portable things like brownies and cookies, which the customers can munch on while they are shopping. Second, you want things they will buy to take home: breads, cakes, and pies.

A variation on the bake booth works well next door to another event that will draw a lot of traffic. For example, one church in a big city is on an alley where the neighborhood association sponsors a two-day antique sale that attracts several thousand people. The church had all the members contribute boxes of brownie mix, then made and sold brownies all day for two days. The fragrance of baking brownies drew the shoppers like bees, and the brownies sold as fast as they could be made. If you wanted to get fancier, you could sell ice cream, too, to go with the brownies. The advantage of selling only one baked good is that you don't have to price them individually, and they will sell themselves.

Another variation on the classic bake sale takes place in Viroqua, Wisconsin, where the bank provides the setting and the charities provide the attraction: the best baked goodies in Vernon County. The bank lets a different nonprofit group run a bake sale in its lobby each Saturday. When the farmers and shoppers come to town, they know they can get mouth-watering goodies like krumkake, rosettes, and donuts, using their good Wisconsin butter in Norwegian family recipes. The bank gets more traffic because of the bake sale, and each organization gets a bigger market without having to worry about publicity or the weather, while knowing well ahead of time which will be its Saturday. By cooperating, both the bank and the local charities make more money.

MORE BAZAAR FOOD

Decide what other food you would like to sell according to your theme, the weather, and your facilities. If you have an outside barbecue, you can cook hot dogs or bratwurst. If you have a kitchen, you can also sell corn on the cob, chili, tacos, pizza, or whole dinners. If you don't have a kitchen, you can sell sandwiches and candy. You can also sell coffee, hot chocolate, lemonade, soft drinks, or fruit juices. If you have a liquor license, you can sell beer in the summer or mulled wine in the winter. You can sometimes get special short-term licenses for special events; check with your local liquor license director, usually in the department of revenue at city hall. If you sell beer or wine, ask your insurance agent about dram-shop insurance and local laws regarding your board's liability.

The major consideration here is how much money you will make on each item. Remember, your bake booth is 100-percent profit, so you want most of your food sales from there. If you also sell donuts, you will only make about 5¢ on each donut and detract from your bake booth sales. Keep the food as simple as possible and have plenty of waste containers around.

ADULT ATTRACTIONS

Offer an exotic-looking fortune teller, palm reader, tea leaf reader, or horoscope caster. Authenticity is less important than entertainment value. Remember, good news is good news.

Button making—buy or borrow a machine for making buttons. Custom-make each with a slogan or photo of the customer's choice.

Calligraphy—A talented art student or professional artist can prepare favorite proverbs, prayers, or sayings suitable for hanging.

CHILDREN'S ATTRACTIONS

Face painting—an artist with a steady hand paints small flowers, stars, ladybugs, etc., on the face of the customer with water-based tempera paint. Charge 25¢ for children, $1 for complicated designs like a dragon or train on adults.

OLDIES BUT GOODIES

- Bean Bag Toss
- Balloon Pop
- Hit the Nail into the Log in Five Hits
- Guess the Number of Beans in the Bottle
- Penny Toss
- Basketball Freethrow Contest

FOR BABIES

For the smallest customers, set up a small pile of clean hay with trinkets hidden near the surface. Babies crawl through the pile until they grasp a trinket—they "win" whatever they grab.

LOSS LEADERS

Offer a special attraction for the kids, because where the kids go the parents will follow. Although you will not make a profit on the attraction, it is an investment to build your crowd. Grocery stores offer special sales called *loss leaders* to get shoppers into the store. You can do the same thing. You can ask for contributions to help underwrite the expense of the attraction.

Some attractions that work well are pony rides (especially in the city), a carousel or calliope, a magician, a puppet show, a band, a ride on the fire engine, or a visit from the most popular children's TV show host or hostess.

GATE

Ask for a modest donation, such as 50¢, at the gate from everyone who comes in. Offer trinkets at the gate for everyone, like
bright neckerchiefs for a western roundup, medallions for the
medieval fair, or balloons. If you print the balloons with "Fargo
Fall Fair" on them, each kid who leaves becomes a walking adver-
tisement for the fair. The income from the gate pays for publicity,
dramshop insurance, and decorations.

Add-On Money Makers

THE ALL-DAY RAFFLE

You can add a raffle to the bazaar. Collect prizes from merchants
and include the best contributions to the flea market, like new
appliances or silver. Sell tickets all day long and have a drawing
every half hour. List the names of all the winners as the day goes
on and post on a large blackboard or sign the time and prize for the
next drawing. You can have several people circulate through the
crowd with raffle tickets.

You can raffle off dinners or lunches at local restaurants. Even
better, combine several prizes into one grand prize. Offer the
"Grand Prize Weekend in Wichita" including lunch on Saturday
with your mayor or senator, a dinner and show for Saturday, a "free
pew" at the church on Sunday morning, Sunday brunch, a guided
tour of the zoo or museum by the director, plus Sunday dinner and
movie tickets. Top it all off with an offer of free baby-sitting for the
lucky winning couple.

SILENT AUCTION

You can run a silent auction anytime you get something that is
very appealing and unusual. You may get more money by auctioning it off than by simply marking a price on it. Good candidates
would be an excellent handmade quilt or valuable antique.

Simply place the item on display with a note about its history and
value. Put a poster next to it with a marker and a beginning (mini-

mum) bid on the top. Then each bidder puts a higher bid under the last:

	Handmade Quilt
Minimum bid	$100
Abigail Adams:	120
Benjamin Franklin:	130
Dolly Madison:	140
Etc.	

Post the final time for bids, say 4 P.M. Make a final announcement at 3:45 that it is your last chance to bid on the quilt. At 4 P.M. whoever has the highest bid gets the quilt.

Sample Report—Urban Church
1976 Fall Fair

Booth	Revenue and Contributions	Expenses	Profit (Loss)	Percent Profit
Boutique (resale clothes)	$202	$— —	$202	100
Baked Goods	515	—	515	100
Candles	99	—	99	100
Herbs	163	—	163	100
Flea Market (resale items)	913	—	913	100
Raffle	507	—	507	100
Handicrafts	1,136	155	981	86
Gate (publicity expenses)	344	63	281	82
Barbecue	236	70	166	70
Kids' Games	128	50	78	61
Ice Cream	91	38	53	58
Beer*	116	108	8	7
Pony Rides**	56	145	(89)	(Loss)
Total	$4,506	$629	$3,877	86%

* Beer was sold at cost to workers, resulting in very little profit.

** Pony rides were the "loss leader" that lost more than expected because they were rained out in the morning. Eliminated the next year and replaced by more games for children.

THE DANCE

A dance can be a fun-filled costume party with a local band, or a formal affair with a big dance band, or a come-as-you-are bash with the latest hits played on a record player. If you have people who like to dance, good music, and fun extras, you can make a lot of money for your cause.

The secret to success is a peppy committee of people who like to plan parties. If they are people who like to go out and have fun, they will plan an event that will leave the guests asking, "When is the next dance?"

The arrangements for a dance can be divided into two parts: first, everything that needs to be done before the dance, and second, everything that needs to happen at the dance to make it a success.

Before the Dance

Before the dance the committee has to choose a date and a theme, book a band and reserve a room, print the tickets, sell ads for the program and print the program, plan the agenda for the evening, and choose the refreshments.

THE BAND

The dance's success depends on a good band. If you get a popular band, everyone will have a good time and will want to come to your next dance. If the band is a bore, it will take a lot of ingenuity to keep the party rolling and even more to sell tickets to the next dance.

How do you find a good band? First consider what kind of band you want for your crowd. Do they want rock and roll, polkas, disco, western swing, reggae, or ballroom dancing? or a combination? The best bands can play a variety of fast and slow numbers, as well as a few group participation songs like "Hava Nagila," "The Bunny Hop," "The Hokey Pokey," and "Zorba the Greek." First, ask everyone on the committee to recommend good bands they have heard at weddings, parties, or other dances and whether they know anyone who either plays in a band or books bands.

Look in the *Yellow Pages* under "Musicians" and call several bands for prices and availability. If there are local clubs that feature live music, the committee could also have a "research night on the town" (at each member's own expense, of course) when they go around and listen to the bands. This is one of the more pleasant aspects of serving on the planning committee, so you might want to do some research even if you already have a band. (As you and your committee members go out during the year, remember always to get a business card from the leader of any good band you hear, for future reference.) You can also call your opposite numbers in other organizations and ask their advice on a band.

You will probably have to reserve a band at least several weeks in advance of the night you want. The more popular the band, the more advance notice they will need. In fact, if there is one band that is outstandingly popular (and still affordable), you should reserve a night as soon as you decide to do a dance. Even if you decide in January to do a dance in September, it is not too early to reserve the best band for the date you want.

It is better to pay more for a band and scrimp on everything else than the other way around. The difference between a $300 band and a $600 band can be the difference between a repeatable event and a flop. Of course, you should always try to get the best for the least money, but if you have to spend more for a popular band, do it.

Free Band: If you have a not-for-profit organization, and you are getting everything else free (the hall, refreshments, etc.), you qualify to get a free band from the Musicians Union. Each local of the Musicians Union has a fund to pay bands to play for nonprofit groups. Call the Musicians Union's local secretary and ask if you qualify. Then find out how to get the band you need. Unfortunately, you seldom get the first-rate bands this way, but it is a great way to get a free band for the after-convention party or other occasions that are more festive than commercial.

CHOOSING A THEME

Although you can always have the "First Annual Friends of the Forests Dance," it is more fun if you choose a theme for the dance. Carry out the theme in the invitations, program, decorations, menu, skits, favors, and costumes.

SAMPLE THEMES

Holidays: Halloween costume party, New Year's Eve, Twelfth Night Elizabethan Revelry, Valentine's Day, Mardi Gras (literally "Fat Tuesday," the day before Ash Wednesday, last chance to feast and revel before Lent), May Day.

Movies: Saturday Night Fever, Cabaret, Showboat, Guys and Dolls, Urban Cowboy, anything with Fred Astaire.

Places: Evening in Paris, A Funny Thing Happened on the Way to the Forum (Rome), South Pacific, Mexican Fiesta, Hawaiian Luau, Carnival in Rio, Emerald Isle, Night on the Nile, Camelot, Arabian Nights (Scheherazade).

Eras: Roaring Twenties, Gay '90s, Happy Days, Hard Times ('30s); 2001, Renaissance, Medieval, Ancient Greece, French Revolution.

Costume themes: Butchers, Bakers and Candlestick Makers Ball (worker's costumes), American Revolution, Best or Worst Politicians, "Enemies Dance" for action groups, Barn Dance, Movie Stars, Villains and Tyrants, Gangsters and Gun Molls.

Fantasy: Wizard of Oz, Lost in Space, Never-Never Land, Lost Atlantis, Garden of Eden.

Seasonal: Spring Fling; Harvest Moon Ball; Saturnalia (Winter solstice, December 21); First Day of Spring, Summer, Autumn, Winter; Midsummer Night's Dream.

PLACE

Once you get a firm date for the band, look for a place to hold the dance. Any large hall with a hard floor will do. It is better if it has a stage and a kitchen, and better still if it has a built-in bar. Other features that are nice but not necessary are a coatroom, nearby free parking, handy public transportation, and few or no stairs. Try to find somewhere free (you may have to do your own cleanup) or as inexpensive as possible. Again, ask your committee members where they have been and what they recommend.

You can use the occasion of the dance to show off your own building, too. Some museums do this to get donors into the building, and many a church kindergarten has become a Roaring Twenties speakeasy for a night. If you do not have a big enough room of your own, consider having a cocktail hour in your offices before the dance so the guests can see firsthand why their money is needed. Then go on to the nearest hall for the dance.

Do not reject your own free but humble hall because of its appearance. As long as it is clean, your clever committee can transform any hall into the Taj Mahal with a maximum of creativity and a minimum of lighting. Or choose a theme like "Fun in the Forties" and call your basement "The Stage Door Canteen." With a simple stage and lots of flags, uniforms, and '40s fashions, it will look like the real thing!

Besides the church basement, the high school gym, or the rented hall, any large space with electricity will do. Some original ideas that have worked well in the past include:

Dices and Pisces (dance with gambling) held at the local aquarium. An action organization could sponsor "Making Waves" at the aquarium.

The Red, White, and Zoo Ball, held at the zoo on the Fourth of July. Or "Zoo La La" at the zoo on Bastille Day, July 14.

Spring Revels on the village square.

Venetian Night Gala on a barge.

Super Circus in a tent.

Harvest Moon Ball in a barn.

"Hard Times" dance in a warehouse.

St. Valentine's Day Massacre gangster-style costume party in a garage.

"Take Me Out to the Ball Game" at a ball park.

"Fabulous Fifties" sockhop at a roller rink.

"Pretty as a Picture" at an art museum.

Wild West square dance at a shopping center mall.

And the ever-popular summertime block party with dancing in the street.

PRINTING

Once you have chosen the date, band, theme, and place, you can print the tickets. A few energetic salespeople can start lining up door prizes and selling ads for the program. The program can be a single page mimeographed in your own office or an elaborate ad book. (See ad book, Chapter 10.) On the program, list the schedule of events, the names of the band and other entertainers, the names of the committee members, a paragraph about the organization and how to join, and a note of thanks for everyone who gave donations.

At the Dance

Once all the advance arrangements are made, the committee moves into phase two, which is a thorough plan of what will happen at the dance. It is the committee's responsibility to make sure everyone is welcomed, the ticket desk runs smoothly, and there is a place with helpers where guests may leave their coats. The committee members set up everything, give precise instructions to the band, sell drink tickets and raffle tickets, and generally mingle to make sure everyone is comfortable. Find someone outgoing to serve as Master of Ceremonies to welcome everyone, introduce the band and any other acts, and give a running report on what happens next. This could include the drawing for the door prizes, the raffle drawing, or introduction of the president. It is the president who "frames" the party by telling the guests what the group is doing and why it needs the money, recognizing the committee and top ticket sellers, and thanking any merchants present who contributed to the event. All of this should be planned in advance, so it all goes smoothly and the president has time to prepare a good *short* talk.

The committee members become the social directors at the dance. They make sure everyone is having fun, start the dancing, and plan games or dances to mix everyone up. They are also the security force if any problems develop. It is the committee's job to remove the problem as quickly, tactfully and quietly as possible. Perhaps you will not have any problems at all, but just in case, decide *beforehand* who will handle it.

REFRESHMENTS

Merry dancers will work up a thirst, so decide what kind of liquid refreshments you will serve. If you choose to have alcoholic beverages, find out if the place has its own dramshop insurance or if you need to get your own. Unless you are expecting several thousand

guests or are holding the dance in a hotel that requires union bartenders, you can recruit your own committee of volunteer bartenders to work the bar. Keep the bar as simple as possible; leave the
fancy blender drinks like brandy alexanders to the pros.

Sell drink tickets at a table near the entrance so that bartenders
only have to serve the drinks. You can buy rolls of tickets at any
novelty store or carnival/bingo supplier. Either sell different colors
for soft drinks, beer/wine, and hard drinks, or get rolls of 50¢
tickets and sell soft drinks for 50¢ (one ticket) and beer and wine for
$1 (two tickets). The other advantage of selling drink tickets is that
the guests will buy more tickets than they will use, and your profit
on the unused tickets will be 100 percent.

You can also offer something to drink for free, like a non-
alcoholic punch or coffee in a self-service urn.

You can put out free salty snacks like pretzels or popcorn, which
you buy in bulk and double-salt to increase the bar revenue. The
committee can recruit a team to bring hors d'oeuvres and finger
food. Specify cocktail-type salty or spicy things that are portable
and can stand at room temperature for several hours. Discourage
sweet dessert-type contributions — they stifle the drink sales. Or you
can sell sandwiches, pizza, or tacos from a table near the kitchen.

Add-On Money Makers

In addition to the regular dance, there are several other money-
makers you can add. As already mentioned, you can sell ads in the
program, run a raffle, sell drinks or sandwiches. For a Roaring
Twenties party, you can have "taxi dancers" selling tickets for "10¢
a dance." (For the Inflation Eighties, sell them for a dollar a dance!)
This also makes a good mixer. You can sell photographs of groups
at a table (as nightclubs do), of posed couples (like the high school
prom), or of corny Tarzan and Jane or American Gothic facades
with holes cut out for the faces (like the grammar school fun fair).
Ask your local camera shop for advice.

Run a dance contest. Charge 50¢ to enter and give ribbons for
first, second, and third place by audience applause. Depending on
the crowd, have a waltz, Charleston, cha-cha, jitterbug, polka,
salsa, or disco contest. Or have an "oldies but goodies" dance con-

test to see who can *still* do the twist, tango, mashed potatoes, soupy shuffle, or lindy hop.

THE HOUSE TOUR

If you have ever walked by an unusual old house and thought, "I wonder what it's like inside?" you are a potential customer for a house tour. The house tour is literally a tour through one or more houses. It gives all the do-it-yourself decorators a chance to get new ideas and gives everyone the chance to satisfy curiosity.

The range of possibilities is endless. The Jaycettes in a small town in Wisconsin sponsored a simple tour of two old homes plus tea at the library to raise money for a flagpole. The women's board of a New Jersey hospital put on a full-tilt, monthlong extravaganza at a redecorated mansion with fourteen boutiques running in the carriage house. They made $260,000. You can put together a combination of interesting homes that will appeal to your community and raise money with very little work.

The first thing you need for the house tour is the houses. You can use your members' homes or ask people outside the organization to let you show their homes. Figure out how many homes you can move people through in a day. You may want to start with two the first year, then go to four, and then to six. You can have them all open all day, or show half in the morning and half in the afternoon.

Successful Tours

HOUSES

Aim for a variety. Show a colonial, traditional, and modern or a big family home, a young married couple's home, an older retired couple's home, and a bachelor's apartment.

THEMES

Show four examples of one architect, examples of the oldest or newest houses in town, or houses in one historical area. You might show houses owned by famous people from the town.

SHOW OFF ONE ROOM

You can have a kitchen tour or a "cook's tour" showing only kitchens and selling your cookbook. Others have run tours of just nurseries, just children's rooms, or just dining rooms.

WHERE PEOPLE WORK

Run a tour of artists' studios in the artists' quarter of the city or executive suites of the top corporations.

GARDENS

Sponsor a garden walk in the spring or summer to show off the prettiest gardens in your neighborhood. This provides an extra boost for people to spruce up their yards. You can also sell seeds, bulbs, and plants at the end.

Once you have several houses for the tour, choose one weekday when you should have good weather. Never attempt a house tour in the winter. Sell a limited number of invitations—usually 500 to 2,000, depending on how many people you can move through the house. Print clear rules on each invitation. Standard rules include: Adults only. No smoking. Be prepared to remove your shoes. Follow the traffic plan. Listen to the hostesses who are wearing the green name tags.

The invitations are also the tickets and the programs. They describe what is special about each house and the history of each house and the town. Include a simple map.

Other Preparation

1. Get extra insurance to cover large numbers of people going through the houses and climbing stairs. Some organizations have run house tours for twenty-five years without an accident, but you still have to get complete insurance to cover anything that might occur. Ask your insurance agent for advice.

2. Get flowers donated for each house from local florists. List the florists' names in the program and put a sign in each house.

3. Notify the police of the day of the tour and the location of the houses. Ask for help in directing traffic where you need it.

4. Give the hosts any cleaning help they want before the tour.

5. Arrange for someone to entertain the host families *away* from home on the day of the tour.

Try to get all the printing, insurance, and flowers donated. Especially if you are doing a historical tour, house tours are great community booster events. They should be supported by your local printer and insurance broker.

Day of the Tour

Get a team of volunteers lined up to work each house. Before anyone comes they set out a marker to mark the house as a tour house, put up a sawhorse to block the driveway, set up a table to check the programs (which are also the tickets), put out a container for cigarettes, and double-check that everything is clean and orderly. Each house needs a greeter to check each ticket/program so each person goes through each house only once. Several volunteers serve as guides. The guides tell guests the history of the house and information about the decor. They are also the security force, keeping an eye on everything in the house. Finally, they clean up the house and yard after the last guest leaves.

The day after the house tour the president delivers personalized gifts to the hosts and thanks them again for the use of their homes.

REFRESHMENTS

If people are on their feet all day seeing the houses, they are going to want to take a break for something to eat. Offer a package of a meal with the tour. You can get a deal from a local restaurant and add $2 to the meal price. You can offer a box lunch in a big yard; serve the lunches and beverage from a decorated garage. Or serve "soup, salad, and sweets" in the church hall.

PRICES

Charge at least $2 a house, that is $2 for a one-house tour and $8 for a four-house tour. Price the luncheon at double the cost to you:

if it costs you $4, charge $8. Sell the luncheon as a package with the tour so that only house tour patrons can attend the luncheon. Limit the luncheon to people who have prepaid tickets so you know exactly how many lunches to make. Do not sell luncheon tickets at the door.

If you are showing only one or two houses, it is easier to have tea and cookies in a free room. Charge $1 for the tea and cookies.

Repeatability

The house tour is a very repeatable event. If people learn you have interesting homes, that you run an efficient tour with little waiting and limit the number of tickets, they will buy their tickets early every year. After you have run your tour two or three years you will find the tickets sell themselves. Do not be afraid of running out of houses. You can always show a house a second time ten years later if it has been redecorated by new owners. And you can add an unusual church or studio for variety.

Variations

THE CHRISTMAS SALE HOUSE TOUR

Use the houses to display your handmade Christmas decorations. Decorate three or four houses with your handmade merchandise. Run the tour in October, and you will find you can sell everything off the walls. Try to have a variety of settings: early American, modern, baby's first Christmas, teenager's Christmas, or ultra-elegant Christmas. Some churches run the Christmas sale house tour every two years. Then they have two years to prepare the merchandise and need to find hosts only every other year.

THE BUS TOUR

Instead of showing people through houses in your own community, you sell them tickets for a tour of another community. This is a dependable fundraiser for small groups of people with spare time, curiosity, and no cars. You can arrange tours of churches, museums, old restored neighborhoods, country places, and gardens. Include lunch and it becomes an all-day adventure. Charge double your expenses. Any travel agent can tell you how to get buses.

THE SHOWCASE HOUSE

The showcase house requires a big investment and an upper-income membership that can get donations of high-priced talent and merchandise. Find an old mansion and recruit professional interior decorators to redo one room each at their own expense. The decorators do it as advertising for new business. If your group is not the kind that can promise a large number of upper-income tourists, the showcase house is not for you because you will not be able to recruit the top decorators.

If you *can* deliver rich tourists, then you can approach the decorators because you can offer what they want: customers. Contact the local chapter of the American Society of Interior Designers (ASID). They can tell you if there is any local competition and can make arrangements to discuss doing a showcase house for your group.

Your group needs to find an available empty mansion and make all the legal arrangements to use the house. It usually takes at least a year of advance work to get the house, choose the decorators, raise the seed money, redecorate the house, do the publicity, sell the tickets, and contract with merchants to sell in the boutiques. If you want more information on showcase houses, contact the local ASID and see the bibliography, Chapter 14, for recommended reading.

THE THEATRE PARTY

The theatre party is the simplest of the medium-sized fundraisers. Since the theatre does all the production and publicity work, all you have to do is sell the tickets.

Preparation

FINDING A THEATRE

First call all the theatre companies and ask to speak to the business manager. Ask if there is any possibility that the company could do a benefit for your group. Make a record of each person's name, the company's policy, and how many seats the theatre has.

There are three systems to make money. You can get all the seats for free, you can buy all the seats at a discount, or you can buy a smaller block of tickets. Your best deal is for the theatre to "give you the house." That is, the theatre donates the performance, and you get to sell all the seats and keep all the money. This is very rare and will probably happen only if the theatre owner or the producer, director, or star of the show is a loyal friend of the group.

The usual system is for a theatre to give you the house on a week-day evening for a discount. For example, if all 300 seats in the theatre usually sell for $8 each, you can get the house for perhaps $5 a seat. Thus your cost is $1,500 (300 x $5). If you sell all the seats at $10 each, you will gross $3,000 and net $1,500.

Profit: Regular Seats

300 tickets x $10.00 = $3,000 gross
300 tickets x $ 5.00 =   − 1,500
                          ─────────
                          $1,500 net profit

Get a written contract explaining exactly what you are paying the theatre. There are actually two ways to buy out the house. In the first case, you buy all 300 seats from the theatre. You owe them $1,500 no matter how many seats you are able to resell. This is the plan the theatre prefers, since it is guaranteed its money no matter how well or poorly you do. Plus, it can mark that night "sold out" on its publicity, which makes the play look good to the general public.

The second case is better for beginners. In this case, the theatre gives you the first chance to sell every seat. These seats cost you $5 each, but you charge $10. If you sell them all, that is fine for both of you. If you sell only some of the seats, the theatre gets to sell the rest at its regular price at the box office the night of the show. For example, if you sell 150 seats for $10 each, the theatre gets $5 per seat, or $750 and you get $5 per seat or $750. The theatre sells the other 150 seats at the regular $8 price. Obviously, the advantage of this system is that you owe the theatre only for the seats you sell. If you were working on the buy-the-house system and only sold 150 seats, the threatre would make its $1,500 and you would make nothing. If you are not confident you can sell the whole house, ask for a discount on all you can sell, with the theatre selling the balance.

A third system for beginning groups is simply to buy a block of tickets. For example, you buy only 150 tickets to resell. You usually get a smaller discount if you take less than the whole house.

Comedies and musicals are the easiest to sell. Avoid depressing plays or very avant-garde pieces with no plot at all. They might be excellent theatre, but they will be hard to sell this year and murder to sell the second year.

Selling the Tickets

Since all you have to do is sell the tickets, concentrate on that. Have one team concentrate on selling patron tickets, priced higher than your regular tickets. Then systematically contact your big donors, politicians, and business executives. Set a goal to have 10 percent of the house as patrons. In our example, if you have a 300-seat theatre, 30 of the seats should be patron tickets. Let's say you price them at $50 each.

PROFIT: Patron seats

30 tickets x $50	=	$1,500	gross
30 tickets x $5	=	− 150	cost
		$1,350	net

This leaves 270 seats to sell at the regular price:

270 tickets x $10	=	$2,700	gross
270 tickets x $5	=	− 1,350	cost
		$1,350	net
Patron ticket profit	=	$1,350	
Regular ticket proft	=	+ 1,350	
		$2,700	

Thus, you make as much money from 10 percent of the seats as you do from the other 90 percent.

Ironically, some of the patrons won't show up. Patron ticket buyers often buy tickets for several events occurring on the same night and obviously cannot be in more than one place. The only patron ticket holders who are *sure* to show up are the politicians who want to work the crowd.

Thus, it is possible in real life to "oversell" the house. This means you gamble that less than 100 percent of the ticket holders will actually show up in person. So you can sell more than 100 percent of the seats. It is usually safe to oversell by about 10 percent, especially for a late show. Thus, if you sell all 30 patron tickets, you can really sell all 300 seats at your regular price, too. You then have 330 tickets sold for 300 seats but will end up with only 300 people for 300 seats.

PROFIT: If You Oversell by Ten Percent:

Patron seats 30 tickets x $50 =	$1,500	gross
30 tickets x $5 =	− 150	cost
	$1,350	net

Regular seats 300 tickets x $10 =	$3,000	gross
300 tickets x $ 5 =	− 1,500	cost
	$1,500	net

Patron seats profit	= $1,350	net
Regular seats profit	= + 1,500	net
Total profit	$2,850	net

If you don't want to gamble your first time out, keep careful records of your first few theatre parties. Write down the total tickets sold and the total attendance. This will tell you the safe margin for overselling. If the committee votes to gamble and oversell, do it with the understanding that *you* are the ones who will stand if you are wrong and everybody comes.

At the Performance

Enjoy! You only need one or two people to take tickets and sell memberships. You can have a speaker during intermission to "frame" the event. The speaker welcomes everyone, introduces the organization, explains its work, and thanks everyone for coming. The president or committee chair should also recognize and congratulate the top ticket sellers.

Add-On Money Makers

If this is too simple, add other money makers. If it is a small theatre (100 to 300 seats), and you are confident you can sell more tickets, ask them to do two performances on the same night. It takes very little additional work to sell the second show. You may be able to get the company to do an early show, say at 6:00 P.M. and 8:00 P.M. rather than their regular 8:00 P.M. and 10:00 P.M. This gives you a chance to sell to your seniors, people with early-morning jobs, and people who have to travel a long way. If you do two shows, you get double the profit, in this example, $5,400.

Add a door prize to produce a sign-up list.

Run a raffle. See Chapter 7 for more advice on raffles.

Print a program with ads if the theatre does not have a program of its own. If the theatre already has its own program, print a one-page insert with information on the group, how to join, the next benefit, and patrons' names.

Ask for a percentage of the bar take if the theatre also serves drinks. Tell the crowd you get part of the money so they drink up.

If you do not get part of the bar revenue, have a do-it-yourself cocktail party before or after the performance. See Chapter 8 for advice on this.

WHERE ELSE TO GO FOR ADVICE

Contact your local arts council, the community arts center, the theatres' organization, or the local Actors' Equity Union. They all work to promote theatre attendance and will have good advice for you about the local theatre scene.

Variations

This format will work for any show business performance just as well as a regular stage play. You can do the same thing to sell tickets to an opera, a concert, a recital, a ballet, a circus, or the legendary dog and pony show.

Some theatres offer other sorts of ready-made fundraising packages as part of their ongoing public relations efforts to introduce new customers to the theatre. For example, the Guthrie Theatre in Minneapolis offers organizations a "Costume Show." Costumes from past Guthrie productions are modeled by volunteers, who also explain the design and construction of theatrical costumes. Be sure to ask all the theatres to explain all the fundraising possibilities they offer.

While you are at it, use this opportunity to get to know the theatre professionals. They can give you invaluable advice since they do professionally as actors what you do voluntarily as a fundraiser: offer people entertainment for money. Everything you do involves theatre, from the simplest presentation to an audience of one to an extravaganza rock concert for an audience of 30,000. Both require theatrical skills: involving the audience, memory, concentration, clarity, and casting. Theatre professionals are the best people to ask to teach you how to give memorable performances.

10

The Big Time

Larger special events allow you to reach a larger audience. They give you a good way to raise money beyond your own members. Although the public at large can support your large benefits, you must still depend on your own members to sell them. You have to recruit and inspire your own leaders to sell tickets or ads, then train them to recruit and inspire other people to do the same.

Here are examples of three large special events: the ad book, cocktail party, and luncheon or dinner. They all require leaders with fundraising experience, from $200 to $2,000 in seed money, three to six months of advance planning, an effective publicity committee, and a commitment to making the event a success. All three can be repeated every year.

Each of these is described briefly because you will be able to get more advice closer to home about the big fundraisers. Ask local politicians and the big charities like the disease associations, art museums, hospitals, colleges, or symphony to give you more suggestions on what works best in your community for big-money fundraisers. Also review Chapter 14 for more books on big-time fundraisers such as concerts and walkathons.

The ad book is the most profitable tool to raise money from people, businesses, and institutions in addition to your own members. You can sell merchants, churches, politicians, corporations, wealthy individuals, and other organizations space in a printed book of advertisements. It is an excellent fundraiser for any organization that covers a specific geographic area, especially community organizations and churches with a parish base. After the first few years you should have enough confident leaders trained to sell the organization's programs to dispense with the ad book and simply ask for corporate donations.

The cocktail party is the opportunity for your leaders to introduce your organization to a small group of wealthy people in the home of someone they know. The host does most of the work of the party; your leaders ask for the money. This is a good way to meet new wealthy people and get their first donation.

A luncheon or dinner gives you a reliable way to reach business people and community leaders to ask for their support. Although it is difficult to make much money on the meal itself, you can use the occasion to ask for corporate contributions or run other fundraisers. Because dinners are a traditional method of raising money for political candidates, you should be able to find experienced people in your own community to give you more advice.

THE AD BOOK

Ad books are a high-profit fundraising device that have been translated effectively from their church and political origins to serve many community organizations. The most profitable ones contain nothing but ads. You simply sell ads to local businesses, politicians, and individuals and then print a booklet. This book can be distributed at a meeting, party, or fundraising event. The biggest advantage of the ad book is that it gives you a way to ask people outside the organization for support.

You can start small by recruiting ads from the churches, merchants, and politicians in your immediate neighborhood. When you have more experience, go after the bigger corporations, institutions, and politicians.

People buy an ad because you *sell* them on the idea of supporting the organization. They know that a $50 ad in your ad book is not going to deliver the customers that the same ad in a local paper will bring. So you have to take the time to plan your sales pitch in the committee. Why is it in the interest of your sales targets to give to your organization? Prepare a sheet on what the organization has done for the community and what it plans to do next year. In addition, match the sellers and customers with care and creativity.

Since you will never be able to offer the advertisers the circulation of the local newspapers, and since they are really giving to support the organization rather than advertise, you can print as few books as possible. You need one for each worker, one for each advertiser, and a stock to take with you when you sell next year. By limiting the number of books you print and limiting the nonadvertising copy, you can make about 90-percent profit on the book.

Besides the all-advertising ad book, there are many other ways you can sell ads to raise money. Many groups sell ads to pay for the expense of printing the convention program. This will allow you to do a classy convention program for a large audience and make a small profit, too.

Some small-town volunteer fire departments sell ads to cover the cost of an attractive community calendar. Each page has a week on one side and ads on the other side. In addition, the book has information on the fire department and the town. Every fall the volunteer firemen go door to door and *give* each household a calendar while other firemen give the kids a ride around the block on the fire truck. Then they ask each person whether they would like to buy two tickets to the firemen's ball. Virtually all say yes. The calendar gives necessary fire information to help the homeowners, a collection of ads from all the local merchants to help the business community, and a pleasant sales gimmick to help the fire department.

You can sell ads on anything you can print. High schools sell ads in the back of the yearbooks, college groups sell ads on desk blotters, and churches sell ads on the back of Sunday programs. Fancy charity ball committees print their big donors' photographs between silver covers and call it a "souvenir journal." You can always print the names of patrons on any mimeographed program for any other fundraising event, too.

See the bibliography, Chapter 14, for inexpensive booklets that share the advice of the experts. *Helping NOW Grow—Fundraising,* by the leaders of the Chicago Chapter of the National Organization for Women, gives the precise details on how they ran their 1973, 1974, and 1975 ad book campaigns. It features foolproof mechanics plus a sample ad book order form, letter of introduction, and volunteer sales instructions. Chicago NOW's net profit was $14,000 in 1973 and $18,000 in 1975. *A Case Study of the COPS Ad Book*, by former COPS staff director Arnie Graf, shares the philosophy that made its sales so successful. Communities Organized for Public Service (COPS) is an independently funded, predominantly Mexican-American, mass-based citizen organization in San Antonio, Texas. This paper shows how they used the ad book sales campaign to teach organizational principles, especially the importance of fundraising. Graf emphasizes that selling ads is not begging. It is 1) collecting dues from everyone in the city who had benefitted from the work of the organization and 2) developing relationships of mutual respect with the banks, businesses, and merchants that took money from COPS members. Asking them to give a small part of that money back to the organization created a feeling of mutual respect. The COPS ad book campaign described in this paper netted more than $47,000 in the first year (1977) and more than $60,000 in 1978 and 1979.

THE COCKTAIL PARTY

The cocktail party as described here is a method for soliciting upper-income people. If your membership includes affluent people, the cocktail party should already be a familiar fundraiser. This is written for organizations with low- or middle-income members who want to take their message to upper-income citizens for support.

Ideally, the way to hold cocktail parties is to find a sympathetic, rich sponsor who will hold a party for you once or twice a year. Your speaker explains that your group is doing the work and that all you want from the rich people is their support, specifically their money. This is similar to the church model for supporting missionaries. Once a year the church's missionary to Outer Bosnia comes back and tells the congregation what the mission has accomplished, how many souls have been converted, and what the mission plans for the next year. Then the group chips in to support the missionary. It works because you are making the program *personal*. Instead of asking for support for "the missions" you are asking for support for your missionary, Gladys Ormphry. In the same way a community organization can send a leader to ask for support for its work. The cocktail party guests then are giving to Joe Smith, president of the Mayfair Community Association, instead of giving to "better neighborhoods."

Cocktail parties are a good way to introduce your leaders and your organization to new wealthy people each year. Once you have their first contributions, the donors can be added to your major donors list, then asked for a large donation every year. By combining special event cocktail parties and a well-planned individual donor program, you will get new big donors every year and get donations from the old donors every year. See Chapter 5, "Getting Money from Believers," for more information on setting up an individual donor program from expert Kim Klein.

People go to cocktail parties for several reasons. They may want to see the house, they may want to meet the host or hostess, they may want to meet the other guests, or they may want to support your cause. Most likely the guests' motivations are more social than idealistic, but that's all right. Your job is not to transform their consciousness; your job is to raise money. If they leave the party a little smarter, too, that is simply an extra benefit.

Preparation

How do you find a rich person to throw a party for you if none of your members is rich or knows anyone who is? Before you do anything, you have to decide that your work is important to the entire community. Everyone will benefit, including the wealthy people. If you have an effective, hardworking publicity committee, the rich folk have probably already heard about your work and are curious about who you are anyway. Now you need to do a systematic search to find one wealthy person to invite others to learn more about you.

It is essential that you overcome any stereotypes about rich people before you start. If you go about your search with a chip on your shoulder, or if you treat the rich sponsor as a frivolous auxiliary to the enemy forces, you will never achieve any ongoing, respectful working relationship with the people you want to reach. Just as you want to be taken seriously for the work you are doing, so the wealthy people want to be taken seriously for the contribution they can make. If you want allies on your team for the long run, treat your wealthy sponsors as equals.

How to Find a Host/Hostess

The first place to look for help is your own contributor list. You have kept careful, complete records of all your donors; now go over them looking for the right names or addresses or simply the biggest donations. You may find you already have a candidate on your list.

Second, talk with any sympathizers you have in the media. Although they cannot ethically throw a party for you, since they need to maintain a facade of "objectivity" for their job, journalists get invited everywhere and know lots of people. Ask them who they would recommend as a host or hostess. They may even set up an introduction for you.

Third, try any sympathetic clergy, especially clergy with upper class congregations. They usually have the best reading on people's budgets, altruism, and networks. In addition, they are surefire door openers since almost no one will turn down a request from a pastor.

Fourth, read the society columns with a careful eye. Clip them regularly so you can go back and see which names pop up with regularity. Most likely the names you see the most are people with "new money" who use their money to meet the people with "old money" and to make an impression on the local social world. These people are the best bet to sponsor an event for you, because they like an excuse to invite other folks they want to know. They can get away with inviting Horace Gotrocks IV to a party for a worthy civic organization, even though H. G. IV would never come to their purely social function.

Fifth, read the business columns. The self-made millionaire is still a reality in America. Financial columnists figure that probably about fifty new millionaires are made every year in a big city. You need to do the same thing the fancy "Director of Development" does for a hospital, disease, or university. Play "Find the Millionaire." Read the gossip column in the business section of the paper and the gossip columns in *Fortune* or *Forbes*. When you find the name look it up in *Who's Who* at the library and see if there is any connection between your leaders and the new millionaire: school, business, or church. If not, you can always just call him cold, introduce yourself, and ask for a meeting.

Sixth, ask politicians for recommendations. Most politicians protect their big funders like a tigress protects her cubs. Look for a politician who has retired recently, one who is midterm in a nonelection year, one who is exceptionally well adjusted, or one who owes you something. Ask the politician to introduce you to a good prospect.

Seventh, cultivate your old school ties. Everybody went to school with somebody who has subsequently struck it rich (usually the person they kicked out for going up the down staircase). Don't be shy. Even if the person doesn't remember you sat behind her in geometry fifteen years ago, she may be curious enough to agree to meet you again.

HOW TO ASK

Obviously, all of these people are virtual strangers. You are going to ask them to throw a party for you in their home at their own expense. Why would they do it? They will do it because they like giving parties, they want a chance to invite bigger shots to their home, or they want to back your work. Mostly, they will give a party for you if they believe in you and like you personally. So it is important who from the group does the asking.

Your most important officer should be the one to ask for the party. Someone else, the pastor or politician, can arrange an introduction, but it is the president who has to go *in person* to convince the host to be a host. Mail information and clippings on the group before the meeting so they know what you have done, why you need the money, and what you intend to do next. If you have another leader who is recognizable from TV, send him or her, too. Consider it from the host's point of view. The host is going to have to tell friends, "I want you to meet so and so." If the host admires you and your work, you may get your party.

Be frank. Explain how much money you need and why. Say that none of your members knows the kind of people the host does and that is why you want the host to have the party. Explain that the host only has to get the people there, that you will ask for the money.

Answer all the host's questions. Say how many people you want to have and which dates you think are best. Leave all the decisions on food and drinks to the host. People who entertain a lot are skilled at estimating the quality and quantity of refreshments needed. They will do it right.

Be clear that you want the host to cover all the expenses. This can run from $100 to $2,000, depending on the size of the crowd and the elegance of the party, so you must both be clear it is the host's donation. Although this is a lot of money, some people think nothing of throwing a party like that but would never just give you a check for an equal amount. Offer all labor for addressing invitations and cleanup.

INVITATIONS

You can print invitations or send a handwritten note on the host's personal stationery. They must look good. Send the invitations about three weeks before the party and follow up with phone calls. It is best if the host and some friends do the follow-up phone calls.

Ask for a specific donation on the invitation (usually $10 to $25). This guarantees a minimum amount from each guest. It also tells the people who cannot attend the right amount for a donation. The callers should urge the no-shows to send in a donation anyway. The invitation should indicate that the guests will be asked for more money at the party. They know it anyway, but it is best to keep everything clear.

Sometimes the host will recommend a very high price per person, say $100, because he or she knows from experience that people will pay that much to get into that particular home. In that case, you need to have a strict but gracious door team to admit only paying customers. Otherwise, cocktail parties run on the honor system. If a guest says he paid, you take his word for it. Even if he did not, you still have a chance to get a check from him at the party. Besides, no one can get away with freeloading for long, because freeloaders will be purged from the invitation list.

Lists. If your host is a veteran party giver, he or she may have a complete list of people to invite. You can add major donors ($50 +) from your own list. In addition, you can mail to any other big donors in the same zip code from lists you can get from politicians or other groups.

REHEARSAL

Try to line up a celebrity to introduce your speaker. A media figure, a sympathetic politician, or a national leader would be good. Practice your pitch before the party. Do it for the host and ask his or her advice.

At the Party

Have the top four to six officers attend the party. They should relax, stay sober, and decide to have a good time. Their job is to tell people about the organization in a low-key way. This is not the time for lectures. It is best simply to *listen* to the guests. Successful people usually consider themselves experts at everything and will want to tell you what you should be doing. As Talleyrand said, "If you wish to appear agreeable in society, you must consent to be taught many things which you know already." Thank everyone for his or her good advice. Try to learn and remember names.

THE PITCH

After everyone arrives, have the host introduce the celebrity. The celebrity explains the issue, what the group is doing, and why it is so important and then introduces the speaker. The president thanks the host and leads a round of applause for such a farsighted, community-minded person.

The pitch must be short, simple, and, above all, personal. More than anything else, the guests want to know who you are. The celebrity has already told them what the organization is doing, and they have your brochure that gives the facts and figures. The speaker's job is to make it personal and real:

"My name is Joe Smith. I was born in the Mayfair neighborhood, and I hope to die there. My first job was selling scorecards right there at the Babe Ruth ball park, when you could still get there for 7¢ on the trolley. I have four kids who all went to the Robert Frost Grade School and Carl Sandburg High School.

"The other folks in the Mayfair Neighborhood Association are just like me. We are working people raising families in a community we love. We are fighting to save that community. We run a bingo every Friday at the Masonic Hall and we run a bazaar every spring. Ninety percent of the families in Mayfair pay dues to support our group.

"But now we find we're up against the toughest fight we've ever had, the Beltway Corridor Plan. That's why we're here tonight, to ask your help. We've gone to the hearings, we've gone to city hall, and we've gone to the capitol. It's clear this is going to be a long, hard fight. We intend to stay in and win. We can do the work if you will help us with a donation. If you can give $25, $50, or $100 tonight, it can mean we can save our neighborhood. And I'll get to see my grandchildren grow up right there, in Mayfair, just like my kids did."

Answer any questions simply and briefly. The celebrity wraps it up and tells how much he or she is giving. Have one or two other people primed to say how exciting this is and how much they are giving, too. Then the organization team and the celebrity collect the checks or pledges. The host does not get involved with the money collection.

RULES FOR THE PITCH

1. Keep it simple.
2. Keep it short.

3. Make it personal.
4. Be proud of yourself, your organization, and your goals. *Never apologize* for who you are, or what you do, or how you do it.
5. Be positive. Paint a picture of determination to win, soon.
6. Don't get bogged down in details. For facts and figures, refer the audience to the written materials.

WRAP-UP

Stay until the last guest leaves. Be sure to thank everyone who gives you a check and make sure that you have their names right. Thank the host again for the hospitality. Offer to do any cleanup, even if there are servants. If there are no servants, *insist* on cleaning up. Don't linger after the cleanup unless invited, and then don't stay too long.

Send a thank-you note and a complete report to the host and the celebrity the next day. Be sure to stay in touch with the host through the year with copies of good clippings, the newsletter, and invitations to social events. A friendly call from the president is good, too. and a request from the fundraiser for advice is superb.

BREAKFAST, LUNCH, OR DINNER— MAKING MONEY FROM FOOD

Serving meals is one of the oldest ways to make money for a good cause. As food prices go up, it is becoming more difficult to make a profit from selling tickets to a breakfast, lunch, or dinner. Especially if you want to keep your ticket price low enough for everyone in your own organization to attend, you will have to add on another more profitable fundraiser such as a raffle or an ad book to make more money.

This section describes meals you buy from a restaurant or hotel and then resell with a program at a higher price to your guests. If your primary goal is getting your own members together to celebrate, sponsor a potluck as described in Chapter 8 instead of a professional meal. If you want to use the meal as a way to present your program to busy executives or community leaders, then it is a good way to prepare them to give. Be sure to get current prices and prepare a complete budget of all your costs with the advice of someone who has done a benefit luncheon or dinner in your community recently. Once you have the current prices, consider if this is the best way to spend your members' time. Committees often suggest luncheons or dinners because they are familiar, festive, and used to be profitable. Be sure you are still making the right choice for your community today.

The Luncheon

Your organization can choose to sponsor any kind of meal that will appeal to its target audience. Politicians and business leaders often use prayer breakfasts to get donors together. A women's organization in Oakland, California, used a "snack and plaque" format for its annual awards ceremony for its business supporters. Local business people were invited in for a snack and given appreciation plaques from the group. It required a minimum of work and expense and gave the merchants the same recognition as a more elaborate affair.

The most popular fundraising meal for office workers, homemakers, and professionals is the luncheon. People figure they have to eat anyway, so they might as well do it and support your organization at the same time. The key to successful luncheons is thorough planning and iron discipline so your meal and program run on time. If you get your crowd fed, educated, entertained, and out the door on time, they will be eager to buy tickets to your next luncheon, too!

You can also run a series of luncheons to get new members or patrons. For example, some big city groups will sponsor a luncheon the second Tuesday of every month. The guests pay for their own meals, so there is no cost to the organization. Then the leaders of the group ask the guests to pledge a monthly amount, usually $10 to $25. This is aimed toward executives and professionals who do not have the time to participate but sympathize with the goals of the group. The advantage to the organization is that it can sell the professionals in a group rather than one at a time. The series builds itself by asking the guests for both money and new names for the next luncheon.

PROFIT FORMULA

It will probably cost you from $5 to $15 for the luncheon. Be sure you set your price based on the total cost: meal plus tax plus tips. Sometimes a restaurant will give you a special price if the owner likes your work or if the owner will get the revenue from the bar. It will be higher at a hotel because you are also charged for setup. Depending on your market, you can charge from $10 to $25. Your profit is the total ticket sales minus the total costs.

Sample: A luncheon at a chic restaurant got a special price for a luncheon of $5.95 because the owner was sympathetic to the cause of the organization. The restaurant got the revenue from the bar. The cost per person was $5.95 plus 5-percent sales tax plus 15-percent tip for a total per person of $7.14. Printing and postage were donated. The group charged $19.76 for the tickets ("in this our Bicentennial year"). The program attracted 170 guests.

$$170 \text{ guests x } \$19.76 = \quad \$3,359.20 \text{ gross}$$
$$170 \text{ guests x } \$ \ 7.14 = \quad - \ 1,213.80 \text{ costs}$$

$$\$2,145.40 \text{ net profit}$$

MECHANICS

The advantage of a luncheon over a dinner is that it is shorter and less expensive. The challenge is to keep the entire meal and program on time, so you must choose a place with good service and run a very well-orchestrated agenda.

It is easiest to schedule the event at a restaurant or hotel that is convenient for most of the guests. Choose a simple menu. Most working people prefer a light lunch so they can stay alert in the afternoon anyway.

People do *not* come to a lunch or dinner event for the food, so don't try to impress them with expensive dishes. They *do* come because of 1) who invites them, 2) who else will be there, and 3) the quality of the speaker and program. See Chapter 7 for more advice on invitations.

The Dinner

A dinner is an overgrown luncheon. You do the same preparation but have more food, a bigger program, and charge higher prices. Because a dinner seems to be more of an "occasion," you can also use it as the basis for a corporate campaign, an ad book, or direct mail solicitation.

Like the luncheon, the draw for a dinner is *not* the food but the person who sends the invitations. Guests come because they want to please the person who asked them. Another gimmick common to dinners is the "honored guest." Many groups choose a beloved recently retired politician, an earnest activist, a dedicated reporter, or a virtuous celebrity to honor at the dinner with an award. This gives you access to the honoree's lists. It also can serve as the bait for a top-notch chairperson if that person wants to be associated with the honored guest. Some groups are crass enough to make their biggest donor the "Man (or Woman) of the Year," because they know he or she has the clout to force other people with money to make an appearance. This does raise money, but it can ruin your credibility as a sincere organization primarily concerned about your program.

Many politicians have run big dinners, and so have many union leaders. Ask them or their fundraisers for advice.

Format

The typical format for a luncheon or dinner is:

1. Greeting by the officers when guests arrive. Fruit juice, wine, or cocktails for the folks who come early. If you want, you can arrange for the hotel to set up a cash bar.

2. Show the guests to their tables. Seating is *not* random. Be sure that you arrange the guests so that they all get to meet someone from your group.

3. You may have a minister or rabbi give a benediction or say grace.

4. A simple meal is served. This needs to be done quickly and efficiently.

5. The chairperson of the luncheon welcomes all the guests and introduces celebrities in the audience.

6. Present your program. This can be a few very short speeches on different aspects of your work, one "state of the organization" speech by the president, or a series of awards. Keep it all as short as possible. Aim for twenty minutes; never take more than forty-five minutes in total.

7. If you are going to ask people for money, have the member at each table armed with pledge cards to distribute to tablemates. You can collect checks at the luncheon or take pledges.

8. Have plenty of written material, fact sheets, brochures, or annual reports for guests to take when they leave.

11

Publicity

Good fundraising is inseparable from good publicity. Your fund-raising campaigns attract public attention to the group, and pub-licity will prepare people to give you money. An enthusiastic public-ity committee will make your organization and its special events easier to sell. Just remember that publicity gets you only attention from the public. If you want to get money from the public, the fundraisers still have to go and *ask* for money. The publicity com-mittee will get you publicity; the fundraising committee will get you money; the membership committee will get you members. Team-work will give you all three!

Publicity will get new donors and volunteers interested in your group, but your leaders need to close the sale. Publicity does *not* raise money. People raise money.

Your publicity committee can be one or two chairpersons who serve for a year or more. They work all year-round to keep your organization in the media. For your big fundraising campaigns such as your membership drive or corporate campaign, they can ex-pand the committee to ten people to reach every volunteer and possible donor. For special events, the committee can expand to twenty to put up posters, pass out fliers, and provide special hoopla such as clowns or town criers.

RECRUITING A PUBLICITY CHAIRPERSON

You need to find a volunteer who will make a commitment to do the job for at least a year. It works well if you have one person who heads the committee for a year and another who is assistant for the same year and becomes head the next year. The ideal person is articulate, well informed, likes to talk about the group, writes clearly, and meets deadlines. He or she must understand that the job is to promote the entire organization, and especially the elected leaders, but not himself or herself. From a practical point of view, news people need to work with someone who is accessible, intelligent, and honest. Your publicity people must be able to make and receive phone calls during the day. Typing and secretarial skills are an advantage. Although the publicity chairperson's job is fun and sometimes even glamorous, it is also hard work. It involves a good deal of monotonous work like typing envelopes and mailing releases. Be sure your candidate realizes this and accepts both parts of the job.

Training a Publicity Chairperson

New publicity people can order and read the books listed in Chapter 14 to learn the mechanics of working with the press. Ask for advice from an experienced volunteer publicity chairperson or a friendly professional publicist. Try to get "adopted" by a veteran to get impartial, objective criticism of press releases and publicity ideas. The most important information to get from a veteran is a current list of the best members of the working press in your town and some indication of their individual interests. Some adult education or college evening classes offer courses on publicity for community organizations. Encourage your publicity people to take one of these and include the cost in your training budget.

WHAT IS PUBLICITY?

Publicity, for our purposes, is all the information about your organization that you can get before the public. You should think of it in two categories. The first is general image publicity—all the work you do to create a positive impression of the organization. The second is fundraising publicity—information used to introduce the organization to potential donors, plus all the promotion you do to boost profits for a specific event.

General Publicity

You need a strategy and an annual calendar for your general image publicity just as you need them for your fundraising. Although there will be spontaneous interviews and stories initiated by the press, most of the press coverage you will get will come because it was planned by your volunteer.

First of all, make a list of what you have to sell to the press—your expertise on the issues, your admirable leaders, your actions, your testimony, your meetings, and your fundraising events. Lay out an annual calendar of events: the convention, election of officers, major hearings and testimony, major fundraising events, and major meetings. After you know what is scheduled, devise a plan for getting the maximum publicity from each event. Be sure to treat the press fairly. If you give the morning paper an exclusive on your nursing home study, give the evening paper the next exclusive on car repair prices. If you give one television station the first interview with the newly elected president, give its rival station the first interview after you win the property tax reform.

In terms of your fundraising efforts, the purpose of general image publicity is to create a positive image of the organization in the minds of the public at large. People should identify the name of the group with the idea of a growing, effective, and efficient organization. You want people to be able to say, "I saw your meeting with the mayor on TV. You know, my taxes are way too high, too. I'm sure glad you're trying to do something about it," or "I read the story about your president in the *Gazette*. Gosh, I'm a working woman, too, and I sure like it when someone tells how it really is for us." You want to make people identify with your leaders and goals. Good publicity makes people realize that your organization is a good investment, because you are doing what they want done and saying what they want said.

The first goal of the general publicity program is this creation of a positive image in the minds of the public at large. The second goal is the creation of a positive image in the minds of the members. It is important that the members think of themselves as winners. You cannot take their attitude for granted. It is human nature for people to wonder "Is this doing any good? Does anyone know what we're doing? Does anyone care?"

The members need to know that what they are doing *matters*. Getting attention from the public via coverage in the newspapers and TV lets members know they are recognized and appreciated. As a side effect, press coverage, especially TV coverage, will deepen the members' commitment to the success of the organization. They gain a sense of responsibility from being — among their friends and neighbors — a spokesperson for that organization that's on the evening news all the time. They want the group to succeed because they are identified with it and their reputations are on the line.

FUNDRAISING PUBLICITY MATERIALS

All that you need to raise money for your organization is the courage of your convictions and the desire to raise money. The rock-bottom bare-minimum fundraising package is a receipt book, which you can buy at any office supply store, or mimeograph your own. Ask someone for money, then give him or her a receipt.

Many organizations choose to give their fundraisers more materials because they give the fundraisers more confidence. The volunteers know they have the answers to any questions, and they also have the support of positive press showing that experts outside the organization think that they are a good investment. Your publicity committee can help the fundraisers by putting together a package of written materials, clippings from the media, helpful brochures, slide shows, and videotapes. Each fundraiser will decide how much of the publicity materials will help make the sale. If you have any doubts about using audiovisuals or a complicated package, leave the props at home. Your own sincerity and experience are always much more eloquent and convincing than brochures or slide shows.

In addition to your general image publicity, you can prepare a package to introduce your group to new people.

Clippings

To introduce your group to people with money, supplement your own material with copies of the good press coverage you have received. Systematically clip stories about the group and mount them on paper. Record the name of the newspaper or magazine, the date, page, and edition. All your clippings should be preserved in chronological order so you can prepare a package of clippings on the organization as a whole or a package of clippings on specific issues. For an introductory fundraising package, include a variety of your best clippings. For example, an effective package would have a neighborhood weekly paper's in-depth article on the leader, a daily newspaper front-page story on your research project, a feature story on the accomplishments of the organization, a national magazine story on your most important issue featuring your group as a good example, and an editorial from a daily newspaper praising the organization's stand on the issue.

Fact Sheets or Brochures

In addition to your collection of clippings, you should prepare a fact sheet or brochure to introduce your group. The information is the same in both cases. Include the history of the organization, the purpose, the current leaders, the current program, significant accomplishments, how to join, and flattering quotes from celebrities. A fact sheet can be typed and mimeographed on paper that will cost about $10 per thousand copies.

A brochure is usually produced on heavier paper, using professional typesetting and design, so it will cost you about $50 per thousand copies. It is perfectly all right to use an obviously low-cost, economy-model fact sheet when you start. People will understand that your group is new and small, so they will admire your economy on the fact sheet as long as they get all the facts. When the group is older, larger, and more solvent, spend money on your paper, especially for brochures that go to new people you are going to ask for money. It is smart in the long run to invest in professional design and good paper products. The brochure introduces you to the public, all of whom can be asked to give you money. If you want to give the image of a successful, effective organization, make up clear, strong, straightforward brochures.

You can round out your introductory package with a copy of your newsletter, copies of original research reports, copies of complimentary letters (used with permission of the author), and copies of your testimony before government committees. A short letter of introduction from the president, the clippings, and the fact sheet are the minimum you need when you write to ask for an appointment with a potential donor. Use all the written materials to give donors background on who you are, what you do, how you do it, and why you need more money. Do the asking in person.

Audiovisual Aids

SLIDE SHOW

The simplest, cheapest, quickest, and most flexible way to tell a story about your group is the slide show. If you can get one or more photographers to donate their services, all you need to pay for is the film and the processing. A slide show is an excellent format for showing contrasts; for example, show the luxurious homes of the county board members and then show the humble bungalows the senior citizens will lose because of extortionate property taxes set by these county board members. The advantage of a slide show is that it is easy to revise and update pieces of the show without having to redo the entire show.

VIDEOTAPE

Another effective publicity piece is a videotape of a TV news show featuring your organization. A TV documentary is much better than your self-produced videotape, especially for an action organization, because the TV news people can usually get access to the people on the other side of the issue. Ironically, the target of an action campaign, especially a corporate target, will often overreact and make your case for you. Even a one-sided news show about the group is excellent because it comes from a believable independent source.

For a local TV station, contact the station manager, the news director, the director of public affairs, or a friendly reporter or producer. Tell him or her what exciting events are coming up and why your group is unique. Watch all your local channels to find out which one would most likely be sympathetic to your program. It will take several calls before you sell the director on a feature story on your group, but it is worth the effort. Make an agreement ahead of time to get a copy of the finished story (you will have to supply a videocassette). Finally, if everything works out, do all you can to give the TV crew complete background information and the best possible working conditions.

For a national news or public affairs show, write the producer at his or her office (usually in New York or Los Angeles) and explain your group and your program. Send a copy of your letter to the star of the show. Mention the local importance of your work but emphasize the national implications.

If a station or network chooses to do a feature on your group on its own initiative, try to get a copy of the tape from the director of broadcasting. Explain that you are a not-for-profit group and say where and how you plan to use the copy. The TV people should be glad to help as long as you are not planning to rebroadcast the show. If one of your members or friends has a videotape recorder, he or she can make you a tape from the television broadcast. You can show the tape on any television set if you have a tuner to adapt the set. A consumer (not industrial) videotape recorder with a tuner cost you about $1,200 (1981 price). Once you own the recorder you can also record news coverage of your work, editorials and your responses, and documentaries about your issue.

You may also want to buy a color video camera (about $1,000 in 1981). Recruit a volunteer who knows how to make good videotapes for the publicity committee or ask one of the committee to learn how to use the camera. Some colleges and some community video organizations offer training. If your city has a new cable franchise, the cable company may have to offer training and equipment to community organizations. If your city is negotiating an agreement for cable, be sure they include access, training and equipment for nonprofit organizations in the contract. Check on what the cable company has offered in other cities and ask other groups what works best for them.

Once you get one or two volunteers trained to make high-quality videotapes, you can produce and show your tapes on your cable network or in people's homes or offices on regular TV sets. If none of your members has an interest in learning to use video equipment, contact your local library, college, or video organization for referrals to video experts you can hire to make a tape for you. The advantage of video is that it is relatively simple to make, it is ready immediately, and it is fun to use. As the technology improves and cable outlets expand, you will be able to do more and more with videotapes in the coming years.

HOW TO PROMOTE AN EVENT

When the organization chooses to do a fundraising event, the publicity people become promoters. Their job is to make the upcoming event the most exciting, unique, and sexy occasion happening that weekend. It should be so attractive that people will drive for miles through a blinding snowstorm to attend.

First, think of how you yourself plan a free weekend. Discuss all the ways you personally decide where you are going to go. Rank them in order. If there is one paper or one column that everyone reads first, put most of your effort into getting into that paper or column. After you have listed all the possibilities and put them in order, work systematically from the top down to get your event prominently promoted in each one.

Start at least two months in advance of the event. You will need to send public service announcements to radio and TV stations at least three weeks in advance, and some magazines need copy six weeks in advance of the first of the month in which your event occurs. Ask a veteran for advice on the best people to call and the deadlines for each medium. If you plan to use specialty advertising like buttons or T-shirts, you will need to order them at least six weeks in advance of the date you want to start selling them.

Here is a list of some possibilities for free advertising and promotion. In addition, if you have the budget for a big money fundraiser, you can buy advertising space and time. Unless you are spending more than $10,000 to put on your event, stick to free publicity. Remember, even "free" publicity will require an investment for printing, paper, and postage.

Press Release

Include description of event, date, goal, celebrities attending, special angles like recipes, chairperson. Send to all local media.

Calendar Notices

Mail one month ahead to the "What's Happening" calendars in daily and weekly newspapers and two months or more ahead to monthly magazines.

Signs and Marquees on Buildings

Write the head of the firm that owns the building and ask for free use of the sign.

Feature Stories

Call and write feature department editors of daily papers. Emphasize photo possibilities. Children and animals still appeal.

Radio-TV Public Service Announcements (PSAs)

See *If You Want Air Time* booklet in the bibliography, Chapter 14.

Free Classifieds

Offered by some weekly newspapers. Read the rules and send early.

Celebrities

Good for column notes or TV/radio plugs dropped ingenuously on talk shows.

Invitations

To local pastors, politicians, and community leaders. It's courteous and promotes word-of-mouth publicity.

Church Bulletins

Mail to pastor two weeks in advance to include in bulletin Sunday before event.

Huge Sign

Make and hang over event site two weeks before event.

Fliers

8½ by 11 inches, printed on bright paper. Tape up on trees and telephone poles around neighborhood, ask other community groups to hand out at their events the weekend before your event, include as stuffers in other programs, and hand out at busy intersections.

Posters

11 by 17 inches on heavier colored paper. Have a team of people hang them up on windows of local merchants, train stations, YWCA, YMCA, and homes near event site. Put up on bulletin boards in schools, churches, bars, theatres, and youth centers.

Coupons

You can add coupons to your own newsletter, fliers, letters, or invitations. Offer free entry, free pony ride, percent discount on merchandise, free glass of wine with dinner, or free dessert.

Radio Show Premiums

Give radio show hosts a quantity of tickets to your sports event, concert, or play. Disk jockeys use them as premiums to give away "to the ninth person who calls 555-5789."

Column Notes

Give an exclusive bit of gossip about a celebrity or unique attraction to a gossip column writer.

Other Organizations' Newsletters

Ask for a paragraph plug on your event in other groups' newsletters. Promise to reciprocate.

Your Own Networks

Mail to *donors list*.

Feature article, photo, and big ad in your own *newsletter*.

Activate your *telephone chain* to be sure everyone is called.

Build up *word-of-mouth* promotion with hoopla. Buttons and bumper stickers promote discussion, as do publicity stunts, like milking a cow on the lawn of the city church to promote the "County Fair" bazaar.

MORE ADVICE

See the bibliography, Chapter 14, for recommended reading on the press and publicity.

12

Making Book

A clear division of labor will help each officer in your organization do a better job. Most groups find that it works best if the fundraiser raises funds and leaves all the bookkeeping, legal, and tax work to the treasurer. However, the fundraiser still needs to understand the accounting system as well as keep track of the general financial strength of the organization.

The first thing to do is get advice from an experienced bookkeeper and lawyer. Second, try to recruit ongoing legal and accounting help from a member or friend of the organization. Third, see the bibliography, Chapter 14, to order more helpful books to improve your financial planning and record keeping.

ACCOUNTING

The clearest explanation of how to set up your records and keep track of your money is in the *Bookkeeping Handbook for Low-Income Citizen Groups,* prepared by the National Council of Welfare of Canada. This is a crystal-clear, step-by-step outline of how to handle your bookkeeping, explained in words nonaccountants can understand. The *Handbook* committee members have made an enormous contribution to small and new community organizations: they explain everything about bookkeeping without using the words

credit and *debit*. Any group in the United States can use this book
perfectly well, too. The only exception is the discussion of how to do
a payroll (the Canadian system is different from the U.S. system).
Since payroll requirements are different in every state, the best
place to get advice on payroll bookkeeping is from an experienced
bookkeeper in your state. See the bibliography, Chapter 14, for
order information.

Best of all, hire or recruit a competent, conscientious bookkeeper. He or she can keep the books, pay the bills, and do the
reports. Then the fundraiser need only keep track of the overall
financial picture.

IDEAS FOR THE NONACCOUNTANT

In addition to the advice from accountants, here are a few tested
suggestions to help you handle money. I am not an accountant, but
these are a few ideas I have found from experience to be helpful for
those of us without accounting skills.

1. Always make a list of your income and expenses from each
event and from the fundraising effort as a whole. You should know
every week where you stand financially — every day in a tight period.
This is your early-warning system to tell you when to step up the
work.

2. Keep track of *all* your money. It can get confusing when you
have money in checking accounts, savings accounts, special funds,
petty cash, and on deposit at the post office for second and third
class postage. You do not have to adopt a complicated double-entry
accounting system (though the bookkeeper may use one). Just keep
track on a chart where all your money is now (today), to whom you
owe money, and who owes you money.

Even if you have an outside accounting firm or a computerized
accounting system, it is important that someone in the group keep
track of the day-to-day financial picture. The best person to do this
is the one who approves expenditures. You need someone to keep a
tight rein on your spending. The smaller the budget, the stingier
you need to be. Every group needs a Scrooge to say, "No, you can't
print two-color posters to help the turnout for next week's meeting.
Use the telephone network, for free, instead."

If you have no one who scrutinizes your money from the moment it comes in to the time it is spent, you will spend more money than you need to. You will order too much paper, permit too many long-distance phone calls, and buy too many supplies. All this happens because you are too busy to have someone figuring out how much paper you actually *need,* as opposed to how much you will use if it is delivered to your door. It is human nature to overproject, overspend, and underutilize what you already have, unless someone controls spending in the context of the yearly and monthly budgets as well as the needs of the moment.

3. Keep all of your bills and receipts from the very first day. Even if you think it will not be necessary to set up books, "because we can win this in three months," keep all your bills *just in case* the fight takes longer or the group decides to move on to a second fight after winning the first. You can never put enough notes on the bills. Write down the number of the check with which you paid the bill, the date, and what the bill was for: "posters for May 5th rally" or "additional wiring to run mimeograph." Then, if you eventually decide to set up books, you can re-create the past from your bills and receipts. Lots of notes on the bills and checks are also a tremendous help to a future treasurer or fundraiser who needs to research any expenses.

4. Shop for a bank. The law sets interest limits, which are the same for every bank. This does not mean that every bank is exactly the same. First, you should look for a bank and a savings and loan that support the community by lending as much money in their primary service area as the people in that community deposit. Ask a bank officer for a report on where the bank gets its money and where it makes loans. In some states this is public information required of all lending institutions. In other states you have to ask each institution for it. If the bank or S&L will not disclose its lending data, assume it has something to hide and give your business to someone else.

You can always have more than one bank. You may want to use a nearby bank for deposits if you handle a lot of cash every day; for example, from a door-to-door canvassing program or if you get large amounts of cash from special events. You can still keep most of your money in another bank with a positive lending record and helpful personnel or invested in another institution at a better rate of interest.

You can also deposit your money in more than one kind of financial institution. For example, you may want to keep a limited checking account at a good bank, a savings account at a good savings and loan or money market fund, and an account in the community credit union you choose to support for political reasons. Your banker can help you compare the advantages of each type of institution.

5. Look for an officer in the bank who will help you. There are many services a bank can give you in addition to a free checking account. You need to find someone who cares about you and the success of your organization to help you get the most the bank has to offer. A bank can give you:

• Advice on the different types of savings accounts and investments.

• Advice on payroll taxes and tax law.

• Advice on employee benefits.

• Lock box service for the returns from a direct mail program. All the returns are mailed directly to the bank itself. Banks will handle the returns and deposit the checks for a fee per check. This means you do not need a person in the office to handle the checks. It makes it impossible to lose checks or have them stolen from the office. Get competitive bids for lock box services, since there is a wide range in bank charges. Also, get advice from other groups that run big mailing programs to assess the quality of the service.

• Advice on establishing a line of credit if you have a lot of money going in and out. This is important for political campaigns, where you get big donations and need to make big expenditures quickly.

• Advice on borrowing money. Especially if your organization deposits large amounts of money in the bank, you can ask for a special rate on loans like other major depositors.

• Help on mundane weekly transactions; for example, issuing and redeeming state lottery tickets.

6. Invest your money so that it makes money for you. If you get any foundation or government grants, your whole annual grant may come in one or two large checks. Many ongoing grass roots fundraising programs have marked seasonal money bulges. Most churches, for example, receive much more money in the winter months than in the summer months; conversely a door-to-door can-

vassing program often nets a lot more in the summer than in the winter, especially in bad climates.

Try to keep only enough money in your checking account to cover two months' expenses. There are two reasons for this. First, all the rest of your money can be earning interest. Second, you won't be tempted to spend next month's money or to think you are richer than you really are. Your banker or accountant can tell you how to balance your long-term income goals and your short-term cash needs.

7. If you want to borrow money, for instance to pay for the postage for your first direct mail campaign or for advertising in a political campaign, always try first to get an interest-free loan from a friend of the group. This is definitely a case of people giving to people. Since the assets of most new community organizations are some secondhand furniture, rebuilt machines, and a lot of paper, the person who lends you money realizes you have no collateral except your word. It *is* possible to borrow interest-free money if people believe in your personal integrity and your organization's chance for success. In the world of high finance, the wheeler-dealers often raise money simply by trading promises with no collateral other than the stock in a fund they hope will work. In other words, you do not always have to have a lot of collateral to raise money. If people with money respect you and your group, you may be able to get an interest-free loan. At least ask your two or three best prospects for such a loan before you borrow from a bank and pay interest.

If you have to borrow money and pay interest, ask your banker what deal the bank can make. Then research your other possibilities: savings and loans, credit unions, or community co-ops that invest in the neighborhood. Some national organizations will lend affiliate chapters seed money for fundraising. Ask other groups in your area what they would recommend.

8. Debt is a drag. It is an enormous drain on your time to keep putting off your creditors. It makes all your fundraising much more difficult because you are limited to smaller events. Worst of all, it is terrible for the morale of the entire organization. Try to set up your fundraising prudently at the beginning to avoid debt at any time.

However, there are reasons why you may find yourself in debt. New organizations that have never had a chance to handle money, gauge the risks of fundraising efforts, and predict the seasonal fluctuations of their income may incur a cash flow problem. This simply means you need to spend more money right now than you have coming in right now. Your goal is to reverse this situation as quickly as possible.

First, step up your fundraising efforts. If you need to cut back on your program to devote more time to fundraising, do it.

Second, cut out all unnecessary spending. If you decide that salaries are necessary, but a photocopier is not, send the machine back.

Third, tell your creditors honestly what your situation is now and what your timetable will be for paying them. Some creditors, like the telephone company, will not wait. If you don't pay, it cuts off your service. Others, like printers or suppliers, may wait if you explain that due to extenuating circumstances you are unable to pay them at this time. Explain that you are launching your membership drive next week and can assure them of payment in sixty days. As long as they have a specific date to anticipate payment, they should wait. It is in their interest to keep you as a customer in the long run, so they may be patient while you are young and learning.

Fourth, make long-range plans to make your income more predictable. This includes formulating an annual strategy for fundraising, regularizing your current fundraising, especially dues renewal, and asking your big donors, whether individuals or institutions, to schedule their donations at the best time for you. Obviously, the best advice on debt is to make accurate plans so you don't fall into debt in the first place.

9. Get a professional audit annually. Although it can be expensive, you can ask the auditor to donate the audit, give you a discount price, or let you pay one-twelfth of the cost each month on a time payment plan. The advantages of an audit are that it gives you an outside professional opinion on your books to show to funding sources, it forces you to get everything completely up to date once a year, and it can give you suggestions for improving your system as the organization grows and changes. Consider an audit as one of your indispensable planning tools and put the cost into your budget each year.

10. Make money by spending less. Every year ask your president, treasurer, and best penny pinchers to take a close look at how you spend your money. Are there any ways you can save by spending less? Every dollar you do not spend is a dollar you do not have to

raise. For a volunteer group, one of your biggest costs is usually printing. Ask a local business or labor union to contribute the printing you need. It may be a major expense for you, but it will be a trivial expense for the big business or union. For a group with paid staff members, salaries are usually the biggest expenses. Consider if there are some jobs that your own leaders and volunteers are eager and able to do. Ask other local organizations in your community that are run by volunteers how they divide the work, then consider practicing what you preach and letting the members literally run the organization and do the work.

What about joining with other organizations to share expenses? For example, the Topeka Tenants Association organized a coalition to take over an empty school. The city gave the association the school and paid for the renovation. The office space is shared by the tenants association, the agency on aging, Big Sisters/Big Brothers, and three other organizations. The local neighborhood association, the Tennessee Town Improvement Association, runs a food concession out of the kitchen, selling coffee and rolls in the mornings and running a soup kitchen at lunchtime. All the groups share the conference room, office machines, and overhead such as insurance, utilities, and upkeep. Ask your secretary to explore ways your organization can cooperate and share expenses with other local organizations. You will all benefit from working together.

LEGAL MATTERS AND TAXES

Be sure that the organization has a firm foundation for fundraising. Ask the president if the group is incorporated in your state and if it has received tax-exempt status from the Internal Revenue Service (IRS) of the federal government. If your organization is incorporated and has a 501(c)(3) tax status, it is easier to raise money because the people who give you donations may deduct that money from their taxable income. If your group has never applied for incorporation or tax exemption, urge the president and treasurer to get the applications and instructions from the secretary of state and the IRS. It usually takes about seven months to get a new group incorporated and tax exempt, so your officers should begin the process immediately if necessary.

Once the organization qualifies, it will be exempt from paying

corporate income taxes, and its donors can deduct the amount of
their donations from their taxable income. A 501(c)(3) tax status
will also make an organization exempt from paying federal unem-
ployment taxes (FUTA). The organization can also apply for
exemption from state sales taxes and local sales taxes and personal
property taxes. Check your own officials because each state, county,
and city has different laws.

A 501(c)(3) tax status will also help you apply for the non-fot-
profit bulk rate postage. This was 6¢ per piece instead of 22¢ per
piece in 1985.

ANNUAL REPORTS

The last responsibility for your group is to be sure the treasurer
files the necessary federal and state annual reports. He or she can
get copies of the federal report forms and instructions from the Internal Revenue Service, which is listed in most telephone books.
Every tax-exempt nonprofit organization must file Form 990. Every
501(c)(3) tax-deductible organization must also file Schedule A of
Form 990. Every charitable organization with unrelated business income must also file Form 990T. The treasurer or bookkeeper can
ask the IRS to send these forms and instructions, then ask an experienced accountant, bookkeeper, or treasurer for more help. Do it today so you will be sure to have the information you will need to file
the reports on time.

Most states and the District of Columbia require nonprofit
organizations to file annual reports. Every state is different, so ask
your own Secretary of State and Attorney General which forms your
organization needs to file; then ask for advice from your lawyer, accountant, and a veteran treasurer or bookkeeper of a well-
established nonprofit. Some states now use the Federal 990 form for
their annual report form. Others require a separate state form from
any nonprofit that solicits funds, does business, or owns property in
the state. Some states require your organization to file one report as
a corporation doing business in the state and a second report as a
charity soliciting funds from the citizens. Be sure you know now
which forms your organization is required to file so you can collect
all of the necessary information and file the annual reports on time.

13

Fundraising Forever

Grass roots fundraising will help you build a successful and permanent organization. To get and keep the members and donors you want, plan ahead when you organize your fundraising work each year. As you get more members and better leaders, the work will become easier and easier. This chapter shares suggestions to help you use your leaders' talents and your members' time to make the most money. Each section illustrates a general fundraising principle.

Grass roots fundraising is do-it-yourself fundraising. Make the fundraising both profitable for the organization and personally rewarding for each volunteer. Use the section "*Teach Yourselves about Fundraising*" to give your people confidence about fundraising. They should find that fundraising is more familiar than they thought.

The goal of your fundraising plan should be to make the most money using the least amount of the members' time. Just as you set long-range goals for the organization's program, make long-range goals for raising money. Use the *calendar* as a guide to help prepare next year's timetable and use the *five-year plans* to make long-range plans.

Democratic planning produces the best plans. Your own members will always invent the most workable and popular plan for

277

your group. In addition, use the list of *where to get advice* to find other ideas you can adapt and improve for your own market.

It is important to continuously build the morale of the group and the momentum of the campaign. If an unexpected crisis befalls the group and you lose money on an event, you must immediately take action to save the campaign. Use the advice and the low-overhead events listed under *"How to Rebound from a Fundloser"* to get back on the right track.

Although this book does not cover grants, they can be an important component of your overall fundraising plan. For the best collection of current information and income tax reports by foundations in your area, use the *Foundation Center Regional Collections.* They are free libraries with a professional librarian to help you.

If you want or need more training for your staff or leaders, consider the list of *training schools* for organizers and leaders. They offer excellent courses in all the skills one needs to build a successful organization.

Last, but not least, decide to have a good time while you raise the budget. Sharing successes, singing songs, and planning parties build the friendships that are the glue of the organization. The fellowship of fundraising festivities is just as important as the income. So have a good time — for fun and profit.

TEACH YOURSELVES ABOUT FUNDRAISING

What do we already know?

Ask each member of your board or committee to make a list of every time he or she gave any person or group money. Include everything from coins in the can to regular dues. Figure out what made you give: cause, asker, habit, or peer group pressure. You will learn that you give money to get something you want. Giving money makes you feel good. This exercise will also give each volunteer a list of names of people who they can ask for money. If you have given money to them, how can they say no to you?

Count the number of ways any one group can get money out of you. For example, your church may get your regular pledge (dues), an extra donation for the seminarian from your parish, another donation for flowers, and a special campaign contribution to protect the stained glass windows; the church may also sell you a calendar, Christmas cards, and numerous small purchases at the Spring Fling and the Fall Fandango. There is no one "right" way to ask for money. You all give to many worthy causes in response to many kinds of requests: personal, mail, or sales. You can also use several styles of asking in your own campaign.

Next, ask the group to make a list of every time a person or group *just missed* getting your money. They moved on too soon, or didn't answer your question, or didn't send the envelope. Make a list of reasons and solutions; then make yourselves a list of dos and don'ts.

Last, ask the group to make a list of people and groups you would *never* give a penny. Make a list of reasons why and add them to your don'ts. Then make a plan for asking for money that will avoid the mistakes that make donors say no.

Begin a File of Fundraising Ideas

Clip the society column and the community calendar from the paper. Send away for free booklets. Write to your friends and relatives and ask them what they do in their towns. Go to the library and see what's available there. Ask the library to order books for you.

Brainstorming

Get your committee together for an evening of brainstorming. If possible, bring in an enthusiastic outsider to chair. Set two firm rules:

1. All ideas are good ideas.
2. You can only give your idea once.

This is not the time to say "We already tried that and it didn't work," or "We've always done it this way," or "We can't afford it," or "That's not our job; X should do it." This is your chance to stretch the imagination of everyone on the committee.

List all the ideas on big sheets of paper. After the meeting, type them up and send them out to all the committee members to consider the possibilities of implementation. Meet again in a month to consider where to go on them.

Sample thought provokers:

"If they find Howard Hughes' will, and we're in it for $1 million, what should we do with it?"

"What could we do to double the membership and/or the budget in five years?"

"What are the needs of the community that no one is filling now?"

A good one to use is the turned-around question:

"What could we do to put the church (the community congress, the hospital) out of business?"

Reverse the answers to learn how to strengthen your organization.

This kind of question was used in a brainstorming session at IBM. The question was, "What could you do to slow down your secretary?" They thought of smeary carbon paper, a typewriter with keys that jam together, and indelible ink that could never be corrected. When they turned these around, they came up with the idea for a typewriter with the correcting tape built in—a feature that will speed things up!

Begin a File of Fundraising Letters

Keep a file of all the fundraising letters you get. Divide them by "membership," "donation," "best" and "worst." Plagiarize freely from the best. Figure out what is especially awful about the worst ones and make yourself a list of don'ts to follow.

You can also ask your friends to pass along their letters to you so you can get more examples. Try to get a Republican and a Democrat, a feminist, a public interest law donor, an ecology freak, your dentist, and your minister to forward their mail. You will be amazed by both the variety and the duplication.

If you or your friends get the same letter and enclosures month after month, that means it works. That letter is making money for the charity that sends it. The best professional direct mail programs

always test their best letter against two or three new letters. When a
new letter produces a higher profit, it becomes the mass letter. The
professionals send the same letter as long as it works better than
others. So study the repeats to learn what works well now.

Selling

All fundraising is selling. Learn how the pros sell. This sounds
corny, but it works. Go to a Tupperware party or any kind of "we
sell our product in your home" party. See how they use incentives,
group pressure, time payment plans, and package deals. Talk to
your local Avon lady or anyone who sells cleaning products or
greeting cards from his or her home. All of them depend on high
sales and repeat customers. Some local chambers of commerce offer
seminars on selling; see if you can get a scholarship or a discount to
attend for your not-for-profit group. Salespeople love to brag about
their successes — ask them.

Volunteer

Volunteer to work on the committee for the next event produced by
the best fundraisers in town. Do as much as possible to see how they
do it. Tell them honestly that you are the fundraiser for the Carson
City Consumers Coalition and want to learn by doing. They should
be flattered and glad to spend some extra time with you.

Volunteer to work for a good political candidate. Electoral campaigns are great examples of involving a lot of people for an intense
short-term effort with high publicity and a definite deadline. You
will learn how to motivate many volunteers to work hard for a short
time. Then you can apply that know-how to your own organization.

GET CONTROL OF YOUR TIME:
PLAN A ONE-YEAR CALENDAR

A fundraising calendar will help you raise more money in less
time every year. It will make sure that you do first things first,

everything gets done, and nothing is forgotten. If you hang a big calendar in your office or meeting space, it shows newcomers the organization has exciting plans and is eager to get new volunteers to help.

Here is advice on making up a fundraising calendar. It will help you take out the bad times and highlight the good times for fundraising. Use this as a sample, then create your own calendar for your own organization. Of course, if your own people are enthusiastic about an event, *any* time can be a good time. In 1981, my Episcopal church, The Church of Our Saviour in Chicago, did a "Midsummer Matrimonial Madness" benefit to celebrate Prince Charles's wedding. Two hundred fifty people paid to see the royal wedding on a rented wide-screen color TV live at 3:00 A.M.! After the wedding we had an English breakfast, Morning Prayers, Holy Communion and then we all went to work. Five volunteers pulled this together in two weeks and made $250 for the restoration fund. If your own people like an idea a lot, *any* time is a good time. If you get a once-in-a-lifetime opportunity, seize the moment!

The goal of grass roots fundraising is to make the most money in the least time, maximizing the dollar return per member hour expended. Long-range plans will increase the profits because you can schedule your campaigns when there will be the most help, the best weather, and the least conflict with other events inside or outside the organization. If you plan your membership drive and special events so they can be repeated every year at the best time, you will be able to make more money each year with less work.

Plan your calendar when you make up your program's budget for the next year. When you complete the budget and know how much money you want to make, you can schedule the campaigns to make the most money in the least time.

You can plan your calendar in the fall if you operate on a regular calendar year (January to December), in the summer if you operate on an academic year (September to June), or in the spring if you operate on a June 30th fiscal year (July 1 to June 30). The president and treasurer can interview other local organizations that do the same kind of work to get their advice on the most effective way to schedule your work. Then the entire board can choose the times it wants to focus on fundraising.

How to Plan

Before the first planning meeting the president will call each person on the board. Ask them to think about the goals of the organization and your opportunities for the next twelve months. Personally invite each person to the planning meeting so everyone knows it is important.

At the first planning meeting, focus on planning. Try to make your planning work the only item on the agenda. Especially during the first year, it will take hard work and concentration to make an effective plan. So allow yourselves the time to do the best job you can.

Give each member of the board copies of monthly calendars for the next twelve months. At the end of the year you can often get nice calendars free from local businesses, banks, and insurance agents. In the middle of the year you may have to buy them. Buy or draw one large calendar with all twelve months on one sheet. Use this to lead the discussion.

Organization Dates

Begin by writing in your most important organizational dates. Enter the work you know you will want to do next year and when you will do it. This includes both monthly events such as your board meetings and yearly dates such as your annual meeting or election.

Write the organizational dates on your calendar in black. These include:

- Regular board meetings.
- Program meetings open to the public.
- Annual meeting or convention. If this includes election of officers, count backward to plan when to appoint a nominating committee and review the bylaws.
- Installation of officers.
- Annual banquets or social events for the volunteers.
- Fiscal responsibilities such as annual tax reports for the IRS and the state and your annual audit.
- Publication of the newsletter and other publications, such as the annual report.

Second, decide when you will want to focus on your program activities. If your organization lobbies, you will give that priority at the end of the legislative session. If you run an emergency food program, you know your work will accelerate in the winter, especially in December. If you organize tenants, you know your work will be greatest when leases run out, such as in April and September. Since you want to get results, plan ahead to have the most time available to focus on your program work.

Fundraising Dates

Third, plan your fundraising. Use a red marker and mark off the *worst* times for fundraising. Base this on what is the worst for your own community. Most groups find that it is more difficult to raise money at the following times.

- Three-day legal holiday weekends.
- State holidays.
- High religious holidays such as Good Friday and Yom Kippur.
- The first and last weeks of the school year.
- Days of major sports events such as the last game of the World Series and Super Bowl Sunday.
- In an election year, election days.
- The end of the month.
- Summer, especially August.

Adapt this for your organization. The B'nai B'rith can ignore Good Friday; the Baptist choir can ignore Yom Kippur. A high school club can ignore election days; senior citizens can ignore the school schedule.

Of course, if you are committed to raising money, any day can be a good day. When I was doing door-to-door canvassing I always tried to weasel out of work on the days when it was pouring rain. I usually said something like, "It's such a terrible day, why don't we stay in and practice instead?" Of course, the field manager said, "Are you crazy! On a day like this? If you can get to someone's door,

how can they possibly say no?" Of course, he was right. The people
at the doors figured that, if we cared so much that we would canvass
in the rain, it must be a good cause, so we all easily made our
quotas.

Best Times for Fundraising

Now take a green pen and put in all the *best* times to raise money
in your community and from your members. First, discuss when
most of your people get paid. That is the time to ask them for
money. For example, senior citizens get their Social Security checks
on the third of the month. The seniors can organize a membership
blitz for the fourth of the month. For salaried workers, when do
they get paid in your community? Pitch them on membership
before payday, then close the sale on payday. If they have income
taxes deducted from their paychecks so they qualify for a refund,
ask them for larger donations when they get their refund checks in
March and April. For people who make more money and itemize
their deductions, ask them early in the year, then ask for another
donation in late November or early December. For corporations,
ask at the beginning of their fiscal year. For students, ask them for
money at the beginning of a new term and when they get their
scholarship checks. For farmers and ranchers, ask them for money
the week they sell their produce. Make a list of the types of people in
your organization, then devise a plan to ask them for money when
they have the most of it. If you are not sure, try the beginning of the
month or simply ask the prospective members when they get paid.

Plan a membership drive and put it on your calendar. Some community organizations schedule their membership campaigns before
their conventions, then use membership figures to assign seating for
delegations on the convention floor. If you are lucky enough to have
a hotly contested race for officers, all the nominees will have their
campaign committees signing up new members to get more votes.
Many direct action organizing and advocacy organizations say it is
easier to attract new members when they are involved in a hot fight
because they get more press coverage and their leaders are more enthusiastic. A good fight also simplifies your sales pitch by giving you

real clarity on the purpose and need for the organization. For this reason, action groups like to combine the membership drive with their action campaigns rather than separate them. On the other hand, service agencies find it easier to schedule the membership drive at a time of the year when the program work is lighter. Then they get a balanced work load for the entire year.

Next, plan your campaign to get large donations from individuals and corporations. This may be spread out over the year or concentrated in one or two months. In either case, your board will need to put it on the calendar in advance so they are sure it gets priority on their own work plans during the best times for asking. Otherwise it is easy to put off asking for big gifts forever. Since this is usually the most intimidating to new leaders, plan ahead so you are sure it will get done next year.

If you want to hold any special events, schedule them last. For new groups, it is often useful to plan several small events to give many people a chance to learn fundraising skills and to bring in new members. After the first two years, choose the one or two events your people like best and schedule them at a time that you can count on using every year. Then you can make more money with less work each year. You may choose to schedule a special event to coincide with an organizational event, such as creating an ad book to distribute at your convention, or you may want to schedule your special events so they are the only important thing on the agenda at that time of the year. Learn the dates of other annual events in your community, so you know if you want to run yours at the same time to get more customers or at a different time to get more workers.

Many groups like to find one holiday and make it their own. For example, public interest law firms organize fundraisers on Law Day, May 1. Women office workers' organizations schedule fundraisers on Secretaries' Day, the last Wednesday in April. Churches organize fundraisers around their patronal feast day. Consider if there is a holiday that would be appropriate for your group, then plan a repeatable special event to make it *your* day.

After you choose the date for your special event, count backward to plan the dates when you will need to make arrangements, book a band or a hall, print the tickets, start and finish sales, and make purchases. Be sure to set aside the week *after* the event to send thank-you notes, write a report, pay the bills, and handle any other follow-up work.

Making It Final

After you have your calendar planned for the next twelve months, review your program plans, budget, and fundraising strategy as described in Chapter 3. The board as a whole can vote to adopt the plan and the calendar, then take personal quotas to raise the budget. In this way, each person knows how much is expected of him or her. You will also assure that the ambitions of the organization will become realities and that *your* projects go into each board member's calendar *first*.

Since your leaders are volunteers giving you their time, you want to respect that time as much as possible. Planning ahead will seem to give you more time, help the entire board agree on the goals, and help you do first things first. Especially if your organization is just beginning its grass roots fundraising efforts, make *that* first until you have confident leaders and a dependable income to support your programs.

FIVE-YEAR PLANS

Five-year plans are usually the most difficult part of planning for a volunteer board of directors because very few of us make five-year plans in our private or professional lives. Like any other skill, you learn to do it by doing it. Especially if your organization has bold program goals or if grass roots fundraising is a new challenge for the leaders, you can help yourselves by having a five-year plan. The work will not happen exactly as planned, but the plan will help you get the most accomplished in the next years. Here is a sample of a five-year plan for a medium-sized group that wants to switch from grant dependency to self-sufficiency and a plan for a brand-new block club that wants to build up its own budget.

Sample Five-Year Plan for Large Organizations

Source of Money	1981	1982	1983	1984	1985	1986
1. CETA	$ 7,000	0	0	0	0	0
VISTA	8,000	0	0	0	0	0
2. Foundation						
Grant #1	10,000	$ 5,000	0	0	0	0
Grant #2	10,000	5,000	5,000	0	0	0
Grant #3	15,000	10,000	5,000	0	0	0
Grant #4	10,000	5,000	5,000	0	0	0
3. Corporate Donations	0	2,000	4,000	$ 6,000	$ 8,000	$ 10,000
4. Dues (Net per member $10)	0	14,400	28,800	43,200	57,600	72,000
5. Direct Mail by Members	0	1,080	4,320	6,480	12,960	16,200
6. Special Events	0	1,500	2,000	4,000	6,000	8,000
7. Speakers Bureau	0	500	500	500	500	500
Total:	$60,000	$44,480	$54,620	$60,180	$85,060	$106,700

GROWTH ASSUMPTIONS AND HOW WE GOT THESE NUMBERS

1. *Government money* will run out.

2. *Foundation grants* will run out over the next two to three years. This assumes these are all first-year grants in 1981.

3. *Corporate money* is there for the asking. In 1979 and 1980 corporations gave more money to nonprofits than foundations. In this strategy, our four best fundraisers will get an average of $500 each from corporations the first year, then get $500 each from new corporations each following year as newer fundraisers get the assignments to renew the older contributions. So corporate giving will grow at a controlled $2,000 a year. This will be easy to do, allows the busiest board members to make the most money in the least time by aiming for $500 per transaction, and assures us that corporate money never makes up more than 10 percent of our budget to eliminate any fears of perceived strings on corporate money.

4. *Dues.* Because our organization wants a dependable, renewable source of income, and because we want political strength in our own community, we decided to make dues from our own members the basis of our budget. We learned in the years that we took foundation grants and government money that we had no incentive to grow and hence had no real power. Changing to a budget based on dues will give us a reason, both financial and political, to recruit more people each year to strengthen the organization.

The plan: we will net $10 per member from their dues. Thus, if our costs go up, we will raise the dues so we are sure to keep our net per member at $10. We have twelve people on our board of directors. Each member of the board makes a commitment to sell twelve memberships a month for ten months. There are no sales in July and August, which we know from experience are the worst months to sell in our community. Board members will turn in the names and money of their new members each month at the monthly board meeting. It will be the job of the president to make sure each person makes his or her quota.

Twelve board members sell 12 memberships for 144 new members per month. At $10 net per member, we will bring in $1,440 per month for ten months, or $14,400 the first year. At the end of the year, we will have 1,440 dues-paying members.

The second year the new board makes the same commitment to raise money by selling 12 memberships per month for ten months. They also now have a base of 1,440 people who are active in committees. One committee will be the Membership Services Committee, which handles the mailing list and renewals. They bill and collect dues from last year's members, as well as finding new people to replace anyone who dies, moves, or quits. Each following year the board takes responsibility for recruiting 1,440 new people, and the Membership Services Committee handles renewals and replacements. At the end of five years the organization will have 7,200 dues-paying members.

5. *Direct Mail.* We know that some of our members can give us more money if we ask them. By asking our own list for money more than once a year, we will get more money from the people who can and want to pay more money to achieve our goals. Assuming we begin our membership drive in January each year, we can begin our

direct mail fundraising to our own list with a holiday mailing in 1982. Assuming conservatively that 5 percent of our people want to give us more money, and they give an average donation of $15, the first year we will make $1,080. The second year we can mail to our own list twice, in the spring and at the holidays (early November for Christmas and Hanukkah.) A 5 percent return and average donation of $15 yields $4,320 the second year and $6,480 the third year. By the fourth year we will have a base of 5,760 members, and we choose to mail now three times a year to our own list every year from now on. This way each person is asked for money four times a year, once for dues and three times for special projects or campaigns. Then the small number of people who want to give us more money will have an easy way to do it. When 5,760 people give us dues, at least 5 percent, or 288, can be expected to give us more through the mail.

6. *Special Events.* The first year, 1982, our board and members will produce three special events to raise money for the organization and help bring in new members. Each of these will average a net profit of $500, for an annual total of $1,500. The second year, 1983, we will evaluate which events were most popular, most profitable, most fun, produced the most new members and the most publicity. We will choose the best two and repeat them in the spring and the fall each year. Two people who are not now members of the board will be chosen to co-chair each event, and two people who are committee chairs this year will move up to be event chairs next year. Net profit for special events double the second year, from $500 to $1,000, so the two 1983 events will produce $2,000. Net profit will double again the third year from $1,000 to $2,000, so our two events will make $4,000. Every year after that the profits will go up $1,000 per event, so we will make $6,000 in 1985 and $8,000 in 1986. Profits go up each year because we have more experienced leadership, more members to sell tickets and do work, and better information on what is most profitable.

7. *Speakers Bureau.* We will ask audiences who want to hear our leaders speak about our program and issues to pay. If we ask a dollar a head per group, we can get $35 for a college class, $50 for a neighborhood group, $100 for a service club, and $150 for a con-

ference on our issues. Assume that we can average $50 per month for ten months, September to June (the school year). This will give us $500 per year. This amount will remain about the same every year unless we develop an exceptionally charismatic leader or if our issues become "the" hot issue for the year and community.

OVERVIEW

The first year we switch from grants to grass roots money our income will go down some; in this case the reduction is the amount we used to get from government money. Every year after that our income will go up. It will take us three years to get back to the amount of money we now get from grants and government money. During that time we will have to do rigorous cost cutting, look for more in-kind contributions, and increase our efforts to develop volunteer leaders rather than depend on paid staff people to do work.

After the first three years our membership base will produce enough money to allow us to increase our program, tackle a bolder goal, and get more results. Once we grow to the size we want, we can simply maintain that level fundraising strategy with a 10- to 15-percent increase to cover the increase in our costs from inflation.

Note: All of these calculations are *very* conservative. These are the lowest possible returns for an average group which makes fundraising a priority. If your group involves leaders with experience in successful fundraising, you will make even more.

Sample Five-Year Plan for a Block Club

	1982	1983	1984	1985	1986
Dues (100 families)	$1@ = $100	$2@ = $200	$3@ = $300	$3@ = $300	$4@ = $400
Block Party (Summer)	− 20	0	25	50	100
Bake Sale (Fall)	100	150	200	250	300
TOTAL	$180	$350	$525	$600	$800

GROWTH ASSUMPTIONS

1. This organization has 100 possible member families. The
easiest, quickest, and most democratic way of increasing their
budget is to increase the dues to cover their subsistence expenses.

2. The block party will lose money the first year and break even
the second, but following years will be a money maker as the club
learns what is profitable and what is not profitable.

3. The bake sale will make money the first year and every year
because it is quick, fun, and 100-percent profit.

HOW TO PREPARE A DONOR CARD

Smart fundraisers always keep complete records. Discipline yourself to prepare a report promptly after each event, keep up-to-date
records on your ongoing fundraisers like direct mail returns, and
always keep the books in order. Then you can quickly answer any
questions from a donor, officer, or committee member. Include an
honest evaluation of mistakes and all the good ideas you always get
after the event in your reports — they will be a boon to the next person.

One of the simplest but most important records to keep is the information on your donors. In addition to giving a receipt for every
donation, you can create a system for keeping track of each donor.
This can be as simple as handwritten notes on four- by six-inch file
cards from the dime store or as complicated as a computerized program. Choose whatever system will be best for your group. Ask
other local groups for advice on the system that is most efficient and
least expensive for your needs.

List on the card name, address, home phone, special interests,
employer, office address and phone, and whether or not the donor
wants to be reached at work. Then note each time the donor gives
you money or an in-kind donation by date, amount, and the source
of the donation. Record each time a member pays his or her dues.
Be sure to record which member first recruited the other, so that
member can encourage renewal of the other's dues.

Keep a cumulative total of each donor's gifts. Honor your loyal donors when their totals reach $500, $1,000, or $5,000. If they reach $10,000, make them life members!

It is useful to have a system for retrieving donors' names four ways: 1) by *name,* alphabetically, 2) by *location,* for example zip code or town, so you can notify residents of local events, 3) by *source,* so you can be sure to invite everyone who bought at the last auction to the next auction, 4) by *amount,* so you can ask everyone who gave you, say, $50 or more to become patrons for a special event.

FRIENDS OF THE PARKS DONOR   Card 1.
OLMSTED, Frederick Law   Phone: 555-6789
                102 Main Street   Recruited by:
                Riverside, II 60546   Sophia Haydn

Work: Park Designer   Phone: 555-1234
        Olmsted, Vaux and Company
        42 East Oak Street
        Riverside, IL 60546

Date	Amount	Source	Cumulative To Date
June, 1976	$15	Dues	15
Dec. 7, 1976	In Kind	Paper cutter for office (= $30)	45
June, 1977	$15	Dues renewal	60
Aug. 3, 1977	$25	Ad: Annual Meeting Ad Book	85
June, 1978	$15	Dues renewal	100
Aug. 7, 1978	$35	Ad: Shakespeare Festival Program	135
June, 1979	$15	Dues renewal	150
Sept. 2, 1979	$100	Honorarium—speech at U. of I.	250
April 3, 1980	$5	Bike maintenance workshop	255
June, 1980	$25	Dues renewal, new rate	280
Sept. 4, 1980	$25	"Save the Elm Trees" mailing	305
April 2, 1981	$50	Patron: Tribute to Duke Ellington	355
May 7, 1981	In Kind	Rakes for Park Cleanup (= $40)	395
June, 1981	$25	Dues renewal	420
Sept. 5, 1981	$50	Patron: Marathon Run	470

WHERE TO GET ADVICE

Experienced Members

First, and always best, ask people in your organization who have done fundraising before. The longer they have worked and the more money they have raised, the better advice they can give you.

Local Talent

Ask the people in your area who do the best membership fundraising. Find out how they do their fundraising. Father Leonard Dubi proposed CAP's first ad book because his church, St. Daniel the Prophet, had just finished one for its twenty-fifth anniversary. CAP's ad book was then copied by Chicago NOW and Women Employed (WE). Bernie Willow set up the bingo game for Our Lady of Grace School. It is one of the most successful bingos in Chicago. He also generously helped set up bingos for the sixteenth District Police Sports Program, the CAP Senior Citizens, a drug rehabilitation program, and Steelworkers Fight Back.

Professionals

Try to contact the best *professionals* in your area. Most large universities and hospitals have professional fundraisers. The president of the women's board of the local large disease association — cancer, heart, multiple sclerosis — often will have more than twenty years of experience and is as knowledgeable as the pros. People like that are usually very gracious and willing to talk. Don't be afraid to ask. When Roger Craver was director of development at Common Cause he invented the most successful direct mail membership program in the country. In two years only five people asked him for advice — and he loves to give advice!

Calendar Keepers

In small towns the chamber of commerce often maintains a calendar to clear events so groups won't duplicate dates. The chamber can tell you who else knows the most about the kind of event you are scheduling. In larger cities, check the daily newspapers, the Voluntary Action Center, the Convention and Tourism Bureau, and the Arts Council.

National Office

If your group is a chapter of a large national organization, find out what fundraising advice and material tailored for your group the national office offers. For example, National NOW offers interest-free loans to local chapters for seed money; the National Women's Political Caucus produces T-shirts and posters of Virginia Slade and Doonesbury by NWPC member Gary Trudeau for sale by local chapters; the League of Women Voters' national office prints excellent pamphlets for use by local leaders.

Similar Organizations

Contact other organizations similar to yours in other parts of the country. Events can be copied from one part of the country to another. The Chicago Junior League began its Paper Peddlers program by flying two women to Texas to learn how the Dallas League did it. Groups in Minnesota, California, and Tennessee adapted Illinois ad book material. You can easily send a letter to another group with the questions you need answered, followed by a phone call to confirm receipt and urge prompt response.

Public Relations Professionals

These people often have to "find a charity" for a promotional event — the opening of a theatre or restaurant, a wine tasting for a gourmet shop, or a showing of new fashions for a department store. If you establish a good relationship with a professional and prove you can deliver the number of people you promise, he or she will enjoy working with you. The Chicago Heart Association had not one, but *two* openings of the same restaurant — its original opening, then the reopening when the first owner bought it back from the second owner. The Heart Association made money each time. All you have to do is sell your tickets. It is the PR person and his or her client who have to make everything work.

Continuing Education

Many local colleges or adult education classes offer excellent courses in public relations for community groups, sales, and accounting. Check the local curriculum. If you will be doing a lot of correspondence without a secretary, you should learn to type.

There are many professional "fundraising," "development," "direct marketing," and "direct mail" seminars for sale. Most are overpriced and aimed at the dinosaurs—hugh national charities with many paid staff people. Representatives of small, rural, minority, ethnic, or women's groups almost always feel the course is not worth the price. *Never* sign up for one of these unless it has been personally recommended by someone you know and trust.

Books

Order and read the volumes listed in the bibliography, Chapter 14, that cover your interest. Ask your library to order them so everyone can use them.

HOW TO REBOUND FROM A FUNDLOSER

Murphy's Law: Anything that can go wrong will.
Flanagan's Corollary: Things that can't go wrong will.

My favorite TV show is Julia Child's "French Chef" cooking show on public television. One reason it is so good is that she not only shows you how to do everything right; she also shows you what to do if something goes wrong. I have seen her drop a poached salmon on the floor and patch it up with cream cheese frosting, poke a hole in her yule log cake and fill it in with meringue mushrooms, and curdle her hollandaise sauce only to save it with some lemon juice. The idea is that beginning cooks cannot afford to waste anything, so there has to be a way to save the ingredients.

The same thing is true in fundraising. Sometimes things go wrong and you have to save the ingredients. In your case, the ingredients are the morale of your members and the momentum of your campaign. Fortunately, there are ways to do this.

The best defense, of course, is a good offense, which is plenty of advance planning. You can't be wiped out by the blizzard of the century if you have already presold the tickets for an event. This is why the foundation of your budget must be the dues of the members rather than income from special events.

But let's say you were counting on the income from one event to carry you through one or two months. Crises happen. I have had the cash box stolen from a costume party and had the bartender get drunk and give away all the liquor at a dance. I have helped throw out 600 pounds of rotten chicken on a hot July day. I have had drunken speakers, stoned bands, and marital fistfights. Believe me, crises happen.

A group in Vermont got a wholesale order of honey that tasted like soy sauce. All the bottles it sold at retail came back. A group in Montana was promised a premier of a big movie only to have the same film open a week earlier across the state line only ten minutes away. A ballet board imported a world-famous French clothes designer to impress big donors ($5,000 +) at an expensive dinner. Unfortunately, the designer had a tantrum and refused to attend the dinner because the airport limousine drove off with all his clothes. Remember Flanagan's Corollary: Things that can't go wrong will.

So let's say you planned an event, worked hard, expected to make $300, and lost money. Psychologically, even breaking even is a loss. What do you do?

The first thing to do is discuss it in the committee as soon as possible. Right after the event is best, but if people are too tired, cross, or inebriated, schedule a meeting for the next day. The chairperson makes sure the committee members all gather to discuss the crisis. They need to talk about 1) what went wrong and 2) what can be done immediately to recoup the money.

The very first thing the chairperson must do is make sure this is not an occasion for pinning the blame on one person. If there were any mistakes of judgment, the chairperson should accept full responsibility. Simply say, "It was my fault." Then you won't debilitate the committee quarreling over who hired the rotten band.

1. What went wrong? Sometimes, it is a combination of causes that all point toward disharmony on the committee and among the membership as a whole. Fundraising reflects the health of the organization. If people are discouraged, or insult the leadership, or make promises they don't keep, it shows the success of the organization is not very important to them. If the causes are organizational, it is time to reorganize. It then becomes the problem of the executive board, not the fundraising committee.

If the members *are* committed to the group and really tried hard but still didn't make money, there are fundraising reasons and solutions. This is the time to discuss what went wrong. Was it that there were only five volunteers killing themselves when there should have been twenty people dividing the work? Was the choice of the event itself wrong—you learned your members really won't buy tickets to a night at the roller rink? Was the price too high or the appeal too low?

Make a list on paper or a blackboard of what went wrong and what to do differently next time. It is a great psychological relief to pin down the precise problem so it doesn't seem like *everything* is a disaster. It is also important that everyone on the committee realizes it is not anybody's "fault" (the chairperson has absorbed that) and that they all agree on what the problems are. This short-circuits the Monday morning quarterback who will want to call all involved to remind them that she never wanted to do a fashion show anyway.

2. What can be done immediately to recoup the money? The best cure for a defeat is a success. The group needed $300. The event lost $50. So now the group needs $350. Instead of dwelling on the problems, set a meeting in three days to decide what you will do immediately to make that $350. Everyone feels better knowing there is a goal in view. Ask each person to collect some ideas for how to raise the $350 right away. The obvious point that will be raised is: "We just tried to make $300 and failed. How can we make $350

next week?" The answer is: 1) Next week we will be older and smarter. 2) It is our responsibility to keep the organization alive. It needs $350, so we need to raise it. If anyone does not want to see the organization succeed or refuses to make a commitment to raise the money, it is time for the slacker to get off the committee and make room for someone else who will do the work. The only plus about crises is they are guaranteed to clear the deadwood off your committee in a big hurry! The chairperson should find fresh faces to replace them before the planning meeting.

Emergency Fundraisers

Here are a few emergency fundraisers you can use to raise the money quickly. They are discussed other places in this book. Depending on your membership, you may have to do two or three to make your goal. They all assume you have no seed money but several willing workers. In addition, there is always the basic level of grass roots fundraising: ask for money. Ask the members who have already given to give again and ask each of them to ask two other people to give. This will at least keep the phones working until you run your emergency fundraiser.

1. Selling memberships, Chapter 4.

2. Canvassing by members, Chapter 5.

3. House meetings, potluck supper, do-it-yourself cocktail party, or raffle, Chapter 8.

4. Dutch auction or memorabilia auction in the auction section or bake sale in the bazaar section of Chapter 9.

FOUNDATION FUNDRAISING

This book does not discuss foundation fundraising, but that does not mean that you should not consider foundations a source of money. Foundations are good for seed money for new projects or one-time grants for equipment or buildings. Unfortunately, most foundation grants run out after one to three years, so they are not dependable for ongoing expenses.

Your own public library will probably have a copy of *The Foun-*

dation Directory, 9th Edition that will tell you about the United States' 4,063 largest foundations—the source of 93 percent of all grant dollars. If you want to learn more about foundations and writing proposals, ask a veteran fundraiser or visit the nearest Foundation Center Cooperating Collection listed below. These are free libraries staffed by excellent professional librarians who can give you help. See the bibliography, Chapter 14, for recommended reading on foundations.

The Foundation Center

The Foundation Center has a nationwide network of foundation reference collections for free public use. These collections fall within three basic categories. The four reference libraries operated by the Center offer the widest variety of user services and the most comprehensive collections of foundation materials, including all of the Center's publications; books, services and periodicals on foundations and philanthropy; and foundation annual reports, newsletters, and press clippings. The New York and Washington, D.C. libraries contain the IRS returns for all currently active private foundations in the U.S. The Cleveland and San Francisco libraries contain the IRS records for those foundations in the midwestern and western states, respectively. The cooperating collections generally contain IRS records for only those foundations within their state, although they may request information or copies of other records from the New York library.

• This symbol identifies reference collections operated by foundations or area associations of foundations. They are often able to offer special materials or provide extra services, such as seminars or orientations for users, because of their close relationship to the local philanthropic community.

All other collections are operated by cooperating libraries. Generally they are located within public institutions and are open to the public during a longer schedule of hours and also offer visitors access to a well-developed general library research collection.

Please telephone individual libraries for more information about their holdings or hours. To check on new locations call toll free 800-424-9836 for current information.

Where to Go for Information on Foundation Funding

Reference Collections Operated by The Foundation Center

The Foundation Center
79 Fifth Avenue
New York, New York 10003
212-620-4230

The Foundation Center
Kent H. Smith Library
1442 Hanna Building
1422 Euclid Avenue
Cleveland, Ohio 44115
216-861-1933

The Foundation Center
1001 Connecticut Avenue, NW
Washington, D.C. 20036
202-331-1400

The Foundation Center
312 Sutter Street
San Francisco, Calif. 94108
415-397-0902

Cooperating Collections

Alabama
Birmingham Public Library
2020 Park Place
Birmingham 35203
205-226-3600

Auburn University at Montgomery Library
Montgomery 36193
205-279-9110

Alaska
University of Alaska,
Anchorage Library
3211 Providence Drive
Anchorage 99504
907-263-1848

Arizona
Phoenix Public Library
Social Sciences Subject
Department
12 East McDowell Road
Phoenix 85004
602-262-4782

Tucson Public Library
Main Library
200 South Sixth Avenue
Tucson 85701
602-791-4393

Arkansas
Westark Community College
Library
Grand Avenue at Waldron Rd.
Fort Smith 72913
501-785-4241

Little Rock Public Library
Reference Department
700 Louisiana Street
Little Rock 72201
501-370-5950

California
California Community
Foundation
1151 West Sixth Street
Los Angeles 90017
213-413-4719

Cooperating Collections (continued)

- San Diego Community Foundation
625 Broadway, Suite 1015
San Diego 92101
619-239-8815

Santa Barbara Public Library
Reference Section
40 East Anapamu
P. O. Box 1019
Santa Barbara 93102
805-962-7653

Colorado
Denver Public Library
Sociology Division
1357 Broadway
Denver 80203
303-571-2190

Connecticut
Hartford Public Library
Reference Department
500 Main Street
Hartford 06103
203-525-9121

Delaware
Hugh Morris Library
University of Delaware
Newark 19711
302-738-2965

Florida
Jacksonville Public Library
Business, Science, and Industry Department
122 North Ocean Street
Jacksonville 32202
904-633-3926

Miami—Dade Public Library
Florida Collection
One Biscayne Boulevard
Miami 33132
305-579-5001

Georgia
Atlanta Public Library
Ivan Allen Department
1 Margaret Mitchell Square
Atlanta 30303
404-688-4646

Hawaii
Community Resource Center
The Hawaiian Foundation
Financial Plaza of the Pacific
111 South King Street
Honolulu 96813
808-525-8548

Idaho
Caldwell Public Library
1010 Dearborn Street
Caldwell 83605
208-459-3242

Illinois
- Donors Forum of Chicago
208 South LaSalle Street
Chicago 60604
312-726-4882

Sangamon State University
   Library
Shepherd Road
Springfield 62708
217-786-6633

Indiana
Indianapolis—Marion County
   Public Library
40 East St. Clair Street
Indianapolis 46204
317-269-1733

Iowa
Public Library of Des Moines
100 Locust Street
Des Moines 50308
515-283-4259

Cooperating Collections (continued)

Kansas
Topeka Public Library
Adult Services Department
1515 West Tenth Street
Topeka 66604
913-233-2040

Kentucky
Louisville Free Public Library
Fourth and York Streets
Louisville 40203
502-584-4154

Louisiana
East Baton Rouge Parish
   Library
Centroplex Library
120 St. Louis Street
Baton Rouge 70802
504-344-5291

New Orleans Public Library
Business and Science Division
219 Loyola Avenue
New Orleans 70140
504-596-2583

Maine
University of Southern Maine
Center for Research and
   Advanced Study
246 Deering Avenue
Portland 04102
207-780-4411

Maryland
Enoch Pratt Free Library
Social Science and History
   Department
400 Cathedral Street
Baltimore 21201
301-396-5320

Massachusetts
• Associated Grantmakers of
   Massachusetts
294 Washington Street
Suite 501
Boston 02108
617-426-2608

Boston Public Library
Copley Square
Boston 02117
617-536-5400

Michigan
Alpena County Library
211 North First Avenue
Alpena 49707
517-356-6188

Henry Ford Centennial Library
16301 Michigan Avenue
Dearborn 48216
313-943-2337

Purdy Library
Wayne State University
Detroit 48202
313-577-4040

Michigan State University
   Libraries
Reference Library
East Lansing 48824
517-353-8816

University of Michigan — Flint
UM — F Library
Reference Department
Flint 48503
313-762-3408

Grand Rapids Public Library
Sociology and Education Dept.
Library Plaza
Grand Rapids 49502
616-456-4411

Cooperating Collections (continued)

Michigan Technological
  University Library
Highway U.S. 41
Houghton 49931
906-487-2507

Minnesota
Minneapolis Public Library
Sociology Department
300 Nicollett Mall
Minneapolis 55401
612-372-6555

Mississippi
Jackson Metropolitan Library
301 North State Street
Jackson 39201
601-944-1120

Missouri
• Clearinghouse for Mid-
    continent Foundations
Univ. of Missouri, Kansas City
Law School, Suite 1-300
52nd Street and Oak
Kansas City 64113
816-276-1176

Kansas City Public Library
311 East 12th Street
Kansas City 64106
816-221-2685

• Metropolitan Association for
    Philanthropy, Inc.
5585 Pershing Ave., Ste. 150
St. Louis 63112
314-361-3900

Springfield–Greene County
  Library
397 East Central Street
Springfield 65801
417-866-4636

Montana
Eastern Montana College Library
Reference Department
1500 N. 30th Street
Billings 59101
406-657-2262

Nebraska
W. Dale Clark Library
Social Sciences Department
215 South 15th Street
Omaha 68102
402-444-4822

Nevada
Clark County Library
1401 East Flamingo Road
Las Vegas 89109
702--733-7810

Washoe County Library
301 South Center Street
Reno 89505
702-785-4190

New Hampshire
• The New Hampshire Charitable
    Fund
One South Street
Concord 03301
603-225-6641

New Jersey
New Jersey State Library
Governmental Reference
185 West State Street
Trenton 08625
609-292-6220

New Mexico
New Mexico State Library
300 Don Gaspar Street
Santa Fe 87503
505-827-3824

Cooperating Collections (continued)

New York
New York State Library
Cultural Education Center
Humanities Section
Empire State Plaza
Albany 12230
518-474-7645

Buffalo and Erie County Public
   Library
Lafayette Square
Buffalo 14203
716-856-7525

Levittown Public Library
Reference Department
One Bluegrass Lane
Levittown 11756
516-731-5728

Plattsburgh Public Library
Reference Department
15 Oak Street
Plattsburgh 12901
518-563-0921

Rochester Public Library
Business and Social Sciences
   Division
115 South Avenue
Rochester 14604
716-428-7328

Onondaga County Public
   Library
335 Montgomery Street
Syracuse 13202
315-473-4490

North Carolina
North Carolina State Library
109 East Jones Street
Raleigh 27611
919-733-3270

• The Winston-Salem Foun-
   dation
229 First Union National Bank
   Building
Winston-Salem 27101
919-725-2382

North Dakota
The Library
North Dakota State University
Fargo 58105
701-237-8876

Ohio
Public Library of Cincinnati
   and Hamilton County
Education Department
800 Vine Street
Cincinnati 45202
513-369-6940

Toledo — Lucas County
   Public Library
Social Science Department
325 Michigan Street
Toledo 43624
419-255-7055 ext. 221

Oklahoma
• Oklahoma City University Library
NW 23rd at North Blackwelder
Oklahoma City 73106
405-521-5072

Tulsa City-County Library
   System
400 Civic Center
Tulsa 74103
918-581-5144

Oregon
Library Association of Portland
Government Documents Room
801 S.W. Tenth Avenue
Portland 97205
503-223-7201

Cooperating Collections (continued)

Pennsylvania
The Free Library of
  Philadelphia
Logan Square
Philadelphia 19103
215-686-5423

Hillman Library
University of Pittsburgh
Pittsburgh 15260
412-624-4528

Rhode Island
Providence Public Library
Reference Department
150 Empire Street
Providence 02903
401-521-7722

South Carolina
South Carolina State Library
Reader Services Department
1500 Senate Street
Columbia 29211
803-758-3181

South Dakota
South Dakota State Library
State Library Building
322 South Fort Street
Pierre 57501
605-773-3131

Tennessee
Knoxville-Knox County Public
  Library
500 West Church Avenue
Knoxville 37902
615-523-0781

Memphis Public Library
1850 Peabody Avenue
Memphis 38104
901-725-8876

Texas
• The Hogg Foundation for
    Mental Health
The University of Texas
Austin 78712
512-471-5041

Corpus Christi State
  University Library
6300 Ocean Drive
Corpus Christi 78412
512-991-6810

Dallas Public Library
Grants Information Service
1515 Young Street
Dallas 75201
214-749-4100

• El Paso Community Foundation
El Paso National Bank Building
Suite 1616
El Paso 79901
915-533-4020

Houston Public Library
Bibliographic & Information
  Center
500 McKinney Avenue
Houston 77002
713-224-5441 ext. 265

• Funding Information Library
507 Brooklyn
San Antonio 78215
512-227-4333

Utah
Salt Lake City Public Library
Business and Science Department
209 East Fifth South
Salt Lake City 84111
801-363-5733

Cooperating Collections (continued)

Vermont
State of Vermont Department of
  Libraries
Reference Services Unit
111 State Street
Montpelier 05602
802-828-3261

Virginia
Grants Resources Library
Hampton City Hall
22 Lincoln St., 9th Floor
Hampton 23669
804-727-6496

Richmond Public Library
Business, Science, & Technology
  Department
101 East Franklin Street
Richmond 23219
804-780-8223

Washington
Seattle Public Library
1000 Fourth Avenue
Seattle 98104
206-625-4881

Spokane Public Library
Reference Department
West 906 Main Avenue
Spokane 99201
509-838-3361

West Virginia
Kanawha County Public Library
123 Capitol Street
Charleston 25301
304-343-4646

Wisconsin
Marquette University Memorial
  Library
1415 West Wisconsin Avenue
Milwaukee 53233
414-224-1515

Wyoming
Laramie County Community
  College Library
1400 East College Drive
Cheyenne 82007
307-634-5853

• Canada
The Canadian Centre for
  Philanthropy
185 Bay Street, Suite 504
Toronto, Ontario M5J 1K6
416-364-4875

Mexico
Biblioteca Benjamin Franklin
Londres 16
Mexico City 6, D.F.
525-591-0244

Puerto Rico
Universidad Del Sagrado Corazon
M.M.T. Guevarra Library
Correo Calle Loiza
Santurce 00914
809-728-1515 ext. 274

Virgin Islands
College of the Virgin Islands
  Library
Saint Thomas
U.S. Virgin Islands 00801
809-774-9200 ext. 487

• England
Charities Aid Foundation
12 Crane Court
Fleet Street
London EC4A 2JJ
1-583-7772

TRAINING SCHOOLS
FOR ORGANIZERS AND LEADERS

Grass roots fundraising is only one of the challenges for membership organizations. You may want or need more training in all the other skills needed to run a successful organization today, such as planning strategy, choosing tactics, building membership, developing leaders, strengthening leader-staff relationships, conducting action research, and maximizing your media campaigns. Fortunately, there are several excellent schools that specialize in training organizers and leaders.

All of them offer training sessions at their own schools, internstyle field placement training, and specialized on-site courses. The courses are taught by experienced professional organizers and veteran leaders of successful membership organizations. All of them also offer ongoing consultation under contract. In addition, they can recommend local individuals for personal consultation.

For information on costs, curriculum, criteria for admission, and applications, write:

Center for Third World Organizing (CTWO)
1459 Columbia Rd., NW
Washington, DC 20009

Center for Urban Encounter (CUE)
3416 University Ave., SE
Minneapolis, MN 55414

Highlander Research and Education Center
Rt. 3, Box 370
New Market, TN 37820

Industrial Areas Foundation (IAF)
675 W. Jerico Turnpike
Huntington, NY 11743

The Institute for Social Justice
4415 San Jacinto
Dallas, TX 75204

The Midwest Academy
600 W. Fullerton Ave.
Chicago, IL 60614

National Training and Information Center
1123 W. Washington Blvd.
Chicago, IL 60607

North County Institute
Box 184
Woodsville, NH 03785

Organize Training Center
1208 Market St.
San Francisco, CA 94103

Pacific Institute for Community Organizing (PICO)
3914 E. 14th St.
Oakland, CA 94601

Resources—Fundraising Training

Many national organizations offer workshops on fundraising at their national or regional conferences. If your delegate likes the workshop, ask the trainers if they do on-site training. If you receive grants from large foundations or government agencies, they may be able to provide or recommend successful trainers.

In your own community you may be able to get good training or advice from the United Way, the Foundation Center Cooperating Collection (see the preceding list), local colleges, or local foundations. In large cities the Small Business Administration offers free workshops on starting businesses, marketing, record keeping, and taxes. These are designed for small for-profit businesses, but they are also helpful to small and medium-sized nonprofit groups. Best of all, ask the experts—leaders who have organized successful funding strategies for similar organizations or similar communities. You know which organizations in your own community are thriving; ask them for advice and where they go for training.

Bibliography

Here are more publications to give you more detailed advice on other aspects of successful fundraising. Many of the best were written by veteran volunteers to help other fundraisers in their own organization. All of them are good values, easy to read, and easy to use.

All addresses are in the United States unless noted. All prices quoted are for single copies as of 1985 and include postage and handling for mail orders. Ask for the quantity discount if you want to order in large numbers. If you are ordering a book from a nonprofit organization, include your check or money order made out to the name of the organization. If the price has gone up, you will be billed for the increase; if the publication is out of print, your check will be returned.

THE BASICS

You must have these volumes and know how to use them. If you cannot buy your own books, the public library will have copies of all of these that you can use.

1. Dictionary: any current and complete paperback.
2. Thesaurus: any current and complete paperback.

3. Etiquette: any paperback such as *Amy Vanderbilt's Everyday Etiquette,* especially useful for letters and invitations.

4. Media directory: a list of the working press in your community, including the names of current staff, with addresses and telephone numbers of newspapers, wire services, radio, and television. This may be published by the local public relations professionals' association, the telephone company, the Newspaper Guild, or a clipping service. Ask a local public relations professional where to get one.

5. Telephone directories for your town and any suburbs or towns that affect your group. If you lobby, you should also get the telephone directories (both white pages and *Yellow Pages*) for your state capital and Washington, DC. All are free from your local telephone company office. In large cities the *Yellow Pages* often include a street guide; a directory of federal, state, and local government offices; professional sports schedules; and other helpful information.

6. Current postal regulations. Free from your local post office, these will tell you how to prepare bulk mailings (second or third class) and first-class mailings.

7. Subscriptions to the daily newspapers, local weeklies, and anything else your membership reads.

8. A current library card. Read magazines and books there. Get to know the reference room librarian. Ask him or her to teach you how to find and use current reference books such as almanacs, atlases, dictionaries, directories, and encyclopedias.

9. Calendars. A twelve-month calendar posted in the office or meeting place with important organizational dates marked on it tells all members that the organization has ambitious goals for the year and that newcomers are welcome. Each member of the board and any staff should also have calendars they can carry at all times.

10. Address book or card file to store and retrieve names, addresses, and phone numbers.

11. Police and fire regulations for crowds. Emergency numbers for local police, fire department, hospital, paramedics, and ambulance.

12. The newsletters from the network, state, regional, or national federation of organizations that work on the same issues as your group.

THE BEST HOW-TO MANUALS

Fund Raising Handbook: A Guide for Ways and Means Chairmen. 1980. 32 pp. 50¢. Consumer Services, The Sperry and Hutchinson Co., 2900 W. Seminary Dr., Fort Worth, TX 76133. Best introduction to grass roots fundraising, special events, and asking for money. Recommended to new fundraisers.

The Grass Roots Fundraising Book: How to Raise Money in Your Community. Joan Flanagan. 1982. 300 pp. $8.95. Contemporary Books, 180 N. Michigan Ave., Chicago, IL 60601. Best book for any group that wants to raise its own budget. Includes information on how to set up a fundraising program, how to choose the right strategy for your group, and how to raise money and build your organization at the same time. Best available bibliography recommends another one hundred books and articles on fundraising.

Helping NOW Grow: Fundraising. Chicago Chapter of the National Organization for Women (NOW). 1975. 20 pp. $2.50 Chicago NOW, 53 W. Jackson, Room 924, Chicago, IL 60604. Good introduction to ad books, budgets, planning, raffles, and door-to-door canvassing by members.

How to Grow a Parents' Group. Diane Mason, Gayle Jensen, and Carolyn Ryzewocz. 1979. 212 pp. $7. CDG Enterprises, P.O. Box 97, Western Springs, IL 60558. Excellent, very readable account of how three women began a Mothers' Hot Line that grew into a comprehensive countywide program for new parents. Excellent chapters on planning, budgets, setting goals and objectives, preparing newsletters, and avoiding burnout and attrition. Recommended to volunteer groups with no staff.

The Nonprofit Money Game. Funding Information Service, Junior League of Washington, DC. 1975. 32 pp. $1.75. Junior League of Washington, DC, 3039 M Street, NW, Washington, DC 20007. Good booklet for beginners. League veterans discuss setting up a successful campaign, proposal writing, benefits, telethons, and personal contact. Features advice on developing a "diversified board of directors representative of the community" including my favorite quote, "Remember the Three G's: Get, Give, or Get off."

The Successful Volunteer Organization, Getting Started and Getting Results in Nonprofit, Charitable, Grass Roots and Community Groups. Joan Flanagan. 1981. 376 pp. $11.95. Contemporary Books, 180 N. Michigan Ave., Chicago, IL 60601. Most complete manual on starting and managing a nonprofit, this book will answer all your questions about choosing a board, long-range planning, holding meetings, and organizing your fundraising. More advice on diversified fundraising plans and how to become self-sufficient.

Survival Planning for the '80s: Fundraising Strategies for Grass-roots Organizations. Tim Sweeney and Michael Seltzer. 1982. 20 pp. $4. Community Careers Resource Center, 1520 16th Street, NW, Washington, DC 20036. Excellent guide to help your board plan their fundraising; features principles of fundraising and planning, the world of money with useful references, and program planning and fundraising.

Best Magazine

The Grassroots Fundraising Journal. Published six times a year. $20. Grassroots Fundraising Journal, P.O. Box 14754, San Francisco, CA 94114. Produced by Kim Klein and Lisa Honig, professional fundraising trainers who specialize in self-suficiency fundraising. Each *Journal* features an in-depth how-to article on fundraising methods such as beginning direct mail, finding major donors, or marketing products. Read first-person success stories from the leaders, fundraisers, and organizers of self-sufficient groups, especially *how* they did it.

How-to Books for Special Audiences

CHILDREN

Note: Both of these books are also good for any adults with low reading skills and for adult groups that want to use service-type fundraisers to make money because they have high energy but low incomes.

Good Cents. Every Kid's Guide to Making Money. The Amazing Life Games Company and friends. 1975. 128 pp. $3.95. Houghton

Mifflin Co., One Beacon St., Boston, MA 02107. My favorite fund-raising book, full of forty-four foolproof ideas for children and teenagers to raise money. Especially good for holidays and services.

How Kids Can Really Make Money. Shari Lewis. 1979. 96 pp. $1.95. Holt, Rinehart and Winston, 383 Madison Ave., New York, NY, 10017. Seventeen plans to make money for children to use to make money for themselves or their clubs.

COOPERATIVES

The Food Co-op Handbook: How to Bypass Supermarkets to Control the Quality and Price of the Food You Eat. The Co-op Handbook Collective. 1975. 382 pp. $4.95. Houghton Mifflin Co., One Beacon St., Boston, MA 02107. Excellent book on organizing food co-ops, from the first meeting to expanding into federations. Take advantage of the firsthand experience of the dozens of people who helped with the book. Recommended to any group that wants to raise money for a cooperative.

Management Manual For Co-operative Houses. Max Kummerow and NASCO. 1972. 18 pp. 75¢. North America Students of Co-operation (NASCO), Box 7293, Ann Arbor, MI 48107. Written for people who want to start or manage a student housing co-op. Recommended to anyone trying to do the long-range fiscal planning if you own (or want to own) real estate that is owned and operated by a group.

PERFORMING ARTS

Subscribe Now! Building Arts Audiences through Dynamic Subscription Promotion. Danny Newman. 1977. 276 pp. $7.95. Theatre Communications Group, 355 Lexington Ave., New York, NY 10017. Foolproof system for building a dependable income for the performing arts through season subscription sales, the theatrical equivalent of dues. This fun, easy-to-read book is packed with ideas for all groups that want to get large numbers of people from their community to support their program. See especially his system for brochures, mailing lists, block sales, and door-to-door sales.

POLITICS

Campaign Workbook. Betsy Wright. 1978. 202 pp. in a looseleaf binder. $15. National Women's Education Fund, 1410 Q Street, NW, Washington, DC 20009. How to put together a winning political campaign. Covers planning; personnel; reaching large, medium, and small donors; budgets; and control.

Also contact your political party for a list of its current publications:

Democratic National Committee, 1625 Massachusetts Ave., NW, Washington, DC 20036.

Republican National Committee, 310 First St., SE, Washington, DC 20003.

PROFESSIONALS

Anatomy of a Counter-Bar Association: The Chicago Council of Lawyers. Michael Powell. 1979. 42 pp. $3. *ABA Foundation Journal* reprint. Vol. 1979, Summer, No. 3. The American Bar Foundation, 1155 E. 60th St., Chicago, IL 60637. Study of the start and early years of an alternative bar association, founded to promote the law—instead of lawyers. Interesting report on its debates on how to set dues, what to offer, what *not* to offer, and how to recruit high-priced professionals for a good cause.

To Light One Candle: A Manual for Organizing, Funding and Maintaining Public Service Projects. Nora Jean Levin and Janet Dempsey Steiger. 1978. 162 pp. $6. American Bar Association, Division of Bar Services, 1155 East 60th St., Chicago, IL 60637. Written to tell state and local bar associations how to raise money from lawyers over and above dues. Recommended to any organization that wants to generate dependable annual income from professionals of high salary.

WOMEN

Dollars and Sense: A Community Fundraising Manual for Shelters and Other Nonprofit Organizations. Marya Grambs, Pam

Miller, et al. 1982. 116 pp. $18.00. Western Center on Domestic Violence, 870 Market St., Suite 1058, San Francisco, CAA 94102. The best manual available for teaching women to raise money for their own programs. Features outstanding chapters on attitudes towards money, the politics of fundraising, planning, membership, special events, capital fundraising drives, starting a business, and even the value of men's auxiliary! Highly recommended to any women's organization.

HISPANICS

Semillas De Prosperidad or How to Cultivate Resources from the Private Sector. Carol Guzman. 1982. 90 pp. $3.95. Neighborhood Housing Service, P.O. Box 7476, Albuquerque, NM 87194. Written in English, this book offers excellent advice on the process of researching and soliciting funds from corporations and foundations. Features excellent section on "Hispanics and Private Funders."

NATIVE AMERICANS

Native Self-Sufficiency. Quarterly newsletter. 16 pp. $6/year. Seventh Generation Fund, P.O. Box 10, Forestville, CA 95436. Every issue shares the best current information from tribes in the U.S. and Canada on building strong, self-sufficient Indian communities that respect their own culture and traditions.

MOTIVATION

Designs for Fund-Raising: Principles, Patterns, Techniques. Harold J. Seymour. 1966. 210 pp. $15.95. McGraw-Hill Book Co., 1221 Avenue of the Americas, New York, NY 10020. Best book on how to design, lead, and maintain a campaign to ask for money in person from large donors. Best section anywhere on how to motivate volunteer fundraisers and potential donors. This is the bible for professional fundraisers and a source of quotable quotes such as

Seymour's (prophetic) quip. "No one ever bought a Buick because General Motors needed the money." Most examples are huge institutions such as Yale and Princeton, but you can adapt the advice to a group of any size.

The Forgotten Heroes of the Montgomery Bus Boycott. Vernon Jarrett. 1975. 12 pp. $2. DuSable Museum of African American History, 740 E. 56th Pl., Chicago, IL 60637. Features the story of Georgia Gilmore who organized her neighbors into "The Club from Nowhere" that began with $14 and ultimately raised $800 a week. This dedicated fundraising paid to operate a free car pool for 40,000 blacks for 381 days in 1955 until they won desegregation of the Montgomery, Alabama, bus system. A powerful story to inspire your fundraisers to aim high.

The Success System That Never Fails. W. Clement Stone. 1962. 280 pp. $2.50. Pocket Books, 1230 Avenue of the Americas, New York, NY 10020. Excellent book on how to motivate yourself and others to achieve your goals. Emphasizes the importance of on-the-job training, setting goals, and self-improvement; it's great for busy people, because it shows you that it takes less work to succeed than to fail. Especially recommended to the board, the fundraising committee, and any fundraising staff.

Success Through a Positive Mental Attitude. Napoleon Hill and W. Clement Stone. 1960. 302 pp. $1.95. Pocket Books, 1230 Avenue of the Americas, New York, NY 10020. Most popular book on how to motivate yourself and others to achieve your goals. Based on Napoleon Hill's principle. "Whatever the mind of man or woman can conceive and believe, it can achieve." Two legends share their tested advice for success and happiness. An excellent book to give your fundraisers.

CHAPTER 4: RAISING MONEY FROM MEMBERS

The Board of Directors. Lisa Honig and Kim Klein. 1984. 14 pp. $6. Grassroots Fundraising Journal, P.O. Box 14754, San Francisco, CA 94114. Best advice on how to evaluate, expand, and inspire your Board of Directors.

Membership Handbook: A Guide for Membership Chairmen. 1977. 24 pp. 50¢. The Sperry and Hutchinson Co., Consumer Services, 2900 W. Seminary Dr., Fort Worth, TX 76133. How to plan and run a campaign to get new members for your organization. How to keep them: "Use a member or lose a member." Useful survey forms and checklists.

Major Gifts Campaigns. Lisa Honig and Kim Klein. 1984. 20 pp. $7. Grassroots Fundraising Journal, P.O. Box 14754, San Francisco, CA 94114. Foolproof advice to train your leaders to ask for large gifts—and get them!

Survey Savvy: A Guide for Understanding Surveys. Marjorie Getchell et al. 1979. 29 pp. 30¢. League of Women Voters of Massachusetts, 120 Boylston St., Boston, MA 02116. Best guide to planning and conducting surveys, verifying and analyzing data, and preparing reports. Use their advice on how to use handmade punch cards for sorting data, popularly known as the poor person's computer, to set up your donor cards. Written by and for skilled volunteers.

Hint: Check with your own network or national organization for publications to make your membership drive a success. Many national and international organizations publish excellent materials tailored for their own local groups such as the *B'nai B'rith Handbook for Membership Growth and Continuity.*

Fees for Services

Fee Management for Noncredit Programs. Bob Wagner 1981. 18 pp. $8. Lifelong Learning Resources, P.O. Box 1425, 1221 Thurston, Manhattan, KS 66502. Good introduction to making budgets, setting fees, determining break-even, and calculating a profit.

CHAPTER 5: RAISING MONEY FROM BELIEVERS

Campaigns for Corporate Contributions

A Case Study of the C.O.P.S. Ad Book. Arnie Graf. 1980. 8 pp. $2. Organize Training Center, 1208 Market St., San Francisco, CA 94102. Excellent account of using an ad book campaign to raise money and teach organizational principles. Emphasizes that selling ads is not begging. It is (1) collecting dues from everyone in San Antonio who benefited from Communities Organized for Public Services (COPS) work and (2) developing relationships of mutual respect with major businesses. Graf was staff director of COPS when it did its first ad book in 1977, net $47,000, and 1978, net $60,000. Suggestions and training can be copied by any citizens' group.

Fund Raising in the Private Sector. Raymond F. Murray et al. 1980. 46 pp. $5.50. National Committee for Prevention of Child Abuse, 332 S. Michigan Ave., Suite 1250, Chicago, IL 60604. See especially the case study by John E. Guth, Jr., vice-president, Data Processing Division of the IBM Corporation, who describes his experience raising money for the Kansas Chapter of the National Committee for Prevention of Child Abuse. A good example for new groups to use to plan their work, because Guth learned that Executives in Kansas City and Wichita "realized something was happening in child abuse, but they didn't know our organization."

The Learning Exchange. G. Robert Lewis and Diane R. Kinishi. 1977. 151 pp. $6.50. The Learning Exchange, 2940 N. Lincoln Ave., Chicago, IL 60657. How to set up and operate a phone referral service to connect teachers and learners. Includes advice on asking for corporate donations useful for any group. Features seventy-eight pages of samples, including the corporate support brochure, sales letters, corporate membership plans, and thank-you letters that raised $76,450 from corporations in five years.

Nonprofit Piggy Goes to Market. Robin Simons, Lisa Farber Miller, and Peter Lengsfelder. 1984. 30 pp. $9.90. Children's Museum of Denver, 2121 Crescent Drive, Denver, CO 80211. Subtitled "How the Denver Children's Museum Earns $600,000 Annually," this clever booklet shares the do's and don'ts of finding corporate partners for income genereateing projects. Loaded with examples, humor, and useful advice from Dr. Richard Steckel, who used this system to take the Denver Children's Museum from grant-dependent poverty to prosperous self-sufficiency in only three years. *Any* group can use this advice, especially good for museums.

Special Events Fundraising. 1975 and 1977. 16 pp. $3.50. The Grantsmanship Center NEWS, 1031 S. Grand Ave., Los Angeles,

CA 90015. Features "Ten Steps to a Million Dollar Fund Raiser," by Sally Berger. This is the best thing in print on how to go to corporations and big businesses for money. Berger directed a yearlong campaign to raise money for a hospital research program. As a volunteer, she asked for a minimum of $500 per company and raised more than $1.4 million. She explains her system for putting together a prospect list, getting appointments, researching the prospective donor, preparing persuasive sales material, closing the sale, and the importance of the thank-you note! Recommended to any group that wants to ask for corporate money.

Ask the librarian at the public library to teach you how to use the reference materials concerning businesses and business people. Some materials that will help you do your homework on local businesses and executives are *Who's Who in America; Who's Who in the West* (or your geographic region); local professional directories for lawyers, accountants, etc.; local and state chamber of commerce business guides; *Moody's Handbook of Common Stocks;* local reference books on publicly held corporations. Ask the librarian in the periodical room to show you *Business Week, Forbes, Fortune, The Wall Street Journal,* and local business magazines and newspapers.

Door-to-Door Canvassing

Knock, Knock . . . Who's There? A Citizen's Guide to Door-to-Door Canvassing. David L. Grubb and David R. Zwick. 1976. 60 pp. $5. West Virginia Citizens Action Group, 1324 Virginia St., E, Charleston, WV 25301. Good introduction to door-to-door canvassing, including sample forms, ads, and pitches. Also check with local groups who canvass for more up-to-date advice.

Direct Mail

A Citizen's Guide to Direct Mail Fundraising. David L. Grubb and David R. Zwick. 1976. 60 pp. $5. West Virginia Citizens Action Group, 1324 Virginia St., E, Charleston, WV 25301. Good introduction to writing, fundraising letters, and choosing packages and lists.

Direct Mail—A Preliminary View. Charlene Divoky. 1981. 5 pp. $3 and self-addressed stamped envelope. Divoky & Associates, 14 Skillings Rd., Winchester, MA 01890. Good introduction to the methods of direct mail fundraising and possible income from a well-planned campaign.

Evaluating Your Fund Raising Program. Roger Craver, Charlene Divoky, and Sanky Perlowin. 1981. Audio cassette, $10. Hoke Communications, Inc., 224 Seventh St., Garden City, NY 11530. Three top professionals illustrate typical questions, asked to begin a direct mail campaign through an interview of the "Executive Director" of the "Fund for the Hairless Raccoons." Features excellent advice from Craver on goal setting and from Perlowin on how to present your cause and how to ask for the largest possible gift.

Payroll Deduction Plans

Introduction to Payroll Deduction Solicitation. Stephen L. Paprocki, 1985. 30 pp. $5.50. Steven L. Paprocki, 1332 C Street, Alameda, CA 94501. How to start a plan for workers in your community to donate money through payroll deduction. Frank discussion of the problems and possibilities by a man who founded one successful fund and advises several others.

Contact the National Committee for Responsive Philanthropy, 2001 S Street, NW, #620, Washington, DC 20009, for a sample of their newsletter, a list of publications about payroll deduction plans, and referrals to plans operating in your area.

Speakers Bureau

Speaking Out: Setting Up a Speakers Bureau. No. 299. 1977. 2 pp. 65¢. League of Women Voters of the United States, 1730 M St., NW, Washington, DC 20036. Good introduction to choosing topics, training speakers, selling speakers, and handling bookings.

How to Talk with Practically Anybody about Practically Anything. Barbara Walters, 1971. 241 pp. $2.25. Dell Publishing

Co., 1 Dag Hammarskjold Plaza, New York, NY 10017. Excellent practical advice for anyone from the experienced speaker to the novice "strangled with panic." Features "the care and handling of a guest speaker" and "you're the speaker."

Newsletters

See also *Editing Your Newsletter. A Guide to Writing, Design, and Production* and *How to Do Leaflets, Newsletters and Newspapers* listed under the section for Chapter 11: Publicity.

CHAPTER 6:
RAISING MONEY FROM THE GENERAL PUBLIC

Starting a Business

FOR-SALE PUBLICATIONS

Small Business Administration Publications. There are many inexpensive booklets available from the Superintendent of Documents U.S. Government Printing Office prepared by the Small Business Administration (SBA). These are all easy to read and very low priced. They include general "how-to" manuals such as *The Handbook of Small Business Finance* ($1.50) and advice on starting and managing specific types of businesses such as a car wash, pet shop, small retail music store, or employment agency. To get the list of current publications and prices, write the Small Business Administration, P.O. Box 15434, Fort Worth, TX 76119 or call the SBA offices in large cities listed in the white pages under "Small Business Administration" or "United States Government." Ask for SBA 115B *For Sale Management Assistance Booklets.* (4 pp.)

Looking at Income-Generating Businesses for Small Non-Profit Organizations. William A. Duncan. 1983. 25 pp. $3. Center for Community Change, 1000 Wisconsin Ave., NW, Washington, DC 20007. Helpful introduction to the risks and responsibilities of starting a business. Good list of questions for the board members to ask when they plan the business.

Starting and Managing a Small Business of Your Own. Wendell
O. Metcalf. 1973. 96 pp. $2.40. Small Business Administration
Publications, U.S. Superintendent of Documents, Washington, DC
20402. Excellent introduction to starting a business, including
many work sheets and questions. Best buy.

Enterprise in the Nonprofit Sector. James C. Crimmins and
Mary Keil. 1983. 144 pp. $7. Partners for Livable Places, 1429 21st
Street, NW, Washington, DC 20036. Excellent study of income-
producing activities by small and medium-sized institutions outside major metropolitan areas, this book provides several case
studies and thought-provoking conclusions about why and how
nonprofit entrepreneurs make a profit. Includes useful advice on
starting a business and other revenue-generators.

See also Chapter 18, "Small Enterprise Development," in *Dollars
and Sense: A Community Fundraising Manual for Shelters and
other Nonprofit Organizations* listed earlier under "How-to
Books — Women."

Hint: Also ask the librarian in the business section of your public
library to help you find the best new books on starting a business
and the type of business you plan to start.

FREE PUBLICATIONS

Small Business Administration (SBA). Write the SBA at the
Small Business Administration, P.O. Box 15434, Fort Worth, TX
76119, or call the SBA office in large cities listed in the white pages
under "Small Business Administration" or "United States Government." Ask for their current publications lists: SBA 115A — *Free
Management Assistance Publications* (4 pp.)

The SBA offers many free booklets to help you plan your budget,
personnel policies, and work plans. Here are a few I recommend to
help you begin planning your business; be sure to check their current publication list to order newer titles, too. Order the following
from SBA, P.O. Box 15434, Fort Worth, TX 76119. All are free.

MA 223. *Incorporating a Small Business.* 8 pp.
MA 231. *Selecting the Legal Structure for Your Firm.* 8 pp.

MA 235. *A Venture Capital Primer for Small Business.* 8 pp.

MA 233. *Planning and Goal Setting for Small Business.* 8 pp. Includes sample work plan.

SMA 71. *Checklist for Going into Business.* 12 pp.

SMA 170. *Thinking About Going Into Business?* 12 pp.

FREE TAX PUBLICATIONS

Internal Revenue Service (IRS) publications. All are free and published each year. Order from your local office of the IRS, listed in the telephone book. To collect and pay taxes:

Circular E. *Employer's Tax Guide.* Publication 15. 48 pp. How to withhold, deposit, report, and pay federal income tax and Social Security (FICA) tax.

Publication 583. *Recordkeeping for a Small Business.* 16 pp.

Publication 509. *Tax Calendar for 19XX.* 12 pp.

Publication 505. *Tax Withholding and Estimated Tax.* 12 pp.

Publication 539. *Withholding Taxes and Reporting Requirements.* 16 pp.

To file annual reports:

Form 990T — "Exempt Organization Business Tax Return." (4 pp.)

Instructions for Form 990T. (10 pp.)

Publication 598 — *Tax on Unrelated Business Income of Exempt Organizations.* (32 pp.)

State and city income tax publications. Contact your state and city departments of revenue to get current state income tax forms and instructions and information on other licenses, permits, and taxes required for your business.

FOR ADVICE ON STARTING A THRIFT SHOP

How to $ucceed in Fund-Rai$ing Today. Helen K. Knowles. 1975. 200 pp. $6.95. Bond Wheelwright Co., Porter's Landing, Freeport, ME 04032. Advice on starting thrift shops, where to get merchandise, and sample consignment contracts.

CHAPTERS 7–10: SPECIAL EVENTS

GENERAL

Special Events Fundraising. 1975 and 1977. 16 pp. $3.50. The Grantsmanship Center NEWS, 1031 S. Grand Ave., Los Angeles, CA 90015. This booklet features the best of both worlds: an in-depth interview with Joan Flanagan on how grass roots organizations can excel at producing special events, followed by advice from Sally Berger on how to produce a big-money, razzle-dazzle event for a major metropolitan hospital. You get helpful checklists for organizing your event and collecting information on corporate sponsors.

Fundraising Events: Making Womanpower Profitable. Lael Stegall and Betsy Crone. 1978. 24 pp. $2. National Women's Political Caucus, 1411 K Street, NW, Suite 1110, Washington, DC 20005. Not for women only, this excellent booklet will help any committee plan a successful event from start to finish. Uses the example of the Caucus's 1977 "Salute to Women in Government" that netted $23,000; features tested advice and sample press release, timeline, response card, tally sheets, mailgram, and instructions for workers.

CONCERTS

Making a Show of It: A Guide to Concert Production. Amy Bank, Cathy Fink, and Sheila Kahn. 1985. 124 pp. $12. Redwood Records Cultural and Educational Fund, 476 W. MacArthur Street, Oakland, CA 94609. Experienced producers share insider's tips on money-making concerts, including sample contracts, checklists, and budgets. This book will help you produce a folk concert for one hundred people or a rock extravaganza for thousands.

FILMS

In Focus. A Guide to Using Films. Linda Blackaby, Dan Georgakas, and Barbara Margolis. 1980. 206 pp. $9.95. Cine Information, 419 Park Ave. S, New York, NY 10016. Excellent manual on producing film showings, with good listing of film sources. Tops for nuts and bolts advice.

Resources. Media Network Information Center, 208 W. 13th St., New York, NY 10011. A clearinghouse for information on social issue films, videotapes, and slide shows. They can help you find the best current media on a particular subject. Sample newsletter available for $1; individual membership is $15.

News from the Film Fund. Quarterly newsletter. $5. The Film Fund, 80 E. 11th St., New York, NY 10003. Useful section of new releases of social issue, third world, and independent films; notices of new films, shorts, and slide shows you can order.

TENNIS TOURNAMENTS

Doing a One-Shot, Big Time Fund Raiser. Christine Pattee. 1976. 5 pp. Free; send self-addressed business-size stamped envelope to Christine Pattee, 50 Forest St., Apt. C-1, Hartford, CT 06105. Excellent report on the 1976 "Rally for the ERA with Billie Jean King" tennis match sponsored by the Iowa Women's Political Caucus.

WALKATHONS AND OTHER MARATHONS

Big Bucks from Bike-A-Thons. Robert A. Loewer. 1981. 34 pp. $3. Miami Valley Regional Bicycle Council, Inc., 1980 Winters Bank Tower, Dayton, OH 45423. Detailed advice, with samples and time-tables, from the Miami Valley Rigional Bicycle Council's Thunder Road Bike-A-Thon that produced $57,000 in 1978 and grew to $150,000 in 1981. More than 70 percent of their funds come from company teams.

CHAPTER 11: PUBLICITY

The Basics

Editing Your Newsletter. A Guide to Writing, Design, and Production. Mark Beach. 1980. 128 pp. $10.95. Coast to Coast Books, 2934 N.E. 16th Ave., Portland, OR 97212. Good advice for new newsletter editors, packed with examples and great tips to help you save money and make your job easier.

The Elements of Style. William Strunk, Jr., and E. B. White. Third Edition. 1979. 85 pp. $2.25. Macmillan Paperbacks, 866 Third Ave., New York, NY 10022. Anyone who writes must have this book. It is the model for any work you do: short, clear, easy to read, full of memorable examples and good humor. A perfect marriage of English professor Strunk's concise commands on usage and composition with author White's eloquent approach to style.

Equality in Print: A Guide for Editors and Publishers. Beryl Dwight et al. 1978. 24 pp. $1.50. Chicago Women in Publishing, P.O. Box 11837, Chicago, IL 60611. A clear, useful guide to help all writers "eliminate obsolete sexist terms, gender assumptions, unnecessary labeling, and anachronistic usages" in letters, newsletters, and reports.

How to Do Leaflets, Newsletters and Newspapers. Nancy Bingham. 1982. 144 pp. $5.75. PEP Publishers, P.O. Box 289, Essex Station, Boston, MA 02112. Wonderful, thorough manual covers, start to finish, the production and editorial work on publications reported and produced by volunteers. Indispensable for the novice; valuable for the veteran. Packed with examples.

If You Want Air Time: A Publicity Handbook. 1979. 18 pp. 75¢. Publications Department, National Association of Broadcasters, 1771 N St., NW, Washington, DC 20036. How to get your message on radio and television, written from the point of view of the stations.

Positioning. How to Be Seen and Heard in the Overcrowded Marketplace. Al Ries and Jack Trout. 1981. 240 pp. $4.95. Warner Books, P.O. Box 690, New York, NY 10019. Two ad men regale you with stories and strategies to make your organization stand out from the other 850,000 charities in the United States.

Publicity Handbook. 1979. 36 pp. 50¢. Consumer Services. The Sperry and Hutchinson Co., 2900 W. Seminary Dr., Fort Worth, TX 76133. Best introduction to press work for volunteers, including a sample press release, photo caption, and radio public service announcement.

Hint: Ask your own national organization or network for publications on publicity. Many offer good. booklets tailored to their members, such as The National Council on the Aging's *Media Relations Handbook.*

Specialized Publicity Publications

To make a slide show:

Projecting Your Image: How to Produce a Slide Show. #296. 1977. 4 pp. 80¢. League of Women Voters of the United States, 1730 M St., NW, Washington, DC 20036.

To make your own television shows:

Doing Community Video. Uptown Community Video Staff. 1979. 30 pp. $2.50. Alternative Schools Network Video Project, 1105 W. Lawrence Ave., Rm. 210, Chicago, IL 60640. Clear introduction to community television. Covers basic equipment and skills.

To write effective letters:

How to Win Friends and Influence People. Dale Carnegie. 1936. 264 pp. $1.95. Pocket Books, 1230 Avenue of the Americas, New York, NY 10020. Now in its 104th printing, this is still the best advice on how to talk and listen to people. Recommended to any leader or staff person who works with the public. See especially Part Five, "Letters That Produce Miraculous Results."

See also *Speaking Out: Setting Up a Speakers Bureau* and *How to Talk with Practically Anybody about Practically Anything,* in the section for Chapter 5: Raising Money from Believers.

CHAPTER 12: MAKING BOOK

Best for Beginners

Bookkeeping Handbook for Low-Income Citizen Groups. The National Council of Welfare. 1973. 104 pp. Single copy free. National Council of Welfare, Rm. 566, Brooke Claxton Building, Ottawa, Ontario K1A 0K9 Canada. Best book for the brand-new treasurer. Covers books, opening the checking account, setting up journals and a petty cash system, reconciling the bank statement, and setting up files. Many helpful drawings of sample forms and journal pages. En français: *Le Poids des Impôts/Le Partage des Bénéfices.* Gratuit.

Recordkeeping for a Small Business. Publication 583. Internal Revenue Service. 1979. 16 pp. Free. Internal Revenue Service, listed in your telephone directory or ask your member of Congress. Good introduction to setting up books for a business that can be used for a volunteer group, too. Includes setting up records; single-entry or double-entry bookkeeping; and sample of checkbook reconciliation, daily summary of cash receipts, monthly summary of cash receipts, check disbursement journal, depreciation record, and employee compensation record. Good if you handle cash every day, pay staff, or run a business such as a thrift shop.

Best All-Purpose Reference

Financial and Accounting Guide for Nonprofit Organizations. Malvern J. Gross, Jr., and William Warshauer, Jr. 1979. 568 pp. $40. The Ronald Press Co., 79 Madison Ave., New York, NY 10016. This is everything you will need in a reference book. Good, clear advice on concepts, financial statements, taxes, control, audits, books, and budgeting. It is worth the price because you will use it often. Indispensable for any medium to large organization.

Useful for the Board, Treasurer, and Fundraisers

Accounting for Culture. A Primer for Non-Accountants. Robin Littauer et al. 1980. 34 pp. $4.45. Accounting, Metropolitan Cultural Alliance, 250 Boylston St., Boston, MA 02116. Excellent introduction to the concepts and vocabulary of accounting and the expectations of accountants. Useful for any treasurer or fundraiser new to accounting terms.

The Audit Process: A Guide for Non-Profit Organizations. 1982. 32 pp. $4. CPA's for the Public Interest, 220 S. State St., Chicago, IL 60604. Excellent introduction to an audit, including advice to make it easier, faster, and less expensive. Includes glossary, checklist, sample letters and reports.

How to Grow a Parents Group. Diane Mason, Gayle Jensen, and Carolyn Ryzewicz, 1979. 212 pp. $7. CDG Enterprises, P.O. Box 97, Western Springs, IL 60558. Best explanation of planning, budgets, and fundraising by volunteers. Appendix B includes an excellent introduction to accounting and budgeting procedures for a nonprofit organization. Includes chart of accounts, income ledger, expense ledger, monthly cash report, and comparing budget and actual figures.

Where Do All the $ Go? What Every Board & Staff Member of a Non-Profit Organization Should Know About Accounting and Budgeting. Gerald G. Bowe, Jr. 1975. 40 pp. $3.75. The New Hampshire Charitable Fund, P.O. Box 1335, Concord, NH 03301. Covers accounting, budgets, and internal control; especially good on clarifying the vocabulary of accounting and introducing double-entry bookkeeping.

Accounting Books for Special Audiences

ARTS

Financial Management for the Arts—A Guidebook for Arts Organizations. Charles A. Nelson and Frederick J. Turk. 1975. 52 pp. $5.95. American Council for the Arts, 570 Seventh Ave., New York, NY 10018. This has the best explanation of how to estimate the "personnel cost by program," or how to figure how much each program costs you in terms of the staff's salaries. Since organizations that employ staff spend 60 to 90 percent of their budgets on salaries, this is the best way to find out if your money is really being spent to accomplish your goals. Explanation of planning, budgeting, cash management, fund accounting, general accounting, and financial organization.

CHURCHES

Money and Your Church. How to Raise More . . . How to Manage it Better. Manfred Holck, Jr. 1974. 189 pp. $7.95. Keats Publishing, 212 Elm St., New Canaan, CT 06840. Holck is both a Certified Public Accountant and former pastor. Especially good on bookkeeping and clear financial systems for small to medium-sized churches.

CO-OPS

The Accountant's Manifesto. Luther H. Buchele. 1977. 86 pp. $2.50. NASCO, Box 7293, Ann Arbor, MI 48107. Recommended for volunteer groups because it was written for housing co-ops in which the treasurer changes every few years. Includes excellent sections on closing the books, what the new treasurer can do before and after training, and proven solutions for "domestic" accounting problems like the long-distance phone bills. For any co-op or other group that depends on each member paying his or her fair share, there is "How to Be an Effective Treasurer Without Losing Friends," which covers collecting money, support of the board, dealing with deadbeats, and confidentiality of the books.

Legal and Tax Matters

INTERNAL REVENUE SERVICE

Call the Internal Revenue Service (IRS) listed in most telephone books or ask your member of Congress for the address of the nearest office. All publications are free.

GETTING STARTED—IRS

Publication 557—*How to Apply for and Retain Exempt Status for Your Organization.* (82 pp.)
Form 1023—"Application for Recognition of Exemption Under Section 501(c)(3) of the Internal Revenue Code." (22 pp.)
Form SS-4—"Application for Employer Identification Number." (4 pp.)

Form 5768 — "Election/Revocation of Election by an Eligible Section 501(c)(3) Organization to Make Expenditures to Influence Legislation." (1 p.)

ANNUAL REPORTS — IRS

All nonprofits:

Form 990 — "Return of Organization Exempt from Income Tax." (4 pp.)
Instructions for Form 990. (8 pp.)

501(c)(3) groups:

Schedule A (Form 990) — "Organization Exempt Under 501(c)(3) Supplementary Information." (4 pp.)
Instructions for Schedule A (Form 990). (8 pp.)

If you operate a business:

Form 990T — "Exempt Organization Business Tax Return." (4 pp.)
Instructions for Form 990T. (10 pp.)
Publication 598 — *Tax on Unrelated Business Income of Exempt Organizations.* (32 pp.)

TO ANSWER QUESTIONS ABOUT DONATIONS

Publication 526 — *Income Tax Deduction for Contributions.* (8 pp.)
Publication 561 — *Valuation of Donated Property.* (12 pp.)

STATE GOVERNMENTS

Ask your Secretary of State and Attorney General's Offices if tax-exempt nonprofit organizations are required to file annual report forms in your state. Some states now use the Federal 990 form, some have their own forms, and some have none. Ask a local nonprofit's treasurer or bookkeeper, your lawyer, and your accountant for more advice on necessary annual reports.

See also *The Successful Volunteer Organization* by Joan Flanagan listed earlier under "The Best How-to Manuals" for the best step-by-step advice on starting a new nonprofit organization.

CHAPTER 13: FUNDRAISING FOREVER

Calendars: How to Get Control of Your Time

Chase's Calendar of Annual Events: Special Days, Weeks and Months in 19XX. William D. Chase. Published annually, 224 pp. $17.45. Best Publications, Dept. C, 180 N. Michigan Ave., Chicago, IL 60601. Every holiday, festival, commercial promotion, and famous person's birthday. You can find an excuse for a party or a theme for a meeting on *any* day from this book.

How to Get Control of Your Time and Your Life. Alan Lakein. 1973. 160 pp. $1.95. Signet Paperbacks, 1301 Avenue of the Americas, New York, NY 10019. Best book on how to stop procrastinating and start getting results. Features Lakein's question "What is the best use of my time right now?" and "IIow to judo fear."

Raising Money from Foundations

Ask an experienced local grant writer for advice on the best people at local foundations. Use the Foundation Center Regional Collections listed in Chapter 13 for the most up-to-date free information on foundations.

Foundation Fundamentals: A Guide for Grantseekers. Carol M. Kurzig. 1985. 148 pp. $9.95. The Foundation Center, 79 Fifth Ave., New York, NY 10003. The best book on how to research foundations, what they are, where they are, and how to apply for their money. Many samples, a good bibliography, and excellent research checklist for proposals.

The Grantseekers Guide: A Directory for Social and Economic Justice Projects. Jill R. Shellow, Editor. 1985. 450 pp. $14.95 prepaid. Moyel-Bell, Ltd., c/o Knaus Reprint, Route 10, Millwood, NY 10546. Excellent book to help social change projects qualify for and obtain grants, includes helpful information on 179 grantmakers and 112 church resources for social justice. Information on funders is indexed by names, geographical area, and subject areas, including "community organizing."

The Grantsmanship Center NEWS. Magazine published six times a year. $28. The Grantsmanship Center, 1031 S. Grand Ave., Los Angeles, CA 90015. Up-to-date information on foundation and government grant writing and helpful tips on management for agencies that take grants. Also sells useful reprints of earlier articles.

Program Planning and Proposal Writing. Expanded Version. Norton J. Kiritz. 1980. 48 pp. $3.00. The Grantsmanship Center, 1031 S. Grand Ave., Los Angeles, CA 90015. Recommended to all grant writers, this booklet is the core of the grantsmanship training course. Easy to read with lots of good examples, it covers each step of writing a proposal, from the cover letter to the budget.

Quest for Funds: Insider's Guide to Corporate & Foundation Funding. Joe Breiteneicher. 1983. 20pp, $2.50. Conserve Neighborhoods, National Trust for Historic Preservation, 1785 Massachusetts Ave., NW, Washington, DC 20036. Written by the executive director of the Bird Companies Foundation, this booklet offers great advice on how to find funders, prepare your case statement, and manage your fundraising program. No-nonsense honesty, easy style, and excellent bibliography make this a good buy for novices.

STEPS in Writing a Proposal. Q-16. 1976. 6pp. 50¢. Citizens Information Service of Illinois, 67 E. Madison St., Chicago, IL 60603. Recommended for new groups planning and writing a proposal for the first time; features "Is your organization ready for a grant?"

See also *Semillas De Prosperidad or How to Cultivate Resources from the Private Sector,* listed earlier under "Hispanics". Contains excellent advice on researching foundations and writing proposals that is helpful for any group.

Ask for the catalog *Publications and Services* from The Foundation Center, 79 Fifth Avenue, New York, NY 10003, for the most complete and current list of directories, guide books, and computer data bases compiled by the national service organization operated by foundations themselves.

Index

A